Preface to
(Here we sat down
(Katav edution)

how we cut O R T
history out O R T
how do people
T about creating
new world.

myth power.

Method and Meaning in Ancient Judaism

11/2 How and use m as daily
guide?

T tells what kind of society
we want on earth.

BROWN UNIVERSITY
BROWN JUDAIC STUDIES

Edited by

Jacob Neusner

Wendell S. Dietrich, Ernest S. Frerichs, Horst R. Moehring

Number 10

Method and Meaning in Ancient Judaism

by Jacob Neusner

Method and Meaning in Ancient Judaism

by
Jacob Neusner

Scholars Press

Distributed by
SCHOLARS PRESS
PO Box 5207
Missoula, Montana 59806

Method and Meaning in Ancient Judaism

by
Jacob Neusner

Library of Congress Cataloging in Publication Data

Neusner, Jacob, 1932-
    Method and meaning in ancient Judaism.

    (Brown Judaic studies ; no. 10)
    Includes bibliographies and index.
    1. Mishnah—Criticism, interpretation, etc.—Addresses,
essays, lectures. 2. Talmud—Criticism, interpretation, etc.—
History—Addresses, essays, lectures. I. Title. II. Series.
BM497.8.N48   296.1'23'06   79-9881
ISBN 0-89130-281-6
ISBN 0-89130-300-6 pbk.

Printed in the United States of America

1   2   3   4   5

Edwards Brothers, Inc.
Ann Arbor, Michigan 48104

For
Lois D. Atwood

TABLE OF CONTENTS

INTRODUCTION

What second-century Jews have to teach the generation of the last decades of the twentieth century is how to make use of imagination and fantasy to confront, defy, and overcome chaos and disorder. The Mishnah, the first and principal document of Rabbinic Judaism, is the work of the second century. It comes to close at the end of that century.

Behind the Mishnah lay the ruins of half a millenium of orderly and systematic Israelite life which had been centered on the regular and reliable offering of the produce of field and flock upon the altar of the Temple in Jerusalem, the ordering of society around that Temple, the rhythmic division of time in response to that cult, and the placing of people and things into their proper station in relationship to that center. One disastrous war ended in the destruction of the Temple. The second, three generations later, made certain it would not be rebuilt in the foreseeable future—nor, as it now appears, ever. In the aftermath of these two terrible wars the Israelite nation entered upon an existence far more precarious in mind than in material reality. Within a century the social and agricultural effects of the wars had worn off. Galilean synagogues of the third and fourth century testify to an age of material surplus and good comfort. But it would be a very long time before the psychological effects of dislocation and disorientation would pass. In some ways they never have. Our age, which looks back upon the destruction of enduring political and social arrangements in the aftermath of two terrible wars (with numerous skirmishes in-between and since), has the power to confront the second century world of ancient Judaism, because, it seems, there is a measure of existential congruence between the two ages and their common problems.

The problems are the kind which challenge the imagination and the will. The power to construct a way of supporting life and sustaining the material needs of society is in hand. The legacy of World War I and of World War II is not death alone or even mainly. Nor has the economy of the nations continued to reveal the costs of war or to pay them. The cities have been cleared and

1

rebuilt. The bonds of war have been paid off by inflation. The dead are buried. The marks of war are gone from Leningrad, Warsaw, Dresden, Berlin, and even Hiroshima. Even the Jewish people has at last entered the time of mourning so that, in due course, that time may pass. Three decades of numb silence are over. Now is the moment of tears for the six million Jews of Europe and the ten million other innocents who perished without cause or justice. We have survived our century. But a precarious order, so painstakingly pieced together and so cautiously maintained by the nations, conceals a chaos just beneath the surface. There cannot be war, but there is no peace. The problem of system and order is not yet solved. This problem must be one of imagination and will, for the material needs of the nations in the main are met or, at least, are not pressing anymore. No more mass starvation exists except in backwaters of the world's economy. But what society is at peace with itself?

The problem of the second century is the crisis of the survivors. The issue which confronted that age is the reordering of a world off course and adrift, an age after the night and fog have passed which does not know where it is. The Mishnah is a document of imagination and fantasy, constructed in part from the sherds and pieces of reality, but in much larger measure from beams of hope. It tells us something about how things were, but everything about how a small group of men wanted things to be. It is an orderly, repetitious, careful, precise document in both language and message. It is small-minded, picayune, obvious, dull, routine—all the things its age was not.

To understand what the document is and what its makers wanted the world to be, we have only to reflect upon the contrast between the document and the world to which it speaks. What it is and what it says are the opposite of its circumstances. Its message is one of small achievements and modest hope. Its meaning is to defy a world of large disorders and immodest demands. The heirs of heroes must build as ordinary, unheroic folk in this age. The Mishnah maintains that what a person wants matters in important ways. It faces an Israelite world which can shape affairs in no important ways and speaks to people who by no means will the way things are.

The Mishnah defies and denies what is because it has a higher view of what can be. It is a practical judgment upon, and in favor of, the power of imagination and will to reshape reality. The Mishnah attempts through imagination and will to regain that system and to reestablish that order upon which a trustworthy existence can be built. The Mishnah's problem is, first, to discover the prerequisites of system and the requirements of order and, second, to state them both in the way the document phrases its message and in what it says. A measured, sustained, balanced, and reliable medium will utter the words by which a world may be re-created and made sensible.

This is, therefore, a book about the world-view of a book—or, more really, a library—which made a world. The book is the Mishnah and Talmud. The world it made is that of Judaism. Specifically, I want to spell out what I believe are fresh approaches to the reading of that 'library' and the

[handwritten margin note:] Is this what created Judaism? Bible?

interpretation of its meanings. I use a number of words to refer to the same general thing, "the Talmud," or "the Talmudic literature," or "rabbinical writings," and the like. Because of the multiplicity and variety of books contained in this library, it is possible to do so. But my specific interest is in only one of those books, the first one, which is the Mishnah. The Mishnah is a code of normative rules, promulgated by Judah, patriarch of the Jewish community of the Land of Israel about the year 200. Most of what I say about a world-view and a way of life refers, specifically, to the world-view and the projected way of life of the second century authorities whose work ultimately finds its way into the Mishnah.

That document, in its turn, laid the foundations for the Babylonian Talmud, a sizable collection of legal, theological, and exegetical materials organized around, and in a measure serving as a commentary to, the Mishnah. This collection, as its name indicates, is the work of rabbis who were located in Babylonia, between the Tigris and Euphrates rivers in what is now Iraq but what was then part of the Iranian empire. There is yet another Talmud, called in Hebrew the Jerusalemite Talmud and, in English, the Palestinian Talmud. Of a parallel character to the Babylonian one, this compilation presents the equivalent materials of the rabbis living in the Land of Israel, particularly in the Galilean part of it. Both Talmuds speak mainly in the names of third and fourth century authorities, although it is generally believed that the Palestinian one came to closure and redaction about a hundred years before the Babylonian one.

In addition to the Mishnah and the two Talmuds, the "library of the Talmud," the corpus of the rabbis of the first six or seven centuries of the common era, includes yet more:

First is Tosefta, a collection of supplements to the Mishnah. These supplements either cite and then gloss a sentence of the Mishnah, or augment its message and its meaning without direct citation but through indirect allusion to the Mishnah's contents. Tosefta ("supplements") seems to have come into being between the end of the second century and the end of the fourth. In many ways, we may speak of Mishnah-Tosefta as a literary and conceptual continuum. The two certainly constitute a formal unity, since Tosefta imitates the language of the Mishnah and is substantively indistinguishable from it, in that it is nearly incomprehensible without reference to the Mishnah.

Second are collections of explanations of the meaning of Scripture as worked out by pretty much the same people who created the two Talmuds. These are of two kinds. One sort tries to link the laws of the Mishnah to the Scripture. The method is to cite the Mishnah's saying verbatim and then assert and demonstrate that the conception of that saying in fact is contained within, and therefore based upon, Scripture. This sort is found particularly in Sifra, on the Book of Leviticus. Sifré treats the Books of Numbers and Deuteronomy. The second sort of biblical exegesis stands independent of the

Mishnah (one of the few types of early rabbinic literature which pretends to do so) and speaks principally of Scripture in its own terms. The exegesis of this kind deals with the books of Genesis and Leviticus and is contained, now, in Genesis Rabbah and Leviticus Rabbah. The first of these two works systematically and in an orderly way comments upon the book of Genesis verse by verse. The second is homiletical. These documents also appear to have come to closure by the beginning of the fifth century.

It follows that the library of which we speak is the work of amazingly creative men who, over a period of approximately two hundred years, took the Mishnah and so shaped it that it might form the foundations of the social and cultural polity of the Jewish people, wherever they might live, for the nearly two millenia to follow. If we add to this period of furious activity the half-century or so in which Mishnah's diverse materials were reshaped into a single, coherent account, then the roughly two hundred fifty years from ca. A.D. 150 to ca. A.D. 400 constitute the formative period of that kind of Judaism—the Rabbinical kind, after the title of its authorities—which predominated for well over fifteen hundred years afterward. So this book addresses itself to the seedtime of Judaism, to the ancient and formative phase of a living and therefore modern religion.

Now what I want to know about that religion is very simple and straightforward: Precisely what is it? I seek to grasp the whole. This means to me to transcend the parts in search of the whole by working through the parts with the claim that each must contain something of the whole. I am keenly interested in the history of the religion under discussion, because it is in part through knowledge of the age and circumstances in which Judaism came into being that the shape and structure of that Judaism are to be described and interpreted. To begin with, after all, the rabbis of the early centuries of the Common Era addressed the world in which they lived. We have to link what they said to the people to whom they spoke (if we can figure out who these people might have been). But history in this setting is an instrument in the practice of a different craft. It helps to shape a picture of the whole; it is not the whole of the story. For beyond is the thing they made: the rabbis' library. And yet further onward in time and in mind is the thing that library made: the religion and culture of the Jewish people for nearly the whole of the rest of the history of the Jewish people and, it is self-evident, a principal source for the formation of that religion and culture even in our own day.

In this book, as I said, I focus upon the earliest of the documents of the Talmudic literature, which is the Mishnah. What I want to know, predictably, is: Precisely what is the Mishnah? I wish to grasp the whole of it and to explain what the document proposes to say through its detailed laws, organized into tractates, with its tractates organized into divisions. Mishnah speaks through remarkably consistent language. It has one voice only. It is anonymous and collective. It clearly means to say how things are supposed to be. To unpack the document, I introduce the notion of *system* (and subsystem), a notion which runs through most of the essays in this book and which is meant to be illustrated by all of them.

My claim is that the Mishnah forms and expresses a system because of its cogency, unitary voice of address, and, clearly, single and whole audience, constituted in Mishnah's conception by the people it calls Israel, the Jewish people. To be sure, a book is not a social system. But this book forms the foundation of, and in fact ultimately creates, a social system, one which endured for a very long time and, as I have emphasized, lives today. Indeed, it is the only social system the Jews have ever known for more than a few hundred years at a time and in more than a few territories of their dispersion. If we can make some sense of the more than five dozen tractates of Mishnah—themselves constituted by more than five hundred chapters—and so specify what it is that we think Mishnah means to say as a whole to the whole of Israel, we shall have a more coherent conception of the character of Judaism as it was created by the earlier generations of rabbis: Precisely what is it which they created?

When properly described and interpreted, this system of Judaism may be brought into juxtaposition, for purposes of comparison and contrast, with other systems within the history of Judaism, on the one side, and with systems formed by other religious-cultural groups as well, on the other. Seen part by part, Judaism yields nothing suitable for comparison. For what is under study will not have been accurately described and adequately interpreted, a point of particular importance in the fourth chapter of this book. But seen as part of a whole, the details of the rabbinic system begin to speak to issues we can grasp. While remaining isolated and majestically alien, they take on meaning accessible to us.

Since this is a book about system and order, I will deal with only one half of one system, three of the six divisions of the Mishnah. In the second part of the book each of these systems is worked out with faithful attention to the specificities of the law, and the character of the linguistic evidence is explained as well. The several exercises on problems of meaning clearly exemplify a rather distinctive set of questions and approaches which, all together, may be deserving of the title, "method." But it is easier to do the work in a given way than to define and explain that way. Perhaps this fact explains the impatience of many scholars, who strongly hold quite distinctive and uncommon opinions on *how* work is to be done, with questions of method. For when we admit that we indeed work in one way and not in some other, that is, when we specify the methods by which we read our texts and construct our problems, we have to face the fact that there are other ways.

It is difficult for scholars to give up the certainty of the givenness of their methods. It is painful for them to face up to the facts that, however ineluctable and right their approaches seem, there are yet others, and that what they take to be based on common sense is not so regarded by everyone else. But no thoughtful person can sustain the claim that the way we do things is how things are supposed to be done. Even the selection of a given text—literary, archaeological, or, in our own day, social and cultural—for study and interpretation constitutes an act of taste and judgment which, together, express a commitment to one method and not to some other. To be sure, the impatience of scholars with discussions of method when these discourses are lacking all attention to problems of inquiry and to concrete, specific texts is well founded. Since, for my part, I share the suspicion of such discussions, I may claim to be stronger on the side of specific studies of concrete things than of general remarks on method. But I do my best to say what I think I am doing. I am not indifferent to the criticism of others outside my narrow range of competence.

In many ways this book constitutes a criticism of historical method as a useful approach to the study of ancient Judaism. I spell out in the first and second chapters what I conceive to be the limitations of historical method, both in theory, and, in the third chapter, all the more, in practice. What has been done seems to me profoundly flawed, for reasons I give in all three chapters. I must make clear that these criticisms of historical method come from a historian. I plan to remain just that. But I want to be a historian who also is other things.

If, moreover, I am silent on the issues of history of religions, it is because I am contented with the way in which these issues are formulated and exemplified in the work of the historians of religions upon whom I depend very heavily, as the fifth and sixth chapters indicate. Jonathan Z. Smith is chief among these. While undertaking to learn something from anthropology and theology, therefore, my commitment to the soundness of the historical and religions-historical approach to learning should be made explicit. Mine is a lover's quarrel with historians. That, too, is why opinions here are so strongly held and fiercely expressed. I do not apologize, regret, repent, or forgive, in matters of mind. I only correct errors—first of all, my own. I most intentionally criticize others, and myself above all, by trying to write a better book than the one I do not like (which, in the nature of things, most commonly is the one I just wrote).

Let me now explain the several chapters, their purpose, and how they relate to one another, because this is a book of essays which is meant to unfold around a single problem and play out the variations of a single theme.

The first two chapters speak to one another. They state as clearly as I can what I conceive to be the promising lines of investigation, for the purposes of the study of religion and culture, into the Talmudic and cognate literature. In the former I outline the program I have laid out for myself and in part effected in the second part of this book. In the latter I explain why I conceive the historical reading of the Babylonian Talmud and related literature to be essentially sterile. "Talmudic history" is bankrupt of interesting questions and fructifying ideas. More than a century has been spent upon the question: What went on in the times of the Talmud? But the question is poorly framed.

First, the Talmud does not define an age, though it is a definitive document. For historical purposes, however, it is merely another source. Second, what is important to the Talmud itself—what the Talmud is about—is not the stories told quite *en passant*, the tales of saints, kings, exilarchs, rabbis, teachers, disciples, and judges. These materials answer important questions. But the questions are not about what things really were like in the centuries in which the Talmud was taking shape. Third, the critical issues of history cannot be worked out along presently available lines. If, for example, we cannot demonstrate that a given authority really said what is attributed to him, then we cannot write his intellectual biography. If we cannot demonstrate that he really did what he is said to have done, then we cannot write his biography in material and concrete terms either. It follows that the Talmud does not permit us to report about the doings of the men who are its heroes, about the practical consequences of the teachings which are its purpose and its point, nor about the age in which it came into being and about which it speaks.

The sort of history we *can* do is important and interesting. This is a history of the unfolding of those ideas which the Talmud takes most seriously, ideas about the normative rules of a supernatural world which, at some few points, intersects with the world of here and now. We can uncover the framing of the Talmud's arcane arguments and trace the sophisticated and brilliant development of its inner, exegetical processes. This and other sorts of intellectual history are entirely feasible. But that is not the kind of history which people have wanted to do and have done. The work they have done seems to me to rest upon exceedingly infirm epistemological foundations. We simply do not know what people assume we know. The sources cannot tell us what people have hitherto taken for granted that they contain. In the opening chapter, I point to a single example of what I believe to be out-and-out meretricious handling of the texts. But it is only chosen because it is current and choice. This unhappy deceit hardly encompasses all of the unfortunate things done in the name of history upon this most unhistorical, indeed anti-historical, kind of literature.

What we have is a literature which tells us not about history but about compulsion, obsession, and fantasy—about the imaginative life of the people who made the literature. The Talmud records their hopes for, and, sometimes, their concrete achievements in, the world in which they lived. It spells out especially their thought-processes. It is a literature which expresses a viewpoint, which delineates the conceptual boundaries of a highly distinctive, profoundly particular, and idiomatic culture—a religious-culture. In my judgment, therefore, the appropriate questions come to us less from history, although—as the second part shows full well—the history of ideas is essential to the larger task, than from anthropology. The reason, as I explain in the opening chapter, is that anthropology teaches us how to ask about those very curious things to which the Talmud and related writings address themselves. Historians and theologians are remarkably cool to questions about what we

eat, how we dress, what work we do on a given day, let alone the unseen realm
of our compulsions, obsessions, fantasies, and phobias. Anthropologists have
taught us not only to take these things very seriously, but also what to make of
them. In the opening chapter I refer rapidly to three contemporary figures
who have, in my view, provided models for the kinds of research and, still
more important, the sorts of interpretation which we must undertake in the
study of the earlier strata of that kind of Judaism contained in the first
rabbinical books. The Talmud organizes its world around subjects like food
and sex taboos, property relationships, and other questions of material
culture which anthropology thinks important, and history and theology do
not. That is why I lay out what I conceive to be fruitful approaches to the
framing of questions in the opening chapter. This program is matched by
attention to unpromising paths to that same question in the second chapter.

The third chapter continues the essential polemic of the second. It spells
out in a concrete instance how historical accounts of the character of Judaism
in the earliest centuries before and after the beginning of the Common Era
have told us about things which, I think, simply were not there. I refer to the
dogma of almost all historians of Judaism of this period that, before 70, there
was a belief in an oral tradition, which was called "the Oral Torah," revealed
to Moses at Sinai alongside the written one. This Oral Torah furthermore
related to, and derived from, the written one. Possession of the Oral Torah is
what marked as distinctive the Pharisees of the period before 70. Now this
conception of a dual Torah is, as I try to show, well founded in the minds of
third and fourth century authorities. I am inclined to see it as a part of the
apologetic created in behalf of the Mishnah promulgated by Judah the
patriarch, an apologetic meant to find a place in the sacred history of Israel for
this important, new document. By linking the generative conceptions of the
Mishnah to Moses at Sinai, the myth of the Oral Torah provided a point of
origin and authority exhibiting impeccable credentials and compelling
universal assent.

When, on the other hand, we read those sources which derive from the
period before 70 without the foreknowledge that they are going to speak of
"the Oral Torah," we find it rather difficult to perceive that those sources
know of any such thing. They do know "traditions of the fathers." They are
well aware of a heritage of tradition external to Scripture. But these ideas in
pre-70 sources do not yield an explicit conception of the Oral Torah. On the
other hand, much later sources, from the end of the Mishnah onward, are firm
in attributing this very concept to authorities who lived before 70—indeed, as
far back as Joshua and the judges and prophets. From the turn of the third
century everyone is sure that Hillel and Shammai, and, before them, Simeon
b. Shatah and Judah b. Tabbai, and before them, Simeon the Righteous, all
were great masters of the Oral Torah. But these same people are equally
certain that Moses was "our rabbi," that David arose at midnight and studied
Torah, that Solomon was a master of Torah, and that all of the great prophets

and other biblical authorities likewise fully realized that ideal of Torah-learning which indeed characterized the masters of the third century and their successors, and which may have characterized even some of their predecessors in the second century. I think it is important to contemplate the issues and the sources as well, so that the true worth of historical research may be assessed. If it is the reader's judgment (contrary to mine) that the issues have been correctly formulated by available historiography ("Since he *really* said it, what does it mean historically?") then it may still be worthwhile to consider whether the results prove to be compelling. In my judgment the wrong questions have been asked and, moreover, the wrong answers given.

The second part of the book continues the opening chapter. It deals with issues of system and order. The fourth chapter makes the main point. If, as I argue, the right questions concern the system and meaning of Judaism as portrayed in the Talmudic sources, then we have to ask about the requirements for the description of a system ("systemic description"). Since a new approach to the learning of these sources is outlined here, we must first set up the alternative. In showing the promise of systemic, as against thematic, description in one subset of the Mishnaic system, I propose to illustrate and explain what is done in the next three chapters as well. The first subset of the Mishnaic system under discussion concerns women. The propositions of that paper both carry forward the program of the opening one and introduce all that follows. I hope its principal claims—that what Mishnah wishes to say on any topic, it proposes to express about every topic, and that the critical issue is why it chooses to speak about the particular six subjects that it has chosen, and not six others—will be given serious thought. I regard Mishnah's treatment of women as a key to Mishnah's understanding of the world. It is a route to the exposition of why Mishnah addresses the topics it chooses and does not speak about the topics it ignores.

The following three chapters—fifth, sixth, and seventh—ask what we may learn about the world created by Mishnah. They deal in substance. The fifth chapter describes the system of sacrifice and sanctuary and the sixth, the relationship of cult and world spelled out in the system of purities. These chapters ask the question: What do we learn about people from *what* they say? The seventh and final one of this sequence raises the complementary question: What do we learn about people from the *way* in which they say things? It is an essay relevant to the (to me most engaging) field of socio-linguistics, to which, I hasten to add, I do not claim to contribute.

The eighth and closing chapter is a very solemn effort to take into account the theology of what I have laid out for scholarly and hermeneutic purposes. My principal and recurring argument is that the world of Mishnah and the Talmud consists of a set of subsystems which, all together, form a whole and complete system. Judaism constitutes a way of viewing the world and of conducting life which fits together in all of its parts and constitutes a harmonious and cogent whole. This system is subjected to interpretation in the first two parts of the book, with questions about its relevance and meaning for the world in which the Jews of ancient times lived out their lives. At the same time, it yields what I conceive to be a claim of considerable importance upon the mind of the Jews of modern times as well—and not only upon their intellect, but also upon their soul. My problem is how this claim is to be stated—the requirements of its description, interpretation, and apologetics all at once.

In general, theologians invoke a "Judaism" which is seldom defined, as if "we all know" the sources and what they mean. The issue of definition is rarely, if ever, addressed, except by those theologians (unhappily, not a few) who determine at the outset to speak in the name of a Judaism which they pretty much make up as they go along. I am not inclined to think this process of *ad hoc* declarations in the name of Judaism is apt to yield interesting, let alone compelling, theological results. The alternative, proposed here, is to continue a path laid out by essentially scholarly methods, into a territory far beyond the reach of scholarship; I mean, the realm of theological instruction and conviction.

So this final chapter spends much time describing precisely how Judaism is to be defined, by which I mean the appropriate hermeneutics for the reading of its received revelation. The reader will notice the recurrence of familiar questions: *How* do these texts convey their message? What is it that we learn from the way they say things, and the way in which people have learned and are taught to hear what they say? At this point, however, the question of relevance is asked. The task of the theologian is to learn the ways of generalization, to undertake the exegesis of the exegesis of life contained within the *halakhic* documents of Judaism—a very difficult undertaking. For this purpose, at the end, I turn back to the work of history, but in a larger enterprise: the description of what I want to call "an ecology of Judaism," *a natural framework in which all elements interact with all other elements to form a stable, coherent, and whole system.* Just as, at the outset, I call into question the legacy of nineteenth and twentieth century scholars and theologians, so at the end I point to the wrong choices they have made. The differences are carefully delineated, so that what is new, and why what is new is promising, may be clearly grasped. I realize that it is not common for a scholar of ancient texts to propose some lines of theological work to be done on those texts, indeed to suggest there are opportunities for theological creativity to be explored in them. But the entire perspective of these essays is uncommon.

My friend and former student, William Scott Green, University of Rochester, originally had the idea of bringing together these particular papers and saw them as a book before I did. He gave me many good suggestions about how to organize the papers and why they belonged together. If, as I think, a book of essays is not merely essays about this and that bound between two covers, but a set of papers which unfold a single thread out of a single skein, then it is to William Scott Green that I owe the recognition of the underlying thread of argument in these papers, which I have written over the past two years. I also enjoyed the good counsel of Richard Samuel Sarason, Brown University, in preparing the papers for press. He was kind enough to review the papers when they were written and to make important suggestions for their improvement.

It is my hope that by bringing out these papers in an inexpensive and well-circulated book, they may find their way into the hands of college and university students of religious studies. They are my audience. If the study of Judaism is going to make its full and appropriate contribution to the study of religions and to the humanities, it will have its impact upon the methods by which other religions are described, interpreted, and compared with one another, as well as with Judaism. It is my high ambition to contribute to the available methods for the study of religions and their comparison. If others, as is their right, declare me to have failed, it will, at least, have been a glorious failure, given what is attempted: method, analysis, theology.

For many years the administrator of our department, Lois D. Atwood, has made life lively and pleasant for the students and faculty at Brown. She is a person who is made happy by making others happy. Her intelligence, wit, and good judgment have sustained and strengthened all of us. I have particularly appreciated her friendship and her perpetual willingness to chat about the affairs of the day. Her good will and excellent counsel transform things which seem otherwise into something tolerable and sensible. This book is a very small token of appreciation and affection, dated on her birthday.

Jacob Neusner

Providence, Rhode Island
December 20, 1978

My thanks go, too, to the exceptionally conscientious and efficient staff of Scholars Press, who did an especially good job on my manuscript.

J.N.

June 18, 1979

ACKNOWLEDGEMENTS

The following chapters originated as lectures:

"Anthropology and the Study of Talmudic Literature," as the Samuel Friedland Lecture, The Jewish Theological Seminary of America, Academic Convocation at Miami Beach, February 28, 1979;

"History and the Study of Talmudic Literature," as the Allan Bronfman Lecture, Shaar Hashomayim Synagogue, Montreal, November 8, 1978; the Hill Professor's Lecture, University of Minnesota, Minneapolis and St. Paul, November 15, 1978, and a plenary lecture in honor of the tenth anniversary of the Association for Jewish Studies, Boston, Massachusetts, December 17, 1978;

"Oral Torah and Oral Tradition: Defining the Problematic," at the Association for Jewish Studies Conference on Jewish Folklore, Spertus College, Chicago, Illinois, May 1, 1977;

"The Tasks of Theology in Judaism" as a lecture upon the occasion of the conferring upon me of the Doctor of Humane Letters (L.H.D.) of The University of Chicago, June 9, 1978.

Prior to the publication of this book, these chapters were printed as follows:

"Anthropology and the Study of Talmudic Literature," under the title, "The Talmud as Anthropology," in *The Samuel Friedland Lectures* (N.Y., 1979: The Jewish Theological Seminary of America);

"History and the Study of Talmudic Literature," under the title, "The Talmud as History," published as a separate pamphlet by Shaar Hashomayim Synagogue, Montreal;

"History and Structure," in *Journal of the American Academy of Religion* 45, 2 (1977) 161–192;

"Map without Territory," in *History of Religions*, November, 1979;

"Form and Meaning," in *Journal of the American Academy of Religion* 45, 1 (1977) 27–45;

"The Tasks of Theology in Judaism" in *The Journal of Religion*, January, 1979.

GLOSSARY AND ABBREVIATIONS

1QS   =   The Manual of Discipline of the Essenes of Qumran.

Aggadah   =   narrative; a story; contrasted to *halakhah*, law; the principal literary categories for the analysis of the Talmudic literature are *aggadah*, in contrast to, *halakhah*, neatly translated as lore and law.

Appointed Times   =   J. Neusner, *A History of the Mishnaic Law of Appointed Times* (Leiden, 1981f.) I–V.

B.   =   Babylonian Talmud.

BASOR   =   *Bulletin of the American Schools of Oriental Research.*

CD   =   Damascus Covenant. The Zadokite Documents, writings attributed to the Essenes of Qumran.

Col.   =   column.

Cor.   =   Corinthians.

Damages   =   J. Neusner, *A History of the Mishnaic Law of Damages* (Leiden, 1981f.) I–V.

Deut.   =   Deuteronomy.

Ed.   =   Mishnah-tractate ᶜEduyot.

Erub.   =   Mishnah-tractate ᶜErubin.

Ex.   =   Exodus.

Hag.   =   Mishnah-tractate Ḥagigah.

Halakhah   =   Normative statement on things a person should do; a law.

Halakhic   =   legal.

Ḥaliṣah   =   removal; rite or removing the shoe of a recalcitrant brother-in-law, described in Deut. 25:10ff.

Holy Things   =   J. Neusner, *A History of the Mishnaic Law of Holy Things* (Leiden, 1978f.) I–VI.

Ipsissima verba   =   his very own words, words really spoken by a given person at a specific moment in history; "the real thing."

15

JBL   =   *Journal of Biblical Literature.*

Lev.   =   Leviticus.

Listenwissenschaft   =   the science of making lists; the organizing of all knowledge in systematic and formally cogent constructions.

M.   =   Mishnah.

Men.   =   Mishnah-tractate Menaḥot.

Mishneh Torah   =   Restatement of the whole corpus of Judaic law and theology by Moses Maimonides.

Ned.   =   Mishnah-tractate Nedarim.

Negaᶜ   =   "a spot" of the disease described in Lev. 13–14.

Num.   =   Numbers.

P   =   The Priestly Code of the Pentateuch, e.g., Leviticus, Numbers (in part).

Par. = Mishnah-tractate Parah.

Purities = J. Neusner, *A History of the Mishnaic Law of Purities* (Leiden, 1974–1977) I–XXII.

Qid. = Mishnah-tractate Qiddushin.

Rabbi = Rabbi Judah the Patriarch, sponsor of the Mishnah, head of the Jewish community of the Land of Israel in the last quarter of the second century A.D. Sometimes: "Our Holy Rabbi."

Rashi   =   R. Solomon Isaac, the standard rabbinical exegete of biblical and Talmudic literature, 1040–1105.

Religionsgeschichtlich   =   having to do with the history of religions; adjective unavailable in American English.

Šelamim   =   peace-offerings.

Shab.   =   Mishnah-tractate Shabbat.

Shulḥan *ᶜArukh*   =   Code of Jewish law for practical purposes created by Joseph Karo.

Sot.   =   Mishnah-tractate Sotah.

T.   =   Tosefta.

Tem.   =   Mishnah-tractate Temurah.

Thes.   =   Thessalonians.

Torah shebeᶜal peh   =   Torah transmitted through memorization, "by memory," "the Oral Torah," the part of revelation at Sinai (="Torah") which was transmitted not in writing but by oral formulation and memorization.

Usha   =   Galilean town which was a center of rabbinic learning in the second half of the second century; "Ushan" refers to a rabbi who flourished in that time.

Women = J. Neusner, *A History of the Mishnaic Law of Women* (Leiden, 1979f.) I–V.

Y. = Yerushalmi; Palestinian Talmud.

Yad. = Mishnah-tractate Yadayim.

Yavneh = Coastal town in the Land of Israel which was a center of rabbinic learning in the last fourth of the first century; "Yavnean" refers to a rabbi who flourished in the period immediately following the destruction of the Temple in A.D. 70.

Yeshiva = Place of rabbinical learning and application of law; a session of lawyers and judges. Pl.: Yeshivot.

Zab = one afflicted by the venereal disease described in Lev. 15:1–15.

Zadokite Fragments = see CD.

PART ONE

PROBLEMS OF METHOD IN THE STUDY
OF EARLY RABBINIC JUDAISM

CHAPTER I

Anthropology and the Study
of Talmudic Literature

I

Gerson Cohen speaks of "the blessing of assimilation in Jewish history," by which he means "the healthy appropriation of new forms and ideas for the sake of our own growth and enrichment." He says, "Assimilation properly channeled and exploited can . . . become a kind of blessing, for assimilation bears within it a certain seminal power which serves as a challenge and a goad to renewed creativity" (1973:257f.). There is no area of Jewish expression more distinctive and intimate to the Jewish people, more idiomatic and particular to its inner life, than the study of the Talmud. In the present age, in my view, it is the study of the Talmud which has experienced[1] and must continue to undergo the fructifying and vivifying experience of assimilation. The reason is that it is precisely there that the Jewish intellect expresses itself.[2]

Now there have been two approaches to learning which already have stimulated students of the Talmudic and cognate literature to ask new questions and, therefore, to understand and perceive new dimensions in that literature. The first is the study of the language of the Talmud in the light of other Semitic languages, on the one side, and of Indo-European ones, Greek, Latin, and Iranian, on the other. Comparative philology in fact is very old,

[1]The ways in which Talmudic scholarship has confronted, if not wholly assimilated, some of the approaches and methods of the nineteenth and twentieth century humanities (and even social sciences) are sketched in J. Neusner, ed., *Formation of the Babylonian Talmud: Studies on the Achievements of Late Nineteenth and Twentieth Century Historical and Literary-Critical Research* (1970) and in J. Neusner, ed., *The Modern Study of the Mishnah* (1973). A broader analysis of the relationship between Jewish learning and the secular university, to which Jewish learning comes only in the twentieth century (and, for the most part, in the third quarter of that century) is in my *The Academic Study of Judaism. Essays and Reflections* (1975) and *The Academic Study of Judaism. Essays and Reflections. Second Series* (1977). Later in this essay I point to two points in which assimilation has been completed, philology and Semitics. The third point at which, I think, assimilation to a fresh mode of thought will be fructifying is in the area of social and cultural anthropology, as I shall make clear.

[2]I hasten to add that that is not the only classic and distinctively Jewish document. The Hebrew Scriptures are still more important and, read as Judaism has read them, equally distinctive. This point should not be given more weight than is intended here.

21

since its first great monument appears in the eleventh century, after the Islamic conquest of the Mediterranean world.[3] The result of the modern phase of that project, which has been continuous since the nineteenth century, has been a clarification of the meanings of specific sentences, the specification of the origins and sense of words used in one place or in another, in all, great improvement upon our understanding of the concrete and specific meanings of the Talmud's various discrete words and phrases. This step forward in exegesis, however, has not vastly improved our understanding of the method and meaning of the Talmud. But it has given greater clarity and accuracy to our search for its method and meaning.[4]

The second approach is the study of the Talmud for historical purposes. It has been in three parts: first, use of Talmudic evidence for the study of the general history of the Near and Middle East of its own times;[5] second, use of historical methods for the study of what was happening among the Jews and especially the people who created the Talmud itself;[6] third, use of historical

[3] I refer to ᶜArukh Hashshalem by Nathan b. Yehiel of Rome, 1035–c. 1110, who gives the meaning and etymology of the Talmudic lexicography in Latin, Greek, Arabic, and Persian. This is not to suggest he is the only important "comparativist" in post-Talmudic times. For their part, Talmudic rabbis themselves are acutely aware of linguistic origins, differences in word choice, and other aspects of what we should now call comparative philology and lexicography. There are, moreover, pericopae in the Babylonian Talmud which can have been composed specifically with the interests of sociolinguistics in mind. But it was in the time of the beginnings of modern Semitics that the true weight and meaning of these facts were grasped and taken seriously.

[4] I do not make reference to important modern and contemporary advances in the exegetical methods brought to bear upon the interpretation of the Talmudic literature because these appear to me to emerge essentially within the limits of classical Talmudic exegesis. They exhibit only casual and, in any event, unsystematic interest in exegetical and hermeneutical experiments outside of Talmudic studies or on its fringes. The reason is that the exegesis of the text is, alas, of interest principally to people who teach in yeshivot and Jewish seminaries or in Israeli university Talmud departments. These scholars have no access to, nor interest in, the work of exegetes in the larger field of hermeneutics in secular universities. Still, the noteworthy achievements of David Weiss Halivni in Meqorot ummesorot (1968, 1975) should be ample evidence of what can be achieved even within an essentially traditional ("aḥaronic") frame of reference.

[5] Historians of the Near and Middle East who have turned to Talmudic materials as a routine part of their examination of the sources are not numerous. In general, well-trained Semitists will be apt to turn to the Talmudic corpus more readily than Classicists and Byzantinists, for obvious reasons. Still, I cannot point to a single major work on the history of the region from Alexander to Muhammed which intelligently and sustainedly draws upon Talmudic evidence. As a general overview, though, I recommend F. E. Peters (1970).

[6] All the historians of the Jews of this period, by contrast, draw extensively upon the Talmud's evidence. But most of them draw solely upon that evidence. The best examples of well-crafted historical accounts of the period making ample and, for their day (which has passed), reasonably critical use of the Talmudic evidence are: Baron (1952), Avi-Yonah (1976), and Smallwood (1976). Each volume in my History of the Jews in Babylonia (1965–1970) opens with a chapter on the political history of the Jews at a given period in the history of the Parthian and Sasanian dynasties; in these chapters the evidences of the Talmudic stories are brought together with those deriving from other sources entirely: Christian, Iranian, Greco-Roman, and the like. The second chapter of each of those books then deals with the inner political history of the Jewish community, and for this purpose Iranian and Talmudic evidences are utilized as well.

perspectives in the analysis and elucidation of the Talmud's own materials.[7] None of these three methods has attracted a great number of practitioners. In a moment I shall explain why use of historical methods for the study of the world of the Talmud has, on the whole, produced results of modest interest for people whose principal question has to do with the discovery of what the Talmud is and means. At this point it suffices to say that the assimilatory process has worked well. The Talmud is no stranger to historical discourse, just as it is a familiar and routine source for the pertinent philological studies.

In my view there is yet a third approach to the description and interpretation of texts and to the reconstruction of the world represented in them. It is the approach of anthropology, the science of the description and interpretation of human culture.[8] Anthropology began its work, as Marvin Harris (1968: 1–7) points out, "as the science of history." It was meant to discover the lawful principles of social and cultural phenomena. In the past half-century "anthropologists sought out divergent and incomparable events. They stressed the inner, subjective meaning of experience to the exclusion of objective effects and relations . . . with the study of the unique and nonrepetitive aspects of history."[9] In our own day there is a renewed interest in generalization and in regularities, for instance, in underlying structures of culture. Now what makes anthropology fructifying for the study of the

---

[7] I am inclined to think that historical perspectives have clouded the vision of those who attempt them for exegesis of Talmudic literature. The most ambitious and, consequently, the most unsuccessful such effort at a kind of historical exegesis of the Talmud and its law is in Louis Finkelstein (1936). But in this regard he merely carried forward the perfectly dreadful approach of Louis Ginzberg (e.g., 1929). My reasons for regarding this approach to the exegesis of the law of the Talmud as untenable and the results as capricious and unsystematic are amply spelled out in my *The Rabbinic Traditions about the Pharisees before 70* (1971). There I review a very wide range of historical writings about the Pharisees and place into context the work of Finkelstein and Ginzberg (among many others). I am able to point to the underlying and generative errors in their approach to the interpretation of the legal materials for historical purposes and in their claim to interpret the legal materials from a historical perspective as well (a totally confused work).

[8] In what follows, I point to the work of a few specific anthropologists. In doing so, I do not pretend to have mastered the corpus of contemporary anthropological theory or to know more than the works I cite. Nor do I even claim fully to grasp all of the writings of the scholars whom I find, at some specific points in their corpus, to be strikingly illuminating for the work of understanding the Talmudic literature. In pointing toward social and cultural anthropology as a source of helpful questions and methods, moreover, I do not mean to take a stand on any of the mooted issues of that field. Nor do those whose names I omit make no or little impact upon me. Indeed, the scholar whose works I should most want to emulate is not cited here at all, namely, Melford Spiro. If I could write for Judaism an equivalent to his *Buddhism and Society* (1972), I believe I could make a contribution of lasting and fundamental importance to the study of Judaism within the study of religions. So, in all, what follows should be understood as a preliminary and tentative account of some of what I have learned from a few interesting people in a field presently altogether too remote from mine.

[9] Harris, *The Rise of Anthropological Theory. A History of Theories of Culture* (1968). It goes without saying that I do not wish to take a position on the controversy generated by this stimulating book. I learned much from Harris's history and critique.

Talmud is a range of capacities I discern in no other field of humanistic and social scientific learning. To me, anthropologists are helpful because they ask questions pertinent to the data I try to interpret.[10] We who spend our lives investigating and trying to master the Talmudic and cognate literature and to gain valid conceptions of the world created by that literature are overstuffed, indeed, engorged, with answers. Our need is for questions. Our task is through the exercise of taste and judgment to discern the right ones.

Information by itself nourishes not at all. Facts do not validate their own importance. Unless they prove relevant to important questions, they are not important. As I shall explain, among anthropologists of various kinds, who would not even agree with one another in many things, I find a common core of perspectives and issues which make their work stimulating for Talmudic learning of a particular sort. It is, specifically, because they show me the meaning of the data I confront that their modes of thought and investigation demand attention and appreciation.

II

Before specifying those things to be learned from anthropology, let me spell out what I find wrong with the approaches of that field which, to date, has predominated in the academic study of the Talmudic literature, I mean, historical study. There are two kinds of problems which in my view call into question the fruitfulness of historical study of the Talmud. It is because of these two problems that I turn to a field other than history to find some useful questions for those many answers which we have at hand.

The first problem is very obvious. The Talmud simply is not a history book. To treat it as if it were is to miss its point. That is to say, the Talmud and related literature were not created to record things that happened. They are legal texts, saying how people should do things (and, sometimes, do do things); or they are exegetical texts, explaining the true meaning of the revelation at Sinai, the Torah; or, occasionally, they are biographical texts, telling stories about how holy men did things. They are put together with an amazing sense of form and logic, so that bits and pieces of information are brought into relationship with one another, formed into a remarkably cogent statement, and made to add up to more than the sum of the parts. Talmudic essays in applied logic rarely are intended to tell us things which happened at some one point. They still more rarely claim to inform us about things that really happened.

For, in the end, the purpose of the Talmudic literature, as Talmudists have always known, is to lay out paradigms of holiness. The purpose is to

---

[10]I cannot overemphasize the priority: anthropology here is important *because* it serves the exegetical project of the Talmud. Whether the Talmud is important for anthropological work I do not know.

explore the meaning of being human in the image of God and of building a kingdom of priests and a holy people. For that purpose, the critical questions concern order and meaning. The central tension in the inner argument lies in the uncovering of sacred disciplines. The Talmud describes that order, that meaning, which, in society and in the conduct of everyday life, as well as in reflection and the understanding of the meaning of Israel and the world, add up to what God wants. The Talmud is about what is holy.

Now in the quest for the holy order, things of interest to historians, that is, the concrete, one-time, discrete and distinctive events of history, are obstacles. For order lies in regularity. But history is the opposite. It is what is interesting, which is what is unusual. That is what is worth reporting and reflection. So it will follow that the last thing of interest to people of the sort of mind who made the Talmud is whether or not things really happened at some point.[11] What they want to know is how things always happen and should happen. If I may project upon the creators of the Talmudic literature what I think their judgment would be, they would regard history as banal. My basis for thinking so is not solely that they wrote so little of it. It is principally that they wrote something else. So history misses the point they wish to make.

Besides the triviality of history there is a second problem, of a quite different order. It concerns how history is done today. For a long time in Western culture we have understood that merely because an ancient source says something happened does not mean it really happened that way, or even happened at all. An attitude of skepticism toward the claims of ancient documents was reborn in the Renaissance and came to fruition, in the religious sciences, in the eighteenth and nineteenth centuries. From that time onward, it was clearly understood that, in trying to figure out who did what and why, we are going to stand back from our sources and ask a range of questions not contained in them. When we come to the Talmudic sources out of which some sort of history (biography, politics, or a history of ideas) may be constructed, so that we have a sense of what came first and what happened then, we have therefore to reckon with the problem of the accuracy and reliability of our sources. That problem would confront us in the examination of any other source of the period of which the Talmud is a part. It is not an insurmountable problem. But it must be met.

Now when we combine these two problems—the first, the problem of the intent of our sources and the meaning they wish to convey, and the second, the

---

[11]I stress that this issue is simply beside the point. It is not relevant to Talmudic discourse. Therefore to accuse the rabbis of lying because they tell didactic tales and moral or theological fables, rather than writing history like Tacitus or Josephus, is to miss the point of what the rabbis of the Talmud mean. By their long arguments of analysis and applied and practical reason they propose to bring to the surface underlying unities of being. It is the most naive sort of anachronism to accuse them of being uninterested in truth because they do not record events, or record them in fanciful ways, since it denies the logicians their task but expects them to work like historians instead.

problem of the accuracy of our sources for the doing of that sort of work which people generally call historical—we realize that the historical approach to the Talmud requires a considerable measure of thoughtfulness. Studying the Talmud as history demands the exercise of restraint, probity, and critical acumen. Unfortunately, these traits, when Heaven divided them up, were not lavished upon the sorts of folk who think that the important thing to ask the Talmud is what really happened on the particular day on which Eleazar ben Azariah's hair turned white or, for that matter, on which Jonah was swallowed by the whale. Let me give just one instance of this fact—the obtuseness of those who ask the Talmud to tell us about people who really said and did the things reported about them—so that I not be thought to exaggerate.

For this purpose I choose the most current book available to me, which is Samuel Sandmel's *Judaism and Christian Beginnings* (1978: 236–51). Sandmel provides an account of what he at the outset admits are "legends" about some of the holy men of the Talmudic literature. These stories he tells specifically in the context of his description of the state of Judaism in the formative century of Christianity. It is self-evident that he would not write about these particular men if he were discussing the Judaism of the third or fourth centuries. But these are the centuries in which the stories he cites first are attested. When Sandmel chooses Hillel and Shammai, he clearly wishes the reader to believe that he is telling about people who are contemporaries of Jesus. When we listen to the fables Sandmel brings in evidence of these contemporaries, what do we hear? This is characteristic of Sandmel's wide-eyed and credulous narrative as a whole:

> Hillel loved his fellow man as deeply as he loved the Torah, and he loved all literature of wisdom as much as he loved the Torah, neglecting no field of study. He used many foreign tongues and all areas of learning in order to magnify the Torah and exalt it . . . , and so inducted his students (1978: 237).

The voice of this paragraph is the historian, that is, Sandmel, claiming to tell us about dear old Hillel (and mean old Shammai). He puts nothing in quotation-marks, and his footnotes lead the reader to unanalyzed, unquoted sources, as though he had any basis whatsoever, other than third and fourth century fables, for every single sentence in this paragraph. But that paragraph in fact is nothing but a paraphrase of materials found in rabbinic sources of a far later age than Hillel. None of the sources emerging from the late second century (a mere two hundred years after Hillel is supposed to have lived) knows about Hillel's vast knowledge. Indeed, in an age in which the sources report conflict on whether or not Jews should study Greek, and in which only a few highly placed individuals are allowed (in the Mishnaic corpus) to do so, no one thought to refer to the "fact" of Hillel's having known many languages. The reason, I think, is that no one knew it, until it was invented for purposes of story-tellers in the age in which the story was told, whatever these purposes may have been. It follows that to represent Hillel in this way (and Sandmel runs on for fifteen pages with equivalent fairy tales) is simply meretricious. If it is the Hillel of legend, then it is a legend which testifies to the state of mind of the story-tellers hundreds of years after the time of Hillel (and Jesus). The stories Sandmel tells us on the face of it record absolutely nothing about the age, let alone the person, of Hillel himself. If they do, Sandmel does not show it. In my judgment, this kind of historiography is deceiving and childish. If Hillel were not interesting to Christians, Sandmel would not tell about him.

But even if this were the true, *historical* Hillel, what difference would it make? By that I mean, what important information, relevant to profound and interesting questions confronting ancient or contemporary culture, should we have, for instance, in the knowledge that "Hillel loved his fellow man," and in similar, didactic statements? The study of stories about saints is interesting, from the perspective of the analysis of culture and society, because it opens the way to insight into the fantasy and imagination of that culture and society. We learn from the hopes which people project upon a few holy men something about the highest values of the sector of society which entertained those hopes and which assigned them to those men. Or we may learn something about the fears of that group. But the one thing which I think is dull and unilluminating is a mere repetition of stories people told because they told them. In other words, when Sandmel claims to tell us about the time of Jesus and then arrays before us perfectly routine third-, fourth-, or fifth-century rabbinical hagiography, he is engaged in a restatement, *as history*, of what in fact are statements of the cultural aspirations and values of another age. It was one in which—in the present instance—some story-tellers appear to have wanted people to appreciate Torah-learning in a broad and humanizing context (if we may take a guess as to what is at hand in these particular allegations about Hillel). But if, for the turn of the first century, we have evidence that the ideal of Torah-study was not associated with the very movement of which Hillel is supposed to have been part, but of a quite different set of people entirely, then I am inclined to think Sandmel engages in deception.[12] If Hillel had not lived in the time of Jesus, Sandmel would not be interested in him for a book on Judaism and Christian beginnings, and he would not be asking us to believe these fairy-tales as history of a particular man, who lived at a particular time, *and who therefore tells us about the age in which he lived*. This is nothing short of an intellectually despicable deceit. But it is how things are among the historians, though, I admit, Sandmel's case is somewhat extreme.

[12]See Chapter III, below. This same argument is made in my *Rabbinic Traditions about the Pharisees before 70* (1971) which, naturally, Sandmel fails to cite. I hasten to add that Sandmel is taken solely to show something acutely contemporary. I could adduce in evidence a great many others over the past two hundred years, as I indicate in *Rabbinic Traditions*, III, pp. 320ff., cited above. That discussion, too, thus far has elicited not a single contrary opinion. I think the reason is that the other side has not got much to say in its own behalf.

III

Of the two problems just now outlined, it is the first which I think more consequential. Merely because historians work unintelligently or without candor is no reason to wonder whether we have to turn elsewhere than to history to find useful questions—appropriate routes toward the center and heart of our sources. But if, as I suspect, historians do not ask the critical and generative questions, then we have to look for help to those who do. Perhaps the most difficult problem is to overcome our own circumstance, our own intellectual framework. For in thinking the Talmud important, we tend to claim it is important for our reasons.[13] We ask it to address questions interesting to us, without finding out whether these are the right questions for the Talmud too. Let me now spell this problem out.

The distance between this century and the centuries in which the Talmud was brought into being is not simple to measure. It is not merely that the rabbis and most others of their day thought the world was flat, and we know it is not. It is that the way in which they formulated the world, received and organized information about life, profoundly differs from that of our own day. We are not equipped to interpret the Talmud's world-view if we bring to it our own. We drastically misinterpret earlier rabbinic documents when we simply seek places on the established structure of issues and concerns on which to hang whatever seems relevant in the Talmudic literature.[14] Let me illustrate the matter very simply.

When the rabbis of the late first and second centuries produced a document to contain the most important things they could specify, they chose as their subjects six matters, of which, I am inclined to think, for the same purpose[15] we should have rejected at least four, and probably all six. That is, the six divisions of Mishnah are devoted to purity law, tithing, laws for the conduct of sacrifice in the Temple cult, and the way in which the sacrifices are

---

[13]Since in my years in rabbinical school and graduate school, the two paramount humanistic disciplines were history and philosophy (philology was a poor third), and since my undergraduate concentration had been in history, it was perfectly natural to me to ask historical questions of the Talmudic sources. I still think these are important questions. In the end, my hope is to contribute to the intellectual and cultural history of the period in which the Talmud came into being. But, as I stress, there are more important questions than the ones with which I (and so many others) began to work.

[14]This is the sort of thing characteristic of theologians of Talmudic Judaism, whose theological categories are imposed upon, and do not flow from, those of the Talmudic literature. I have spelled this problem out, in one concrete instance, in "Comparing Judaisms" (1978) and, in another, in my essay-review of Urbach's *The Sages* (1976). I think the only modern student of Talmudic Judaism to confront this problem and to try to overcome it is Max Kadushin (e.g., 1964). My impression is that his failure lies in his trying to do too much, on too broad a canvas; for his results are entirely unhistorical and undifferentiated. But the effort is impressive and not to be forgotten.

[15]As if we knew their purpose!

carried on at festivals—four areas of reality which, I suspect, would not have found a high place on a list of our own most fundamental concerns. The other two divisions, which deal with the transfer of women from one man to another and with matters of civil law—including the organization of the government, civil claims, torts, and damages, real estate and the like—complete the list. When we attempt to interpret the sort of world the rabbis of the Mishnah propose to create, therefore, at the very outset we realize that that world in no way conforms, in its most profound and definitive categories of organization, to our own. That is why we need help in interpreting what it is that they propose to do, and why they choose to do it that way and not in some other.

It follows that the critical work of making sense and use of the Talmudic literature is to learn how to hear what the Talmud wishes to say in its own setting and to the people addressed by those who made it up. For that purpose it is altogether too easy to bring our questions and take for granted that, when the rabbis of the Talmud seem to say something relevant to our questions, they therefore propose to speak to us. Anachronism takes many forms. The most dangerous comes when an ancient text seems accessible and clear.[16] For the Talmud is separated from us by the whole of Western history, philosophy, and science. Its wise sayings, its law, and its theology may lie in the background of the law and lore of contemporary Judaism. But they have been mediated to us by many centuries of exegesis, not to mention experience. They come to us now in the form which theologians and scholars have imposed upon them. It follows that the critical problem is to recognize the distance between us and the Talmud.

The second problem, closely related to the first, is the work of allowing strange people to speak in a strange language about things quite alien to us, and yet of learning how to hear what they are saying. That is, we have to learn how to understand them in their language and in their terms. Once we recognize that they are fundamentally different from us, we have also to lay claim to them, or, rather, acknowledge their claim upon us. The document is there. It is interesting. It is important and fundamental to the definition of Judaism. When we turn to the humanities and social sciences of our own day with the question, Who can teach us how to listen to strange people, speaking in a foreign language, about alien things? I am inclined to look for scholars who do just that all the time. I mean those who travel to far-off places and live with alien tribes, who learn the difficult languages of preliterate peoples, and who figure out how to interpret the facts of their everyday life so as to gain a picture of that alien world and a statement of its reality worth bringing back to

---

[16]I think theologians and historians of Talmudic theology most consistently commit the sin of anachronism. In this regard the list of examples covers the bibliography of available monographs and books. I cannot think of a single theologian who begins with consideration of the character of the sources and what he proposes to say about them. Everyone works as if "we all know" what we are doing.

us. Anthropologists study the character of humanity in all its richness and diversity. What impresses me in their work is their ability to undertake the work of interpretation of what is thrice-alien—strange people, speaking a strange language, about things we-know-not-what—and to translate into knowledge accessible to us the character and the conscience of an alien world-view.

When I turn to anthropology for assistance in formulating questions and in gaining perspectives on the Talmudic corpus, what I am seeking is very simple: fresh perspectives, fructifying questions.[17] To illustrate what I have found, let me now take up three specific problems solved for me by anthropologists, all three problems directly related to the study of early Rabbinic Judaism and its classic texts.[18]

IV

First, the most difficult task we have is to learn how to decipher the glyphs of an alien culture. For example, in the case of the Talmud, if we have a story about how a holy rabbi studied many languages and mastered all knowledge in his pursuit of Torah—as we do about Hillel—what is it that the story-teller is trying to express? And what communion of language and forms, perceptions and values makes it possible for him to speak to his listener in just this way about just this subject? In other words, once we concur that we want to create more than a paraphrase of the sources, together (in the case of the historians of conscience) with a critical perspective upon them, what is it that we wish to discover? We need to learn how to read these stories and so how to become sensitive to their important traits and turnings, both those of language and those of substance. Literary critics make their living on their sharpened mind and eye; for the purposes of ancient Jewish and Israelite sources, so, too, do people who learn to think like anthropologists.

Let me cite, as a stunning example, the perspective of the great structuralist-anthropologist, Edmund Leach, upon the story of the succession of Solomon to the throne of Israel. This is how he introduces his work:

> My purpose is to demonstrate that the Biblical story of the succession of Solomon to the throne of Israel is a myth which 'mediates' a major contradiction. The Old Testament as a whole asserts that the Jewish political title to the land of Palestine is a direct gift from God

---

[17]It is far from the truth that historians do not bring fresh perspectives on ancient or medieval sources. I point for contrary evidence to the splendid work of Peter Brown (1971), for instance. There is a certain insightfulness in Brown's work which some may call *ad hoc* and impressionistic, but I think it is genius.

[18]Once more I emphasize that I do not pretend to be a master of contemporary anthropological thought or research. I point only to a few of the writings of a handful of people who have given much to me and made me see things in a fresh way. I have no news to bring to anthropologists and little enough to Talmudists.

to the descendants of Israel (Jacob). This provides the fundamental basis for Jewish endogamy—the Jews should be a people of pure blood and pure religion, living in isolation in their Promised Land. But interwoven with this theological dogma there is less idealized form of tradition which represents the population of ancient Palestine as a mixture of many peoples over whom the Jews have asserted political dominance by right of conquest. The Jews and their 'foreign' neighbors intermarry freely. The synthesis achieved by the story of Solomon is such that by a kind of dramatic trick the reader is persuaded that the second of these descriptions, which is morally bad, exemplifies the first description, which is morally good (1970: 248–92).

This brief statement of purpose tells us that Leach will show us, in stories we have read many times, meanings and dimensions we did not know were there. When we follow his analysis, we realize that we have been blind. For he shows us what it means to see.

V

Second, the most difficult question is to find out what are the right questions. Precisely what we want to know when we open the pages of the Talmud is not simple to define. To be sure, these documents have been studied for centuries by people who knew just what they wanted to find out. The questions shaped and brought to the Talmud by the rabbinical scholars of earlier ages made sense both for the Talmud and for the social and intellectual circumstances of the scholars of the Talmud.[19] But, as I have made clear, the information and insight we seek, the problems we wish to solve, and the questions we find urgent are not those which flow, directly and without mediation, from the pages of the Talmud itself. It is one thing to point out that history provides us with the wrong questions. It is quite another to lay forth right ones.

[19]The *yeshivot* in Europe trained masters of the Talmud able to exemplify and apply its teachings (in that order of importance) and who could serve as judges and clerks for the Jewish community. That is why the Talmud was studied by them as it was; for instance, it explains the tractates they chose. Their larger cultural tasks—to perpetuate the relevance of the text through continuing and extraordinarily brilliant work of exegesis, and application—were wholly successful. So what they did was congruent to their social and cultural context. Indeed, in large measure, because of their success, they imparted to that context its distinctive social and cultural traits. (If universities in the Western countries should enjoy an equivalent success, then the populations of those countries would enjoy the power to think clearly and analyze an issue critically.) Precisely why *yeshivot* and Jewish seminaries in the USA and Canada study the texts which they do and ignore the texts they ignore (out of the same corpus of Torah-writings) is not so clear. My impression is that the curriculum, once crucial to the formation of Jewish culture, has not changed, so that the things the students might know in order to have something worth sharing with their own age are not given to them. The result among *yeshiva*-alumni I have known is rather sad, people who cannot, for example, operate in a world in which statements are verified by reference to empirical testing, not by what sounds right or seems reasonable (let alone what some holy rabbi tells them). In the end they tend to make things up as they go along and call it Torah-true.

For this purpose, I am much in debt to theorists of social anthropology for showing, in the study of other artifacts and documents of culture, the sort of thing one might do, too, with this one. I refer, for important example, to the conception of religion as a cultural system. This conception proposes that we view a document of a culture as an expression of that culture's world-view and way of life.

In this context, for example, there is much to be learned from the statement of Clifford Geertz (1973: 87–88):

> . . . sacred symbols function to synthesize a people's ethics—the tone, character, and quality of their life, its moral and aesthetic style and mood—and their world-view—the picture they have of the way things in sheer actuality are, their most comprehensive ideas of order. In religious belief and practice a group's ethos is rendered intellectually reasonable by being shown to represent a way of life ideally adapted to the actual state of affairs the world-view describes, while the world-view is rendered emotionally convincing by being presented as an image of an actual state of affairs peculiarly well-arranged to accomodate such a way of life.[20]

What Geertz's perspective contributes is the notion that the world-view and way of life laid forth by a religion together constitute a system, in which the character of the way of life and the conceptions of the world mutually illuminate and explain one another. The system as a whole serves to organize and make sense of all experience of being. So far as life is to be orderly and trustworthy, it is a system which makes it so.

Now it would be difficult to formulate a more suitable question to so vast, encompassing, relentlessly cogent a document as the Talmudic literature than this simple one: How does this document inform us about the ethos of the community it proposes to govern? For this document does present a picture of the proper conduct of life, expressive of a cogent ethos. In this immense mass of ideas, stories, laws, criticism, logic, and critical thought, we are taught by Geertz to look for the center of it all, and to uncover the principal conceptions which unite the mass of detail. Geertz for his part emphasizes that there is nothing new in his perspective: "The notion that religion tunes human actions to an envisaged cosmic order and projects images of cosmic order onto the place of human experience is hardly novel." But, he notes, it is hardly investigated either.[21] And, it goes without saying, all those who have spoken

---

[20]I may point out that this is not the first point in my work at which I have drawn upon Geertz's thoughtful proposals. His "Religion as a Cultural System" (1973) originally appeared in Michael Banton, ed., (1966). It made an immediate impact upon my approach to the history of the Jews in Babylonia, which I made explicit in the preface to the concluding volume of *A History of the Jews in Babylonia* V. *Later Sasanian Times* (1970: xvii). In fact, it was from Vol. III onward that the shape of the work changed in some part in response to what I was able to learn from Geertz.

[21]I think the most difficult thing to investigate in the Talmudic ethos is also the most obvious: the character of the literature, its logic and the sorts of arguments and analyses it presents. I have tried to present such an analysis in my *Invitation to the Talmud. A Teaching Book* (1973, esp. 223–46), and in Chapter VII, below. But these papers, I should claim, only scratch the surface.

of the Talmud as an ocean share a single failing: none has offered us much by way of a chart.[22]

VI

While the contributions of Leach and Geertz serve to make us aware of the potentialities of our sources, we may, third, point to yet another anthropologist, who has realized a measure of these potentialities. Some of the work of Mary Douglas already has made a considerable impact upon the analysis of students of the Hebrew Scriptures and earlier strata of the rabbinical literature. *Purity and Danger* (1966),[23] for example, opened new perspectives on the issues and meaning of the laws of Leviticus. Her contribution is both to the theory and the substantive analysis of a society's culture. Her stress is upon the conception that, "each tribe actively construes its particular universe in the course of an internal dialogue about law and order" (1975: 5). So, she says,

> Particular meanings are parts of larger ones, and these refer ultimately to a whole, in which all the available knowledge is related. But the largest whole into which all minor meanings fit can only be a metaphysical scheme. This itself has to be traced to the particular way of life which is realized within it and which generates the meanings. In the end, all meanings are social meanings (1975: 8).

These judgments, which I think form a common heritage of social analysis for the work before us, present a challenge. It is how not only to decipher the facts of a given culture, but also to state the large issues of that culture precisely as they are expressed through minute details of the way of life of those who stand within its frame. Mrs. Douglas has done a fair part of the work. So she has given an example of how the work must be done. This is in her work on the Jewish dietary code, especially as it is laid out in the book of Leviticus. She introduces one of the most suggestive examples of her work in the following way:

> If language is a code, where is the precoded message? The question is phrased to expect the answer: nowhere . . . . but try it this way: if food is a code, where is the precoded message? Here, on the anthropologists' home ground, we are able to improve the posing of the question. A code affords a general set of possibilities for sending particular messages. If food is treated as a code, the messages it encodes will be found in the pattern of social

---

[22]Though, as I said, some have tried, Kadushin (1964) being the one worth noting. Among *yeshiva*-trained Talmudists none even tried.

[23]I point out, also, that Mrs. Douglas was kind enough to read in manuscript and to write an important critique of my *Idea of Purity in Ancient Judaism* (1973: 137–42). This critique was my first exposure to the interesting perspective of anthropologists. Further discussions with her and (of a quite different order) with Melford Spiro have proved stimulating.

relations being expressed. The message is about different degrees of hierarchy, inclusion and exclusion, boundaries and transactions across the boundaries (1975: 249).

What should be striking is that she treats as suggestive and important those very rituals in which the Talmud and the form of Judaism created and expressed in it abound.

VII

While I have pointed to three specific contributions of anthropologists, I do not ignore a more general contribution of anthropology as a mode of thought. When we speak to anthropologists about the details of the Talmud's laws, not merely about its intellectual results, we do not have to feel embarrassed or apologetic as we do when we talk to historians and theologians. Let me spell this out.

A critical problem facing us when we come to the Talmud is that it simply does not talk about things about which people generally want to know these days. The reason that historians have asked their range of questions is in part a counsel of desperation: let us at least learn in the Talmud about things we might want to know—wars, emperors, or institutions of politics. The theologians and historians of theology similarly bring a set of contemporary questions—for instance, about the Talmud's beliefs about sin and atonement, suffering and penitence, divine power and divine grace, life after death and the world to come—because people in general want to know about these things. Both kinds of scholars do not misrepresent the results when they claim that the Talmud contains information relevant to their questions.

But neither the historian nor the theologian and historian of theology would ask us to believe that the Talmud principally is about the questions they bring to its pages. As I said, it is not divided into tractates about kings and emperors nor about rabbis and patriarchs, for that matter. It also is not organized around the great issues of theology. There is no tractate on the unity of God or on prayer, on life after death or on sin and atonement. Nor does the Talmud speak openly and unambiguously on a single religious and theological question as it is phrased in contemporary discourse. So the two kinds of work done in the past, theology, including history of theology, and history, have asked the Talmud to speak in a language essentially alien to its organizing and generative categories of thought.

What does the Talmud tell us? To take three of its largest tractates: it speaks about who may and may not marry whom, in Yebamot; about what may and may not be eaten, in Hullin; and about the resolution of civil conflict, courts of law, property claims, and similar practical matters, in Baba Qamma, Baba Mesia, and Baba Batra. If, to go on, we speak about yet another vast tractate of Mishnah, we address the issues of Kelim, thirty chapters, longest of them all, which analyze the questions of what sorts of objects are subject to cultic uncleanness, and of what sorts of objects are not subject to cultic uncleanness. What follows is an amazing agendum of information, answers to questions no one would appear in our day to wish to ask: marriage, food, property-relations, cultic cleanness.

Yet it is not entirely true that no one wants to know about these things. When an anthropologist goes out to study a social group, these are the very questions to be asked. As Mary Douglas says, "If food is a code, where is the precoded message? Here, *on the anthropologist's home ground*, we are able to improve the posing of the question" (1975: 249). The stress is in her words, *on the anthropologist's home ground*, because when we want to tell scholars of religious studies and theology about the things important to the Talmud, their interest perishes at the frontiers (however wide) of their courtesy. How I slaughter an animal is not deemed a question relevant to religion among philosophers of religion and theologians. But it is a critical question to an anthropologist of religion. The difference lies in the understanding of the task. The anthropologist wants to understand the whole of a social and cultural system, the group's way of living and its world view. As Geertz points out, the anthropologist seeks to tell us important things about how these interrelate and define a coherent system. Douglas points out that we uncover a cogent set of conceptions and social events, which, when uncoded, tells us something important about the human imagination. Viewed in this way, things which seem trivial are transformed into the very key to the structure of a culture and the order of a society.

Matters are not to be left in such general terms. When we speak about the human imagination, we are addressing a particular issue. It is how people cope with the dissonances and the recurrent and critical tensions of their collective existence. What lies at the heart of a group's life, and what defines both its problem and its power? In the case of ancient Israel, it is the simple fact that a small people lives upon a land which it took from others and which others wish to take from it. So what is critical is the drawing and maintaining of high walls, boundaries to protect the territory—both land and people— from encroachment. As Douglas phrases matters:

> Israel is the boundary that all the other boundaries celebrate and that gives them their historic load of meaning.

In the very next sentence, she says:

> Remembering this, the orthodox meal is not difficult to interpret as a poem (1975: 272–73).

It is this mode of thought which I think makes us see the pages of the Talmud in a way in which we have never seen them before. It makes us realize we have never seen what has been there all the time. And it gives us confidence that others too should see what we do. Douglas concludes:

It would seem that whenever a people are aware of encroachment and danger, dietary rules controlling what goes into the body would serve as a vivid analogy of the corpus of their cultural categories at risk. . . . the ordered system which is a meal represents all the ordered systems associated with it (1975: 272–73).

This is the sort of thesis which, I think, we are able to explore and analyze by reference to the documents of early Rabbinic-Judaism. For this purpose they are perhaps more compelling than some more theological ones.

VIII

Yet a second more general contribution accruing from the anthropological mode of thought is to be specified. We have to learn not only how to describe and make sense of our data. Once we have discerned the system which they evidently mean to create, we have the task before us of comparing that system to other systems, yielded both by Judaism in its various stages and by other religious and cultural contexts entirely. For a system described but not juxtaposed to, and compared with, other systems has not yet been interpreted. Until we realize what people might have done, we are not going to grasp the things they did do. We shall be unable to interpret the choices people have made until we contemplate the choices they rejected. And, as is clear, it is the work of comparison which makes that perspective possible. But how do we compare systems?[24]

In fact, whenever we try to make sense for ourselves of what alien people do, we are engaged in a work of comparison, that is, an experiment of analogies. For we are trying to make sense specifically by comparing what we know and do to what the other, the alien culture before us, seems to have known and to have done. For this purpose we seek analogies from the known to the unfamiliar. But the work of comparison is exceedingly delicate, for by using ourselves as one half of the equation for a comparative exercise, we may turn out to impose ourselves as the measure of all things.[25] That, of course, is something anthropology has taught us not to do which is another reason for its critical importance in today's labor. In fact, matters prove more insightful when we reverse the equation and regard the other as the measure and ourselves as the problem. That is, we have to recognize that these are the choices those people made which help us to understand that we, too, make choices. These are the potentialities discerned and explored by those folk who

---

[24]Much that is called 'comparative religions' compares nothing and is an exercise in the juxtaposition of incomparables. But it does not have to be that way.

[25]It seems to me any pretense that we stand outside of the equation of comparison is misleading. When we teach a foreign language to our students, it is, in significant measure, by trying to locate analogies to facilitate memorization and, at the outset, to relate the unknown to the known. That is so in any sort of interpretive enterprise, I think; and it is best to admit it at the outset. But it is specified not as what must be, only as what is anachronistic and must be avoided.

have made this document and this system. Now we may measure ourselves by whether, for our part, we too recognize potentialities beyond our actuality, whether we see that we also have the capacity to be other than what we are. These are critical questions of culture and sensibility.

That is the point at which the Talmudic literature proves especially interesting to students of culture, on the broad stage of the humanities, and to scholars of contemporary Judaism, on the narrow one of theology of Judaism. It provides us with the richest documentation of a system of Judaism among all the Judaic systems of antiquity, from the formation of the biblical literature to the Islamic conquest. When we consider that the Talmud also is formative for the systems of Judaism of later times, we realize how promising it is as a fulcrum for the lifting of that unformed mass of the ages: the making sense of the Judaic tradition in all its diversity, complexity, and subtlety. Clearly, I deem anthropology to be a useful instrument. Let me conclude the argument by specifying that thing I wish to make with diverse tools, one (but only one) of which is the anthropological instrument.

IX

What I seek is insight into the world of ancient Judaism.[26] This is in part so that contemporary Jews may have a clearer picture of themselves but in still larger measure so that contemporary humanists may gain a more ample account of a tiny part of the potentialities of humanity: that part expressed within the Judaic tradition in its rabbinical formulation. We have to find out what others have made of that system, what it is that that Talmudic system contains within itself, so as to find yet another mode for the measure of humankind. The human potentialities and available choices within one ecological frame of humanity, the ancient Jewish one, are defined and explored by the Talmudic rabbis. (As it happens, we know a great deal about the results.) This same question—the possibilities contained within the culture of ancient Judaism—is to be addressed to the diverse formations and structures of Judaism, at other times in its history besides that of late antiquity. But we have to learn how to do the work in some one place, and only then shall we have a call to attempt it elsewhere. What we must do is first describe, then interpret. But what do we wish to describe?

I am inclined to think the task is to encompass everything deemed important by some one group, to include within, and to exclude from, its holy book, its definitive text: a system and its exclusions, its stance in a taxonomy of systems. For, on the surface, what they put in they think essential, and what they omit they do not think important. If that is self-evident, then the affirmative choices—which are not the only ones about which we know—are the ones requiring description and then interpretation. But what standpoint

[26]In a moment I make this banal statement much more specific.

will permit us to fasten onto the whole and where is the fulcrum on which to place our lever? For, given the size of the evidence, the work of description may leave us with an immense, and essentially pointless, task of repetition: saying in our own words what the sources say, perfectly clearly, in theirs. That is not an interesting task, even though, in some measure, it must be done.

So when I say that a large part of work is to describe the world-view of the rabbis of the Mishnah and the Talmud, at best I acquire a license to hunt for insight. But I have to come closer to the definition of the task. What brings us closer, indeed, what defines the work as well as I am able, is the conception to which I have already alluded, the idea of a system, that is, a whole set of interrelated concerns and conceptions which, all together, both express a world-view and define a way of living for a particular group of people. (That word, system, yields a useful adjective, systemic: the traits pertinent to a system.) The work I do is to describe the system of the rabbis of the Mishnah and the Talmud. That is, I propose to bring to the surface the integrated conception of the world and of the way in which the people should live in that world. All in all, that system both defines and forms reality for Jews responsive to the rabbis.

Now all worth knowing about the rabbis and the Jews around them is not contained within their system as they lay it out. There is, after all, the hard fact that the Jews did not have power fully to shape the world within which they lived out their lives and formed their social group. No one else did either. There were, indeed, certain persistent and immutable facts which form the natural environment for their system. These facts do not change but do have to be confronted. There are, for instance, the twin-facts of Jewish powerlessness and minority-status. Any system produced by Judaism for nearly the whole of its history will have to take account of the fact that the group is of no account in the world. Another definitive fact is the antecedent heritage of Scripture and associated tradition, which define for the Jews a considerably more important role in the supernatural world than the natural world obviously affords them. These two facts, the Jews' numerical insignificance and political unimportance and the Jews' inherited pretentions and fantasies about their own centrality in the history and destiny of the human race, created (and still create) a certain dissonance between a given Jewish world-view, on the one side, and the world to be viewed by the Jews, on the other. And so is the case for the rabbis of the Misnah and the Talmud— and that seems to me a critical problem to be confronted in the Talmudic system.[27]

But, as I have stressed, we cannot take for granted that what we think should define the central tension of a given system in fact is what concerns the people who did create and express that system. If we have no way of showing

---

[27]The conception of an 'ecology of religion' is spelled out as best I can in the third edition of my *Way of Torah: An Introduction to Judaism* (in press for 1979).

when our surmise may be wrong, then we also have no basis on which to verify our thesis as to the core and meaning of our system.[28] The result can be at best good guesses.[29] A mode for interpreting the issues of a system has therefore to be proposed.

One route to the interpretation of a system is to specify the sorts of issues it chooses to regard as problems, the matters it chooses for its close and continuing exegesis. When we know the things about which people worry, we have some insight into the way in which they see the world. So we ask, when we approach the Talmud, about its critical tensions, the recurring issues which occupy its great minds. It is out of concern with this range of issues, and not some other, that the Talmud defines its principal areas for discussion. Here is the point at which the great exercises of law and theology will be generated—here and not somewhere else. This is a way in which we specify the choices people have made, the selections a system has effected. When we know what people have chosen, we also may speculate about the things they have rejected, the issues they regard as uninteresting or as closed. We then may describe the realm of thought and everyday life which they do not deem subject to tension and speculation. It is on these two sides—the things people conceive to be dangerous and important, the things they set into the background as unimportant and uninteresting—which provide us with a key to the culture of a community or, as I prefer to put it, to the system constructed and expressed by a given group of people.

X

I have outlined what must appear to be a formidable and serious agendum for scholarly work. Yet the truth is otherwise.

The work of learning is not solemn but is like the play of children. It is an exercise in taking things apart and putting them back together again. It is a game of seeing how things work. If it is not this, then it is a mere description of how things are; and that is not engaging to active minds. If I do not have important questions to address to the facts in my hands—the documents which I study—then I am not apt to discover anything interesting. I am unlikely to make of the documents more than a statement of what already is in them. But the Talmud and its cognate literature have exercised a formidable and continuing power over the minds of the Jewish people for nearly twenty centuries. They contain the artifacts of a foreign culture, exhibiting distinctive traits and capable of sustaining quite searching scrutiny by scholars of culture.

---

[28]Furthermore: *if we cannot show it, we do not know it.* I am tired of the appeal to "it seems reasonable to suppose," and "this has the ring of truth," which fills the pages of Talmudic history. It is just as weighty an argument as is the common criticism, "not persuasive."

[29]That is, pure subjectivity and impressionism. These can be avoided.

Therefore, merely saying what is in the Talmud and its cognate literature is not sufficient.

The central issues, those questions which generate insight worth sharing and understanding worth having, therefore, are to be defined in these terms: What does the Talmud define as its central problems? How does the Talmud perceive the critical tensions of its world? We want to describe the solutions, resolutions, and remissions it poses for these tensions. We propose to unpack and then to put back together again the world-view of the document. When we can explain how this system fits together and works, then we shall know something worth knowing.[30]

[30]I do not mean to suggest there are no problems in anthropological approaches and methods. For one thing, we address ourselves to historical data and seek to accomplish the interpretation of a world known through its literary remnants. But anthropologists tend to do a better job on living societies than on books. Leach and Douglas are exceptional, I think. Further, there is a range of questions I have not confronted here, specifically, about whether, when we speak of systems, we mean merely philosophico-religious ones (that is, intellectual constructs) or we refer to social-cultural groups ("real people"). The Talmudic literature begins in Mishnah, which is an essentially theoretical account of a non-existent world (see Chapters V and VI, below); but it ends in the Jewish community formed under rabbinical authority and governed by the Talmud. So there are more ambiguities than I have suggested—many more.

CHAPTER II

History and the Study of Talmudic Literature

I

Enduring works of the intellect last because they speak to minds beyond limits of space and boundaries of time. The mark of greatness is the vision and will to transcend all frontiers and address an age one can scarcely imagine. But what is heard beyond the bounds of space and time is not always, and perhaps not ever, what the original mind meant to say. Like a diamond, which reveals a different light to the eyes of each of those who see it, these lasting works of mind, whether in art or music, philosophy or literature, religion or science, enjoy a diverse reception. People hear what they are capable of perceiving. One generation reads Shakespeare in light of one set of issues and another, in light of a different set. The history of the reception of the thought of Socrates is shaped by Plato and of that of Plato, by Aristotle. As Harold Cherniss points out, Aristotle's criticism of pre-Socratic philosophy, of Plato, and of the Academy is complicated by Aristotle. For he attributes to Plato a theory which is not in Plato's writings (1935, 1944, 1945). On this basis, Cherniss (1935: ix) accepts the possibility that "Aristotle was capable of setting down something other than the objective truth when he had occasion to write about his predecessors."[1] The discovery of that possibility, however, had to await the coming of Harold Cherniss, twenty-three hundred years after Aristotle. The reason for the delay explains much about the consciousness and culture of the West in the intervening centuries. So it is self-evident that the great

---

[1]Compare my *History of the Mishnaic Law of Purities* (1977, XVII: 202–220) on the Houses of Shammai and Hillel as represented by second-century authorities such as Meir, Judah, Simeon, and their contemporaries. I am able to show that attributed to the ancient Houses are positions on issues moot after Bar Kokhba's War, and that the opinions assigned to the Houses by the second century authorities are suspiciously similar to those held by the second century masters. The second century figures play an active part in the formation of the "tradition" of the Houses. Since the same authorities give in their own names what they also state in the names of the Houses, there can be little doubt that the attributions to the Houses are, in fact, invented and fictitious. This is especially likely because the authorities of the period after 70, which intervenes between the Houses and their epigones, are remarkably ignorant of the principles espoused by the Houses and even of the basic issues debated by them. A gap of over a century in a continuous tradition is curious.

intellectual accomplishments of humanity, the ones which endure for centuries, not only transcend the limits of time and space,[2] they also overcome the barriers of their own composition: the mind of the maker, the world to which the maker spoke and which, to begin with, received the work and accepted (or rejected) it. This is so for the diverse collections of the Hebrew Scriptures, for Plato, for the traditions of Chinese and Indian philosophy and Christian theology, and for that document distinctive to the inner life of the Jewish people for nearly two millenia, the Talmud.

A history of the study of the Talmud, from the Talmud's formative period in the first and second centuries of the common era down to the present day would provide insight into the intellectual history of Judaism, of which the Talmud is the principal component. It also would give us important facts about the sociology of the Jewish people, the character of its religious life in diverse dimensions, the nature of the educational and cultural institutions which express and shape that life. The reason is that the conditions of society define the things society wants to know. The shape of the program of study of the inherited monuments of culture is governed by the people who propose to

[2]See S. C. Humphreys (1975). She states:

> One of the factors influencing the intellectual to adopt a transcendental perspective appears to be the need to make his work comprehensible to an audience widely extended in space and continuing indefinitely into posterity. How far is our own appreciative response to these works—and especially to the rationalism of the Greek philosophers— due to the authors' deliberate intention of transcending limitations of social structure and temporal horizons? How far is this successful transcendence due to content and how far to form, to the structuring of the communication in such a way that it contains within itself enough information to make it immediately comprehensible? Is this a common quality of rational discourse and of "classic" works of art?

What I believe Miss Humphreys wishes to emphasize is that when we respond to a document such as Mishnah and Talmud and enter into its world, we do so because the people who make it as it is so framed it that we *should* do so. Our response to the aesthetics of Mishnah in particular—our recognition of how it is that matters are stated to facilitate memorization and, thereby, shape processes of cognition—is a tribute to the work of Rabbi and his colleagues. By stating Mishnah in terms essentially neutral to their own society (though, to be sure, drawing upon the data of their context), Rabbi sees to it that his part of the Torah will pass easily to other places and other ages. Through patterned language, Mishnah transcends the limitations of its own society and time. And, I have argued, a great part of this extraordinary creative achievement is in form, in the "structuring of the communication in such a way that it contains within itself enough information to make it immediately comprehensible." And yet, there is a second side to the matter. What makes Mishnah useful not only is its comprehensibility, but also its *incomprehensibility*. It is a deeply ambiguous document, full of problems of interpretation. Easy as it is to memorize, it is exceptionally difficult to understand. Mishnah not merely permits exegesis; it demands it. We can memorize a pericope of Mishnah in ten minutes. But it takes a lifetime to draw forth and understand the meaning. Mishnah contains within itself, and even in its language, a powerful statement of the structure of reality. But that statement is so subtle that for eighteen hundred years, disciples of Mishnah, the Talmuds, and the consequent literature of exegesis, have worked on spelling out the meaning (not solely the concrete application) of that statement. Compare my "Transcendence and Worship through Learning: The Religious World-View of Mishnah" (1978).

carry out that program and the interests of the people who are supposed to contemplate the results of the work.

To take one very current example, Christopher Lasch explains the reason that The University of Chicago became the great center for sociology which it did—the place in which, for a long time, the issues of sociology were defined—and also the reason that sociology done in Chicago took up the very questions it asked:

> The presence in other departments of the university of such important thinkers as Veblen, John Dewey, and Mead; the enterprise of Jane Addams . . . and other settlement workers in accumulating empirical data on urban life and insights into its pathology; the many-sided intellectual awakening known as the "Chicago renaissance"; the existence of the city itself as a laboratory of industrial conditions—all these made Chicago almost inevitably a center of sociological studies. Nor is it surprising that those studies addressed themselves especially to the sociology of urban life. From the perspective of Chicago, which had grown from a frontier settlement to a huge industrial metropolis in less than a century, completely rebuilding itself after the fire of 1871, rapid urbanization loomed as the central fact of modern society. . . . Accordingly, the city should be studied as a total environment that gave rise to a distinctive way of life (1977: 33–34).

I quote Lasch at length because he provides a model for two propositions. First of all, he shows that the conditions of society generate the data to be examined by the intellectuals. Second, he indicates that the character of the studies carried out by them is defined by those same conditions. Sociology took up the questions of society and family, in the place in which the work was done, by the people by whom the work was done, specifically because the context defined both what was to be studied and who should do the work.

If then we ask how the Talmud was studied, we transform a question of intellectual method, superficially a formal question about traits of logic and inquiry. We find ourselves asking about the world in which Jews lived, the values they brought to the Talmud, and the reasons that moved them to open its pages to begin with. So, as I said, when we contemplate the study of the Talmud, we find ourselves examining the history of the inner life of the Jewish people and, self-evidently, the intellectual history of Judaism.

I argue this proposition with some care so that my basic perspective on historical interest in the Talmud will be clearly defined. The questions I wish to answer are these:

First, why was the Talmud studied as a historical document?

Second, what was the intellectual program of the people who originally decided that the Talmud should be studied as a historical document?

Third, why is the Talmud studied today, in a very considerable measure, as a historical document?

Fourth, what is the intellectual program of the people who today do the work?

Persuasive answers to these four questions will give us a clearer notion of the work we do and a firmer definition of the work to be done in the future. So when we speak of the Talmud as history, we address ourselves to questions of acutely contemporary character and cultural consequence.

II

The beginnings of the study of the Talmud as history, like the beginnings of nearly all of the methods and ideas of the "Jewish humanities," lie in nineteenth-century Germany. Ismar Schorsch (1975: 48) points out that the definition of the modern debate about the Talmud, in mostly historical terms, was supplied in a single decade, the 1850s. Four books were published in less than ten years, which defined the way the work would be done for the next one hundred years. These are Leopold Zunz's publication of Nahman Krochmal's *Moreh nebukhe hazzeman* ("guide to the perplexed of our times"), 1851; Heinrich Graetz's fourth volume of his *History of the Jews from the Earliest Times to the Present*, which is devoted to the Talmudic period, 1853; Geiger's *Urschrift und Uebersetzungen der Bibel*, 1857; and Zechariah Frankel's *Darkhe hammishnah* ("ways of the Mishnah"), 1859.[3] These four volumes place the Talmud into the very center of the debates on the reform of Judaism and address the critical issues of the debate: the divine mandate of Rabbinic Judaism (Schorsch, 1975: 48).[4]

The Talmudic period defines the arena of the struggle over reform because the Reform theologians made it so. They had proposed that by exposing the historical origins of the Talmud and of the Rabbinic form of Judaism, they might "undermine the divine mandate of rabbinic Judaism" (Schorsch, 1975: 48). As Schorsch points out, Geiger's work indicates the highwater mark of the attack on Rabbinic Judaism through historical study.[5] Krochmal, Graetz, and Frankel present a sympathetic and favorable assessment. In so doing, however, they adopt the fundamental supposition of the Reformers: the Talmud can and should be studied historically. They

---

[3]I pay little attention to Geiger in what follows because his work had little influence on the course of Talmudic historiography. The main lines of research followed from Frankel, for biography, and Graetz, for narrative history.

[4]*Ibid.* Historical study also served as an instrument in the attack on Talmudic tradition and defense of Reform Judaism in Poland in the same period. See Biderman (1976: 19–44).

[5]*Ibid.* On this point, Professor Jakob Petuchowski provides the following comment:

I suppose that, as seen from Ponevezh or Slobodka, Geiger's work might be seen in that light. But, within the setting of 19th-century inner-Jewish polemics in the West, I get quite a different picture. Unlike some of his contemporaries (e.g., Holdheim, the British Reformers, the Frankfort Friends of Reform, etc.), Geiger does *not* attack Rabbinic Judaism *per se*. He does attack the modern, self-styled "guardians" of Rabbinic Judaism—precisely because they have closed their eyes to the dynamics inherent within that system. As for Rabbinic Judaism in its own period (period #2 in Geiger's periodization of Jewish historical development), Geiger is full of praise for it; and, in fact, he sees in the dynamics of Rabbinic Judaism the legitimization of his own Reform attempts.

concede that there *is* a history to the period in which the Talmud comes forth. The Talmud itself is a work of men in history.

The method of Graetz and of Frankel, therefore, is essentially biographical. One third of Frankel's book is devoted to biographies of personalities mentioned in the Talmud. What he does is collect the laws given in the name of a particular man and states that he appears in such and such tractates, and the like. His card file is neatly divided but yields no more than what is filed in it (Gereboff, 1973: 59–75).[6] What is important is not what he proves but, as I said, what he implicitly concedes which is that the Mishnah and the rest of the rabbinic literature are the work of men. Graetz likewise stresses the matter of great men. As Schorsch characterizes his work:

> Graetz tried valiantly to portray the disembodied rabbis of the Mishnah and Talmud as vibrant men, each with his own style and philosophy and personal frailties, who collectively resisted the disintegrating forces of their age. . . . In the wake of national disaster, creative leadership forged new religious institutions to preserve and invigorate the bonds of unity. . . . He defended talmudic literature as a great national achievement of untold importance to the subsequent survival of the Jews (1975: 48).

Now why, in the doing of history, the biographies of great men should be deemed the principal work is clear: the historians of the day in general wrote biographies. History was collective biography. Their conception of what made things happen is tied to the theory of the great man in history, the great man as the maker of history. The associated theory was of history as the story of politics, thus of what great men did. Whether or not the Jewish historians of the "Talmudic period" do well, moderately well, or poorly, the sort of history people did in general I cannot say. The important point is that the beginnings of the approach to the Talmud as history meant biography.

What was unimportant to Graetz, Frankel, and Krochmal, was a range of questions of historical method already thoroughly defined and worked out elsewhere. So the work of Talmudic history was methodologically obsolete by the standards of its own age. These questions had to do with the reliability of

---

[6]Gereboff concludes as follows:

For Frankel Rabbi was the organizer and the law-giver. He compiled the Mishnah in its final form, employing a systematic approach. The Mishnah was a work of art; everything was "necessary" and in its place. All these claims are merely asserted. Frankel gives citations from Mishnaic and Amoraic sources, never demonstrating *how* the citations prove his contentions. Frankel applied his theory of positive-historical Judaism, which depicted Jewish Life as a process combining the lasting values from the past with human intelligence in order to face the present and the future, to the formation of the Mishnah. The Mishnah was the product of human intelligence and divine inspiration. Using their intelligence, later generations took what they had received from the past and added to it. Nothing was ever removed. Frankel's work has little lasting value. He was, however, the first to analyze the Mishnah critically and historically; and this was his importance.

sources. Specifically, in both classical and biblical studies, long before the mid-nineteenth century a thorough-going skepticism had replaced the gullibility of earlier centuries. Alongside the historicistic frame of mind shaped in the aftermath of the Romantic movement, there was an enduring critical spirit, formed in the Enlightenment and not to be eradicated later on. This critical spirit approached the historical allegations of ancient texts with a measure of skepticism. So for biblical studies, in particular, the history of ancient Israel no longer followed the paths of the biblical narrative, from Abraham onward. In the work of writing lives of Jesus, the contradictions among the several gospels, the duplications of materials, the changes from one gospel to the next between one saying and story and another version of the same saying and story, the difficulty in establishing a biographical framework for the life of Jesus—all of these and similar, devastating problems had attracted attention. The result was a close analysis of the character of the sources as literature, for example, the recognition—before the nineteenth century—that the Pentateuch consists of at least three main strands: JE, D, and P. It was well known that behind the synoptic Gospels is a source (called Q, for *Quelle*) containing materials assigned to Jesus, upon which the three evangelists drew but reshaped for their respective purposes. The conception that merely because an ancient story-teller says someone said or did something does not mean he really said or did it goes back before the Enlightenment. After all, the beginnings of modern biblical studies surely reach into the mind of Spinoza. He was not the only truly critical intellect in the field before Voltaire. But as a powerful, socially rooted frame of mind, historical-critical and literary-critical work on the ancient Scriptures is the attainment of the late eighteenth and nineteenth centuries. And for the founders of Talmudic history, Graetz, Frankel, and Krochmal, what had happened in biblical and other ancient historical studies was either not known or not found to be useful. And it was not used.

No German biographer of Jesus by the 1850s could have represented his life and thought by a mere paraphrase and harmony of the Gospels, in the way in which Graetz and Frankel and their successors down to the mid-twentieth century would paraphrase and string together Talmudic tales about rabbis, and call the result "history" and biography. Nor was it commonplace, by the end of the nineteenth century, completely to ignore the redactional and literary traits of documents entirely, let alone their historical and social provenance. Whatever was given to a rabbi, in any document, of any place or time, was forthwith believed to provide evidence of what that rabbi really said and did in the time in which he lived. Even Christian "Fundamentalism" approaches the Biblical literature with greater shame than this!

III

Now why these people did what they chose to do is no more important than why they refrained from doing what they chose not to do. Just as they chose to face the traditionalists with the claim that the Talmud was historical, so they chose to turn their backs on the critical scholarship of their own day with that very same claim that the Talmud was historical. I think the apologetic reason is self-evident and requires no amplification. We may now answer our first two questions. The Talmud was first studied as a historical document because, in the war for the reform of Judaism, history was the preferred weapon. The Talmud was the target of opportunity. The traditionalists trivialized the weapon, maintaining that history was essentially beside the point of the Talmud: "The historians can tell us what clothes Rabh wore, and what he ate for breakfast. The Talmudists can report what he said." But, it goes without saying, polemical arguments such as these, no less than the ones of the Reformers, were important only to the people who made them up.

The weapon of history in the nineteenth century was ultimate in the struggle for the intellect of Jewry. And the intellectuals, trained as they were in the philosophical works of the day, deeply learned in Kant and Hegel, made abundant use of the ultimate weapon. The Reformers similarly chose the field of battle, declaring the Hebrew Scriptures to be sacred and outside the war. They insisted that what was to be reformed was the shape of Judaism imparted by the Talmud, specifically, and preserved in their own day by the rabbis whose qualification consisted in learning in the Talmud and approval by those knowledgeable therein.

But the shape of the subject and its results, paradoxically, also reveal the mind of the traditionalist Reformers, Graetz and Frankel. Their intellectual program consisted of turning the Talmud, studied historically, into a weapon against the specific proposals and conceptions of the Reformers. And for the next hundred years, with only one important additional area of study, the history of the "Talmudic period" would be the story of rabbis, paraphrases of Talmudic and midrashic units strung together with strings of homilies— where they were strung together at all.

This additional area of study need not detain us for long, for what is done in it is essentially what is done in biography. I refer to the study of what was called "Talmudic theology" or "Talmudic thought" or "Rabbinic theology." In English the pioneering work is Solomon Schechter's *Studies in Judaism*, three volumes beginning in essays in the *Jewish Quarterly Review*, 1894 through 1896. The next important work in English is George F. Moore's *Judaism*, published in 1927, then C. G. Montefiore's and H. Loewe's *Rabbinic Anthology*, 1938, and Ephraim Urbach's *The Sages. Their Concepts and Beliefs*, in Hebrew in 1969 and English in 1975. There were parallel works in German as well.[7] In all of these works the operative method is the same as in biography, but the definitive category shifts to theology. Each work takes up a

---

[7]These are briefly summarized and criticized by Urbach (1975:1-18). My review of Urbach is in *Purities* (1977, XIV: 206-220).

given theological category and gathers sayings relevant to it. The paraphrase of the sayings constitutes the scholarly statement. Urbach correctly defines the work which was not done: "the history of *the beliefs and concepts of the Sages against the background of the reality of their times and environment*" (italics his) (1975:5). The use of evidence for the theological character of Talmudic Judaism is just as gullible and credulous as it is for biographies of Talmudic rabbis. What is attributed to a given rabbi really was said by him. What he is said to have done he really did. No critical perspective is brought to the facts of the Talmud. And the Talmud always supplies the facts, all the facts, and nothing but the facts.

We need not dwell on the historical study of the Talmud for theological purposes, therefore, because the methods were no different from those taken to be essentially sound for the study of the Talmud for biographical purposes. And these two purposes—biography and theology—define the character of nearly all of the historical work done in Talmudic literature for the century from the decade of foundation onward. Graetz set the style for such history as was attempted; Frankel for biography. The greatest achievements of the next hundred years—I think of the names of Buechler and Alon, for example[8]—in no way revised the methods and procedures or criticized the fundamental suppositions laid forth in Graetz and Frankel. When we realize the conceptual and methodological history of biblical studies in that same century, when we gaze upon the stars which rose and the stars which fell, when we remember the fads and admire the lasting progress, we realize that the Talmud as history is a world in which the clock started in 1850 and stopped in 1860. That of course is an exaggeration. Even those who could find no better methods and suppositions than those used for a hundred years could at least propose better questions. A clearly historical, developmental purpose is announced, though not realized, for example, by Urbach, when he says:

> The work of the sages is to be viewed as a protracted process aimed at the realization of the Torah and the ideals of the prophets in the reality and framework of their time . . . (1975:17).

Now while this is a clearly apologetic and theological proposal, it does make a place for the notion of change and development, that is, a genuinely—not merely a superficially—*historical* proposal.

At the end let me quote Schorsch's (1975: 61–62) judgment of Graetz, which forms a devastating epitaph to the whole enterprise of Talmudic history from the 1850s to the 1950s:

> Above all, Graetz remained committed to the rejuvenation of his people. His faith in God's guiding presence throughout Jewish history, as witnessed by two earlier instances of national

---

[8]See. A. Buechler (1956, 1912, 1928) and G. Alon (1957–58). Alon's lecture notes were published as *Toledot havvehudim be eres visra el betequfat hammishnah vehattalmud* (1954–55). These are uneven, and most of the work on ancient history is seriously out of date.

recovery, assured him of the future. His own work, he hoped, would contribute to the revival of Jewish consciousness. He succeeded beyond measure. As a young man, Graetz had once failed to acquire a rabbinic pulpit because he was unable to complete the delivery of his sermon. There is more than a touch of irony in the remarkable fact that the reception accorded to Graetz's history by Jews around the world made him the greatest Jewish preacher of the nineteenth century.[9]

IV

The second century of the historical study of the Talmud and related literature is marked by the asking of those questions ignored in the first: What if not everything in the Talmud happened as it is narrated? What if the attribution of a saying to a given rabbi does not mean that that rabbi really said what he is supposed to have said? Then what sorts of historical work are we able to do? What sorts can we no longer undertake?

At the outset let me specify the answers to my third and fourth questions, raised earlier: What is the intellectual program of the people who today do the work? Why is the Talmud studied today as a historical document?

Answering these questions requires attention to the character of the people who do the work. These are all university people. Talmudic history may be taught in some Jewish theological institutions—not in Yeshivas at all—but no books or articles in Talmudic history emerge from these schools. The books and articles in this field over the past twenty years have been written by university professors in America and Canada (and even in the State

---

[9]Professor Petuchowski comments on the foregoing discussion as follows:

This attack is, I think, just a little bit too sweeping. If I think of men like Manuel Joel (*Blicke in die Religionsgeschichte*), of Arthur Marmorstein, and even, to some extent, of Graetz himself (in *Gnosticismus and Judenthum*), I think of men who, with all of their simplistic acceptance of attributions, were aware of the necessity of matching rabbinic statements with the currents and crosscurrents in the wider world around the Rabbis, such as Christianity, Gnosticism, etc. In other words, as far as they were concerned, the Talmud itself did *not* "supply *all* the facts." I am also thinking of Marcus Petuchowski, a Hoffmann disciple, who, in his admittedly pietistic and hagiographical *Der Tanna Rabbi Ismael* (Frankfurt a. M., 1894), could say, on page 108:

"Wenn wir auch im allgemeinen die Glaubwürdigkeit der Ueberlieferung in den talmudischen Quellen nicht anzweifeln dürfen, . . . so ist es doch natürlich, dass im Laufe der Jahrhunderte, da der Talmud nur mündlich gelehrt wurde, manche Angaben schwankend und zweifelhaft werden mussten. Wir finden daher oft in den verschiedenen Quellen für dieselben Aussprüche verschiedene Autoren, ohne dass es immer möglich wäre, aus den mannigfachen Varianten den Urheber mit Sicherheit herauszufinden."

He then proceeds to some textual criticism, pointing out passages which, in his opinion, have been wrongly attributed to Rabbi Ishmael. Not, of course, the kind of standard we would expect from our students; but also not bad for an Orthodox rabbi at the end of the nineteenth century.

In other words, what is said about both theology and biography is absolutely right in its general thrust. But, as I said, the formulation is a little bit too sweeping.

of Israel). The reason this particular aspect of Talmudic studies is important to professors in diaspora-universities should be made clear.

Among those engaged in the teaching of the "Jewish humanities," the Talmud is a particularly important document. It is distinctively Jewish. The Hebrew Scriptures are not; they are a splendid literature and a self-evidently important one. Much of the medieval philosophical and mystical literature is of very special interest. The Talmud, by contrast, speaks of the formative years of Judaism as we know it; and it addresses itself, also, to the centuries in which the two other religions of the West (Christianity, for the earlier phases of the Talmud, and Islam, for the very last phases) were taking shape. Consequently, there is a genuine interest in Talmudic learning among a wide audience of scholars and students. It is natural, therefore, for people in the setting of secular universities to turn to Talmudic studies as a distinctively Jewish, important, and welcomed topic.

But what people in universities want to know has little to do with the ritualistic repetition of hagiography. They are not apt to sit still very long for edifying tales of ancient rabbis (or other sorts of holy men either). There is a contemporary program of research, a set of questions which just now appear urgent and pressing, as much as the issues of the reform of Judaism through historicism appeared urgent and pressing a century ago.

Of still greater importance for the present part of the argument, there is a considerable and shared program of criticism, historical, literary, anthropological and philosophical, as well as *religionsgeschichtlich*. This program is naturally attractive. One question which to New Testament scholars is deemed unavoidable is how to tell what, if anything, Jesus really said among the sayings attributed to him, and what Jesus really did among the deeds assigned to him. There is no way that what is perceived as "fundamentalism" will find a serious hearing in the study of Judaism when that same attitude of mind is found barbaric and irrelevant in the study of Christianity of the same place and nearly the same time. It follows, as I indicated at the outset, that the pressing problems of this second century of Talmudic studies for historical purposes are not, Did Rabbi X really say what is attributed to him? but, What do we know if we do *not* know that Rabbi X really said what is attributed to him? What sort of historical work can we do if we cannot do what Frankel, Graetz, and Krochmal thought we could do?

V

Since the contribution of the nineteenth and early twentieth century historians in the Talmudic area was to biography, let me now report the results of a considerable scholarly program of the past nearly two decades. I refer, specifically, to the study of the lives and thought of the rabbis— "Tannaim"—who are supposed to have flourished between the destruction of the Second Temple in 70 and the advent of Bar Kokhba in 132 and who are therefore associated with the period, if not the locus, of Yavneh. My *Life of Yohanan ben Zakkai* (1962) marks the end of an old epoch in methodology, and my *Development of a Legend: Studies on the Traditions concerning Yohanan ben Zakkai* (1970) signals the beginning of the new one in this area of study. A series of studies and dissertations has been successfully accomplished. These have repeatedly produced a few significant results.[10]

First, in the study of the traditions attributed to, and stories told about, the earlier rabbis, we have to take account of three wholly distinct types of material which seem to have no influence upon one, or connection with, another. These are legal, exegetical, and "biographical."

The legal materials attributed to all of the rabbis of Yavneh occur in the earliest rabbinic documents, Mishnah and Tosefta. In general they unfold, where the history can be assessed, in a disciplined and orderly way. As I showed in *Eliezer ben Hyrcanus*, what is attributed to Eliezer b. Hyrcanus by his immediate disciples and contemporaries will unfold and be subjected to development in later strata, literary or attributive. But it will never then be contradicted. Moreover, pericopae bearing evidence of later origination in documents after Mishnah, or bearing attestations of authorities of the third and fourth century, fall nearly wholly within the thematic framework established by materials bearing earlier attestations or occurring in Mishnah. This means that in the area of legal sayings there was no tendency promiscuously and without clear warrant to attribute to Eliezer whatever people wanted. On the contrary, there seems to have been a rather disciplined effort to amplify and augment materials assigned to him solely within the conceptions and principles already established in his name. This is a sign that the unfolding of the legal tradition in the three or four hundred years after the turn of the second century was governed by attention to what is said in the name of the earlier authorities and will not be characterized by attribution to an early authority of an idea first invented later on, for instance, for the purpose of securing for that new idea the prestige of the name of the revered and ancient master.

When, by contrast, we come to exegetical materials, that is, sayings on the meaning of Scriptural verses given in the name of Yavnean authorities, we find it simply impossible to relate what is said on Scripture to what is said on law. Time and again, the students of the traditions assigned to Yavnean rabbis have been stymied by the problem of how to relate the exegetical to the legal corpus. What they find in Genesis Rabbah or Leviticus Rabbah, the earliest

---

[10]These studies and dissertations are as follows: J. Neusner (1973), Gary Porton (1976), William Scott Green (1979), Shamai Kanter (1979), Charles Primus (1977), Jack N. Lightstone (1979), Tzvee Zahavy (1977), and Joel Gereboff (1979). In addition, shorter studies on traditions attributed to the men of the Great Assembly, Ṣadoq, Eleazar Ḥisma, and some other minor figures are analyzed by several authors in William Scott Green, ed. (1977). My *Rabbinic Traditions about the Pharisees before 70* (1971) treats all figures assumed to have been Pharisees and to have lived in the period before the destruction.

compilations of exegetical sayings, and what they find in Mishnah and in Tosefta, or even in the two Talmuds, are simply without apparent relevance to one another. Nor are the exegetical materials themselves susceptible to the sort of study of development and disciplined amplification referred to in connection with the legal ones. In the exegetical compilations, Eliezer, Ishmael, Tarfon, and Gamaliel simply supply names to which exegeses are assigned without (as-yet-perceived) rhyme or reason. The exception will be reference in the legal exegetical compilations, particularly Sifra and Sifre, to legal rulings of Mishnah-Tosefta, in which case the point is to demonstrate that said rulings derive from exegesis, not from reason. These self-evidently are secondary to, and dependent upon, Mishnah-Tosefta and in no way change the picture.[11]

As to "biographical" materials, by which is meant sayings or stories in which a rabbi's name is mentioned, these are of two kinds. In the first, a rabbi's name is used without any clear claim that a particular individual and his intellectual or moral traits come under discussion. There will be set sequences of names, e.g., Eliezer, Joshua, Gamaliel, ᶜAqiba. But what is said about, or done with, those names bears no relationship whatever to biography, that is, to what a particular individual said or did. In the second, a particular rabbi's name is used in a clearly homiletical story, e.g., how Tarfon tended to his mother's needs. Even if we were to believe all of the stories presented to us as "biographical," we should have very little biography for the earlier rabbis. The reason is that the homilies all together add up to no effort, even casual and unsystematic, to record what a given authority really said or did through a significant part of his lifetime. The blatant homiletical purpose precludes nineteenth century biography in these "biographical" materials.

A further insuperable barrier to biography is the absence of a generally accessible framework of biography for individual rabbis. There is no effort to report the outlines of a single authority's career, beginning to end. Because of that fact, even if all the sayings could be shown really to have been said by the rabbi in whose mouth they are set, and all the deeds really to have been done by him, we still should not have a hope of writing the sort of biography which Graetz and Frankel and their successors proposed to do. Their failure was apparent even at the outset: they really had nothing much to say and, when the sermons came to an end, so did their biographies.[12]

Since the three kinds of materials given in the name of a particular rabbi bear virtually no internal interrelationships, on the one hand, they must be used for purposes other than the composition of biographies. For even if we concentrate on the legal sayings, inclusive of the stories of various types, whether precedents or illustrations, we come to insuperable problems. These

[11]Compare my *History of the Mishnaic Law of Purities. VII. Negaim. Sifra* (1975:1–12, 211–30).

[12]I owe this point to Morton Smith.

are generated by the documents in which said sayings occur. If we were to propose to describe a given authority's legal ideas, that is, his religious philosophy expressed through concrete teachings on the conduct of ordinary life, we should want to begin with some evidence that what a given authority is supposed to have said really has been said by him. Otherwise, our account of his legal ideas is really not intellectual biography at all. But when we approach the diverse documents of the law, we find that the sayings attributed to all authorities are given in highly patterned and stereotype language, so that it is hardly possible to claim that, to begin with, we have in our hands anything like *ipsissima verba*. We may have access to what an authority thought. That has yet to be demonstrated, and I think it is beyond proof. But we rarely can show, *and therefore do not know*, that what he thought has been preserved in the words in which he expressed his thought.

We often can demonstrate the opposite. For Mishnah and Tosefta are documents formulated in the processes of redaction. What the redactors have done to create Mishnah, in particular, is to revise the whole of the received corpus into the language and redactional constructions of their own preference.[13] I am inclined to think that, prior to the time of "Our Holy Rabbi," Judah the Patriarch, materials were collected along the lines of a single authority's name, or of a single formal pattern, or of a single principle of law affecting diverse topics of law. But Rabbi's preference clearly is to group materials not in the name of a given authority, form, or abstract principle, but, essentially, topically, even though the sherds and remnants of materials brought together along other lines do remain in our hands. It follows, in any event, that while what is attributed to a given authority may or may not derive from him or his circle of disciples, we have no hope of presenting sizable bodies of sayings in the exact words spoken by a given authority.

VI

Since these are the facts, it must be concluded that the effort to recover the biographies of individual rabbis of the late first and early second centuries is not feasible. It seems to me that the same conclusion holds for the rabbis who lived in the later second century, since the literary facts pertinent to ᶜAqiba apply without much variation to Judah, Simeon, Meir, or Yosé. The state of the question for the rabbis of the third and fourth century is apt to be shaped by the nature of the quite different processes of literary formulation and transmission which produced the Talmuds in which their materials in the main are preserved, on the one side, and those same processes which yield the

---

[13]This is demonstrated at some length and systematically in my *History of the Mishnaic Law of Purities. XXI. The Redaction and Formulation of the Order of Purities in Mishnah and Tosefta* (1977: Chap. VII). I do not engage in similar studies for *A History of the Mishnaic Law of Holy Things,* and *of Women* which are now in press. I must say I find these results disturbing.

Midrashic compilations, on the other. These have not been critically assessed in detail, so we cannot yet come to conclusions on the promise of rabbinic biography for the "Amoraic" period.

We hardly are justified, however, to conclude that we learn nothing about earlier Rabbinic Judaism from the study of the sayings and stories assigned to its founding generations. On the contrary, once we ask the correct questions, we find we learn much worth knowing. In the study of the history and character of the traditions in the names of Yavneans, for example, we learn what it was important to say about those authorities in the times in which those responsible for the later compilations did their work. We notice, first of all, that in the third and fourth and later centuries, the telling of stories about earlier rabbis was deemed an important part of the work of traditioning and handing on the Tannaitic corpus. Men who, in their own day and for a century thereafter, are important, e.g., in Mishnah-Tosefta, principally in connection with opinions in their names on mooted topics of Mishnah-Tosefta, now, in the strata of the Talmuds and in the Midrashic compilations require yet another treatment entirely. They must be turned into paragons of virtue and exemplars of the values of the growing rabbinic movement. Long after their legal traditions had come to closure, their "biographies" continue to grow in response to a self-evident need to expand the modes by which Rabbinic tradition would express itself and preserve and impart its teachings. The histories of the traditions of the several authorities of Yavneh[14] prove beyond doubt that it is in the third and fourth centuries that the telling of stories about rabbis of the first and second centuries, the making up of homilies about their deeds, and the provision of a more human visage for the ancient authorities became important to Rabbinic circles of both Palestine and Babylonia.

It furthermore should not be supposed that the attribution of sayings to authorities of the late first and second centuries bears no consequences for the study of the history of earlier Rabbinic Judaism. The contrary is the case. For we are able to devise a method by which we may test part of what is alleged in those attributions, which is that the saying belongs at a given point in the history of Rabbinic legal thinking, and not later. If to ᶜAqiba is assigned a saying which in conception and logic is prior to one attributed to Judah or Meir, of the next generation, and which furthermore appears to generate the conception attributed to Judah or Meir, then we may fairly conclude that to

---

[14]These histories have not been entirely worked out yet since, as is clear, the analysis of the traditions is still in process. My *Development of a Legend. Studies on the Traditions concerning Yohanan ben Zakkai* (1971: 265–301) indicates the sort of work to be done. But that early work also explores a number of other kinds of problems entirely, e.g., the issue of how to deal with diverse versions of what appears to be a single story; how to contend with the versions of a single saying in several successive documents and how to construct the necessary tables and charts to come to grips with the state of the entirety of a given rabbi's tradition. I have supplied an extended critique of *Development* in *Eliezer ben Hyrcanus* (1973, II: 437–58).

the *time* of ᶜAqiba belongs the conception of the saying given in his name. That sort of conclusion may not appear so satisfying, but upon that basis a fairly firm and solid history of the law and its religious and philosophical conceptions is to be worked out.

That kind of history[15] in no way depends upon whether or not ᶜAqiba really said what is attributed to him, but only whether we are able to find evidence that what is assigned to ᶜAqiba or any other Yavnean is prior in conception or principle to what is assigned to Judah or Meir or any other Ushan after Bar Kokhba. Upon that basis a history of the unfolding of the law is to be founded. The consequent history of ideas further may be correlated with the great events of the age to which, it would seem reasonable, the rabbis' thinking upon any important question necessarily responded, for instance, the Temple's destruction or Bar Kokhba's catastrophe. Once the history of the law is worked out for Mishnah-Tosefta, we should have a fair picture of the foundations of the earlier stages of Rabbinic Judaism.[16] These in turn will delineate the work which must follow.

VII

A sign of a field of study in flux is the incapacity of scholars to find common grounds for disagreement. At the present time the Talmud is read as history in two completely different ways. Those who do it one way cannot communicate with those who do it the other. For example, those who maintain the established theory of the character of the Talmudic sayings and stories as facts of history, pure and simple, will present to those who do not the following arguments: 1) the rabbis were scrupulous about the truth; 2) facts

[15]It is exemplified in my *History of the Mishnaic Law of Purities* (1974–1977, I–XXII), *History of the Mishnaic Law of Holy Things* (1978–1979, I–VI), *History of the Mishnaic Law of Women* (in press) and my students' *History of the Mishnaic Law of Agriculture*. In addition, see Richard S. Sarason (1979). The other tractates are presently underway, as follows: *Berakhot*, Tzvee Zahavy; *Peah*, Charles Primus; *Kila⁾im*, Irving Mandelbaum; *Shebiᶜit*, Leonard Gordon; *Terumot*, Alan Peck; *Maᶜaserot*, Martin Jaffee; *Maᶜaser Sheni*, Peter Haas. The others in that Order will soon find their commentators within the present framework. A set of studies about the shape of ideas at given periods, e.g., from the destruction of the Temple to the disaster of Bar Kokhba, will now be worked out by me.

[16]The interplay between ideas held at a given period and the events of that period will allow for some interesting and fresh perspectives on the character of the ideas now encapsulated in Mishnah itself. Ultimately a history of Judaism from 70 to 200, that is, the formative century of Rabbinic Judaism, will be constructed and built upon exceedingly solid critical foundations. If it is a success, then a hundred years from now, it will be found primitive and incompetent by some new generation, with new questions and new reasons for asking them. So in the end all that will — and should—endure is the Talmud itself. Our contribution will be that, in our time and for our place, we showed why it should be received and studied as a monument of human culture and an enduring ornament to the human intellect. But, it goes without saying, that is not to be said. It can only be demonstrated in the hard work of asking questions and shaping answers relevant to the wider range of interests of the world of learning as we know it. That is the point of Chapter I.

incorrectly reported were challenged; 3) the holy rabbis of the Talmud surely would not lie. To these assertions, a master of the contrary viewpoint—that Talmudic stories, like biblical ones, have to be read in a critical spirit—will reply with such words as "sometimes" and "probably." That is, the rabbis *sometimes* were scrupulous about the truth. Facts *sometimes* were challenged when reported incorrectly. The holy rabbis of the Talmud *probably* would not lie. But, this master will add, "Rabbinic literature is full of obviously contradictory and grossly false statements. Contradictory reports stand unchallenged as often as they are corrected. The rabbinic literature contains innumerable nonsensical and obviously incredible statements." So, this master concludes, "If the rabbis were so scrupulous and painstaking as you pretend, how do you account for the enormous mass of claptrap they handed down?"[17]

Clearly, an argument phrased in the language of piety provokes the language of anti-piety, as well it should. But it appears to me that the argument is poorly phrased when the "veracity" of "the rabbis" is made the issue. What really requires attention is the identification of the things we shall concur to regard as facts and the questions to which these facts are claimed to be relevant. An Israeli graduate student (of American origin) who attended a conference at which issues such as those under discussion here were raised made the following comment:

> I am used to historians who argue with one another by showing that the hypothesis suggested by competitors is either contradicted by some known datum or unnecessarily involved or extravagant to explain the known data, as a simpler hypothesis would equally do. That is, everyone assumes that the few known data, which by themselves do not give us an understandable picture, are the surviving fragments of a 'building' which once stood. The historian's job is to suggest what that building looked like.

Now this conception of the writing of history confuses history with mathematics. It is, indeed, a conception possible only for a graduate student who has heard lectures but given none, read and criticized many books but not yet formulated even his own thesis-topic.

But the insight that no longer is there any agreement whatever on what constitutes facts and how facts are discovered and defined is significant. I think it is entirely sound and accurate, not only for the conference on which the student comments, but also for the state of the field of the Talmud as history. That is why the sort of discourse about "the holy rabbis' not telling lies" is possible. For, as I think is clear from the perspective of historical

---

[17]I here paraphrase a correspondence between a distinguished American scholar and an equally accomplished Israeli one about the veracity of Talmudic stories about rabbis and attributions of sayings to rabbis. Language in quotation marks is drawn from the actual correspondence. I am not free to reveal the names of the participants. The argument did take place in precisely the terms in which I represent it.

studies, we are not entirely sure what we mean by the truth. That is why we cannot say what is an untruth. We in the humanities do our work in an age of powerful, conflicting currents of thought. There is little agreement on fundamental issues of method and theories of knowledge. It is no wonder that the character of the work done in this first quarter of the second century of the study of the Talmud as history should appear to be diverse and lacking a common core of consensus and concurrence. Since that is so of society at large, why should it *not* be so of scholarship?

CHAPTER III

Oral Torah and Oral Tradition: Defining the Problematic

What complicates the definition and analysis of the oral traditions of ancient Judaism is the claim that Moses received at Sinai a dual Torah, part in writing and part not in writing. This latter part is called Oral Torah. In consequence, it is fairly widely assumed that the whole of rabbinic literature, correctly designated Oral Torah, falls within that more general category of oral traditions subject to investigation by scholars of folklore. My small contribution to the present discussion is to distinguish Oral Torah from that much larger and more encompassing category of oral traditions. This I shall attempt to accomplish by a definition of the point at which the conception of Oral Torah enters Judaic theological thinking and, still more important, the *locus* of that conception.[1] In doing so, I restate conclusions advanced elsewhere (Neusner, 1971:III, 143–79), but not fully exploited to this time, in the field of Jewish folklore. To state the result at the outset: the conception that ideas were reduced to fixed mnemonic formulas and transmitted through memorization and not in writing is specific to Mishnah. That conception, so

[1]It generally is supposed that the oral formulation and transmission of materials characterize the whole of the rabbinic corpus: Midrash, Mishnah, Talmud, and the like. For example, Alexander Guttmann (1940:16.140–41) writes:

> . . . the Jewish schools differed from those of other people in that not only were the lessons taught orally, but also the entire material studied was transmitted in the same fashion. The existence of other religious writings alongside of Holy Writ *was not countenanced* [italics supplied]; nor was the use of either notes or books allowed in the oral teaching of the material studied. [Here Guttmann refers to B. Git. 60b, cited below.]
>
> By virtue of this rule, the extra-biblical traditions were transmitted essentially by word of mouth, and no (official) fixing in written form of any of the material used in the teaching of religious law was possible. It is not difficult to discover from the literary-historical point of view the impression that such an oral method of teaching made upon style. While an authoritative written text takes on a static character with fixed norms and conventions, the method of oral transmission has a certain natural flexibility which remains with it even when later on it is reduced to writing. The notes which were prepared in secret and the traditional teachings which were collected and later written down clearly reveal the style of an oral discussion. *The Midrash, Mishnah and similar sources of traditional Jewish literature were, in like manner, records of the work which developed in the schools.* [Italics supplied.]

far as Mishnah is concerned, is absolutely sound, because the internal evidence of Mishnah itself most certainly confirms it. But the criteria for mnemonic formulation and transmission established through the internal analysis of Mishnah reveal that Mishnah's most closely related document, Tosefta, is not so formulated as to facilitate transmission and reveals traits associated with written, not oral, tradition. It will follow that when we speak of Oral Torah, we do not mean the whole of the rabbinic tradition, nor do all, or even the bulk, of the materials of the Talmuds fall into the category of oral tradition. We speak principally of Mishnah. Put most simply: Mishnah is Oral Torah.

I

To begin with, let us ask: At what point, and for what purpose, is the conception of Oral Torah first formulated? The answer to that question lies not in assessing the attributions of conceptions of Oral Torah to various authorities. For these begin with Moses himself, so the absurdity of that position is self-evident. What we must ask is: Where do we find the earliest claim, in the documents of rabbinic Judaism in particular, that some traditions or ideas are alleged to have been formulated and handed on through memory and not through writing?

Since, it is generally agreed, Mishnah is the first document of rabbinic Judaism, to begin with we turn to Kosovesky's *Oṣar lashon hammishnah* (II:886–88) in quest of a single instance in Mishnah at which we may find the precise language, *torah shebeᶜal peh*. There we find no such language. There are, to be sure, many references to Torah in the sense of "learning traditions of Torah." Most of these are grouped in Abot. But the conception phrased in the archetypal language, *torah shebeᶜal peh*, is not present in Mishnah. The closest we come, in Abot, brings us to Mishnah's first important apologetic. If we ask Tosefta for its evidence (*Oṣar lashon hattosefta* [III:582–85]), we find none. True, as we shall see, it is alleged more than a few times that traditions come down in oral form and that these traditions have been stated in some sort of standardized language. Thus some few debates between Eliezer and Joshua (e.g., M. Par. 1:1, T. to M. Nid. 1:1ff.) find one party citing a fixed formula, subject to the interpretation of the masters. But this allegation pertains solely to materials in Mishnah. It is a far cry from the allegation that Moses has received two Torahs at Sinai, that one of them was transmitted orally, and that that very Torah is now contained within the rabbinic writings. The stratum of the rabbinic literature represented by the Babylonian Talmud, by contrast, contains all three relevant phrases: *Written Torah, Oral Torah,* and *whole Torah.* But even here the references are remarkably thin.[2] The bulk

---

[2]Written Torah: B. Shab. 31a (stories of Hillel, Shammai, and a prospective convert), B. Yoma 28b, B. Qid. 66a; Oral Torah: the same; whole Torah: B. Baba Batra 116a, Menahot 65b.

of the relevant stories, moreover, represents the dual Torah in a polemical context: Yoḥanan ben Zakkai and the Sadducees (B. Men. 65b), Hillel, Shammai, and a prospective convert to Judaism (B. Shab. 31a).

That fact leads us to ask: At what point is the conception of the two Torahs, one oral, the other written, a central issue of Judaic theological polemic? Babli's evidence clearly suggests that the conception, while present, is hardly important, since recourse to the claim is seldom and unimpressive. It must follow that while what is in Mishnah soon after its promulgation is given a central place in the divine revelation at Sinai, the allegation that Mishnah is part of Torah at that early time is not joined to the closely associated claim that Mishnah represents, whole or in part, *ipsissima verba* of Sinai. We shall see in a moment that the claim of oral formulation and transmission pertinent to Mishnah is quite different and speaks of an entirely separate matter. In point of fact, so far as I can see, it is in the polemic with Qaraism that the claim of origin at Sinai in behalf of Mishnah, indeed, the whole of the rabbinic tradition constituted by both Talmuds, becomes crucial. In his famous letter on the history of the Talmudic tradition (ca. 987), Sherira claims that while Judah the Patriarch produced the Mishnah, he relied upon a chain of tradents going back to Sinai. The early generations did not put their names on the laws; there were no disputes. Each master preserved exactly what he had learned as a disciple, in exactly the words of the master, back to the Great Assembly (see Lewin, 1921:4–35; Neusner, 1973:xii–xiii). This notion, that the rabbinic version of Torah goes back to remote antiquity, is meant to strengthen the rabbinists' claim, rejected by Qaraism, to authority and authenticity advanced in behalf of Mishnah and its Talmuds. It is an essentially historical argument about a theological issue of revelation.

Yet, as we note, even Sherira does not formulate the historical claim in its most extreme form, which is to allege that the path of Mishnah leads all the way back to Sinai. That claim, while implicit here and there, is not made explicit even in the document which purports to give a history of the rabbinic Torah. This observation brings us back to the point at which we began: Precisely what is the nature of the claim laid forth in behalf of Orah Torah? What document is particularly alleged to have been orally formulated and transmitted?

To answer that question, we turn to a story in which rabbis describe precisely what they believe Moses, "our rabbi," did when he formulated and transmitted the other half of his Torah. The first thing we shall notice is that the pericope speaks explicitly of Mishnah. Self-evidently, it also will attribute to Moses and Aaron the modes of formulating and transmitting traditions familiar to the story-tellers themselves, that is, to rabbis of the late first and second-centuries. It is as follows:

> Our rabbis taught: How [was] the Mishnah order[ed]?
> A. Moses learned from the mouth of the Almighty. Aaron entered, and Moses repeated to him his [Aaron's] chapter (PRQW). Aaron departed and sat at the left hand of Moses.

His sons entered and Moses repeated to them their chapter. His sons departed. Eleazar sat at the right hand of Moses and Itamar at the left of Aaron.

R. Judah says, "Aaron surely sat at the right hand of Moses."

Again the elders entered, and Moses taught them their chapter. The elders departed, and all the people entered, and Moses taught them their chapter.

So it came out that in the hand of Aaron [were] four, in the hand of his sons three, and in the hand of the elders two, and in the hand of the whole people one.

His sons taught them their chapter. His sons departed. The sages taught them their chapter.

So it came about that in everyone's hand were four.

B. On this basis

R. Eliezer says, "A man is required to repeat to his disciple four times . . ."

R. ᶜAqiba says [sic], "How do we know that a man is liable to teach his disciple until he learns it? As it is said . . ." (b. ᶜErub. 54b)

Judah b. Ilai's interpolation supplies a firm *terminus ante quem* for the pericope: Usha. Eliezer's and ᶜAqiba's lemmas, appropriately attached (MKᵓN), stand independent of the story which conforms to Eliezer's view. Indeed, one might have formulated the story on the basis of the dispute of Eliezer and ᶜAqiba, thus supplying a precedent for the position of the former. We therefore have firm evidence that the pattern of oral formulation and transmission of traditions was well established, indeed taken for granted, by Usha (Judah). We may push the date back to middle-Yavnean times, ca. 100, and even earlier. Eliezer's and ᶜAqiba's argument suggests that the procedures of oral instruction had not yet been fixed. A second such story, also in the stratum of the Babylonian Talmud, is at B. Git. 60b (B. Tem. 14b). I shall show that its exegetical proposition is original to the authority to whom the story is attributed, a third century master.

R. Judah b. Naḥmani, the *Meturgeman* of R. Simeon b. Laqish, expounded (DRŠ), "It is written, *Write for yourself these words* (Ex 34:27), and it is written, *For according to the mouth* (ᶜL PY) *of these words* (Ex 34:27). How now [to reconcile writing with memorizing] (ᶜL PH)? Things which are in writing you are not permitted to state from memory. Things which are memorized (DBRYM ŠBᶜL PH) you are not permitted to state in writing . . ."

R. Yoḥanan said, "God made a covenant with Israel only for the sake of things which are oral (DBRYM ŠBᶜL PH), as it says, *For by the mouth* (ᶜL PY) *of these words I have made a covenant with thee and with Israel* (Ex 34:27).

The exegetical tradition on Ex 34:27 does not conform to Judah b. Naḥmani's tendency. Judah the Patriarch derives from the Scripture the lesson, "Great is circumcision, for it outweighs all the other commandments of the Torah" (B. Ned. 32a). Yosé b. R. Ḥanina proves from the same Scripture that the Torah was given only to Moses and his seed, but Moses generously gave it to Israel (B. Ned. 38a). Ḥaggai in the name of Samuel b. Naḥman sees in the Scripture the lesson that things orally transmitted are more beloved than things in writing. Yoḥanan and Yudan b. R. Simeon prove from it that one must observe oral as well as Scriptural traditions (both: y. Peᵓah 2:4; y. Meg. 4:1; y. Ḥag. 1:8). (Late Amoraic and medieval compilations are of no interest here.)

Judah b. Naḥmani's interpretation therefore is unique, moves far beyond the point made by Samuel and Yoḥanan, and possibly is new with him. All others understood the verse to mean that oral traditions are especially beloved—standard rabbinic polemic against those Jews who did not accept the authority of Oral Torah (meaning, the rabbis' Mishnah), and they were many. The allegation in connection with Ex 34:27, that it is strictly forbidden to write down oral traditions in any form, is not found before this time. It therefore hardly seems warranted to extend the rule back to Moses[!].[3]

II

Thus far we have seen that the allegations that there is a mode of formulating and transmitting traditions through oral, not written, means is particular to Mishnah. Let us turn back to the evidence of Mishnah itself and ask how that document formulates the claim. The first allegation that someone has a tradition formulated and transmitted orally in precisely the language in which that tradition now is repeated pertains to Yoḥanan b. Zakkai, *via* Eliezer b. Hyrcanus and Joshua b. Ḥananiah. The pertinent passages are as follows:

> R. Joshua said, "I have received as a tradition from Rabban Yoḥanan b. Zakkai who heard from his teacher, and his teacher from his teacher, as a *halakhah* given to Moses from Sinai, that Elijah will not come to declare unclean or clean, to remove afar or to bring nigh, but to remove afar those that were brought near by violence, and to bring near those that were removed by violence." (M. ᶜEd. 8:7)

This is the *first* reference to exact words supposedly orally formulated by a master (Moses), then orally transmitted, and now set down in writing. Joshua likewise alludes to words of Yoḥanan b. Zakkai (M. Soṭ. 5:2, 5), but in that instance those words in fact were not formulated in a fixed, oral lemma;

[3]The most extreme claim in behalf of the view that the rabbinic traditions now in our hands comprise originally orally composed and orally transmitted materials comes from Birger Gerhardsson (1961). Gerhardsson repeats and embellishes the views of nearly all scholars of Jewish literature of the past century, who routinely quote Judah b. Naḥmani's and other sayings as entirely valid testimonies for the Second Temple period and even earlier. Gerhardsson relies upon unexamined allegations in the literature rather than on a close examination of internal evidence. If something is said about oral transmission, it is assumed that that saying not only was true when said, which is possible, but also characterized earlier processes of redaction and transmission, which is unlikely. This reading of pertinent sayings seems to me conceptually primitive. It requires the assumption that the conditions for the formation and transmission of traditions were constant from remote antiquity. The way in which the Mishnah was published is likewise the way in which everything before Mishnah was given substance and form. My teacher Morton Smith (1963) has said the last word on Gerhardsson's theory. He comments, "To read back into the period before 70 the developed rabbinic technique of . . . [the year] 200 is a gross anachronism." Smith's judgment is that there was a general failure to preserve *ipsissima verba* of the early teachers.

indeed, Yoḥanan's statement was either lost or suppressed, or it was not given any sort of official formulation at all. So when Joshua heard something along the lines of what Yoḥanan had allegedly said to him, he referred to the tradition but not to a fixed lemma in which the teaching was formulated. The same allegation concerning Yoḥanan derives from Eliezer:

> On that day . . . they voted and decided that Ammon and Moab should give Poorman's Tithe in the Sabbatical Year.
> And when R. Yosé the son of the Damascene came to R. Eliezer in Lydda, he said to him, "What new thing did you have in the house of study today?"
> He said to him, "They voted and decided that Ammon and Moab give Poorman's Tithe in the Sabbatical Year."
> R. Eliezer wept and said, "*The secret of the Lord is with them that fear him, and he will show them his covenant* (Ps 25:14). Go and tell them, 'Be not anxious by reason of your voting, for I have received a tradition from Rabban Yoḥanan b. Zakkai, who heard it from his teacher, and his teacher from his teacher, as a *halakhah* given to Moses at Sinai, that Ammon and Moab give Poorman's Tithe in the Sabbatical Year.'" (M. Yad. 4:3)

Eliezer's assertion, in the same words as the decision, comes in reference to the *on that day*-traditions concerning Gamaliel's deposition. This case is better evidence than those deriving from Joshua's circle that to Yoḥanan were attributed orally formulated and orally transmitted traditions and that those traditions were alleged to have derived in exactly their present form from Sinai. But the very sayings of Moses through Yoḥanan never survived in their original form! We should not have known them had not Eliezer and Joshua quoted them. And Eliezer quoted his only when able to do so, after Gamaliel II was out of power. So if Yoḥanan's saying had earlier been given fixed form and if this was done orally and if it was thereupon taught to Eliezer for memorization and oral transmission, then that saying nonetheless was not published, for only Eliezer knew about it. The others were in the dark, so had to vote. This pericope hardly conforms to the picture of the oral formulation and transmission of a *public* tradition, the Oral Torah.

III

Let us now shift the focus of argument and make explicit a distinction which heretofore has been implicit, a distinction I believe may prove useful to students of folklore. We have to separate generalized traditions—stories, sayings, ideas—passed on orally, on the one hand, and tradition which is, to begin with, carefully formulated orally and then orally transmitted, word for word, with the help of mnemonic schemes and by that means only, until written down in exactly its earliest, original, oral form. Clearly, the rabbinic stories even in Mishnah itself claim that that is what has been done by Yoḥanan ben Zakkai and his principal disciples. But the issue is *not* whether there were traditions, or even oral traditions. We have no reason to doubt there were. The issue is: Do the written traditions before us contain meticulous reproductions of exactly the words originally spoken by the masters to which they were attributed in precisely the form given them by those very masters—*ipsissima verba*?

That issue must forthwith be divided into two parts. First, did the masters originally say what now is attributed to them? This we cannot know. Second, does the present literature contain exact replications of materials originally formulated orally and transmitted orally? It is a fact that the Mishnah does exhibit mnemonic patterns, some formal, some substantive, precise, and striking.[4] What inferences are to be drawn from that fact? Shall we conclude

[4]It is when the sayings alleged to have been formulated for oral transmission exhibit concrete characteristics attesting to such a purpose that scholars in other fields have—in my view, persuasively—alleged the proposition herein advanced in behalf of Mishnah in particular. For example, Milman Perry states (1930: 31, 138; also in Lord, 1948: 52, 36):

> It is of course the pattern of the diction which, as in the matter of the authorship of the style, proves by its very extent that the Homeric style is oral. It must have been for same good reason that the poet, or poets, of the *Iliad* and the *Odyssey* kept to the formulas even when he, or they, had to use some of them very frequently. What was this constraint that thus set Homer apart from the poets of a later time, and of our own time, whom we see in every phrase choosing those words which alone will match the color of their own thought? The answer is not only the desire for an easy way of making verse, but the complete need of it. Whatever manner of composition we could suppose for Homer, it could be only one which barred him in every verse and in every phrase from the search for words that would be of his own finding. Whatever reason we may find for his following the scheme of the diction, it can be only one which quits the poet at no instant.
>
> There is only one need of this sort which can even be suggested—the necessity of making verses by the spoken word. This is a need which can be lifted from the poet only by writing, which alone allows the poet to leave his unfinished idea in the safe keeping of the paper which lies before him, while with whole unhurried mind he seeks along the ranges of his thought for the new group of words which his idea calls for. Without writing, the poet can make his verses only if he has a formulaic diction which will give him his phrases all made, and made in such a way that, at the slightest bidding of the poet, they will link themselves in an unbroken pattern that will fill his verses and make his sentences.

The question, who is the author, is therefore false: "An oral poem undergoes two kinds of creation, that of the man who first makes it and that of the man who sings it each time" (Lord, 38).

Parry's argument about the oral composition and transmission of poetry bears no relationship to the materials before us. The reason is that the formulaic patterns, particularly those exhibiting affinities with the characteristics referred to by Parry, do not characterize whole pericopae, but only apodoses in disputes. Perhaps formalization of the Houses-apodoses was intended to ease the burden of decision-making. Once someone knew the protasis [*If*] *a seah of unclean Terumah falls into a hundred seahs of clean*, and also knew that the Houses discuss the matter, he would need no great effort to rule: "House of Shammai prohibit. House of Hillel permit." The apodoses of Houses-lemmas do, therefore, tend to be fixed, but also are apt to be moved from one protasis to another, as in the Ushan stratum. This seems to me to signify that the small units of tradition were memorized with precision—it was easy enough. But the cases to which they were to be assigned were entirely fluid and not set forth with equal precision. And mnemonic patterns in which the Houses-apodoses are carefully arranged look to be the creation

that the traditions were *based upon* orally formulated and transmitted materials? On the face of it, that conclusion is unwarranted. *Clearly many traditions before us were formulated so as to facilitate their memorization.* But whether or not the redacted pericopae derive from originally oral materials is a question that obviously cannot be settled, one way or the other, by the character of materials which we have only in written form.

The sole fact in our hands is that Mishnah has been so formulated as to facilitate memorization. But then other rabbinic documents, not exhibiting the redactional as well as formulary mnemonic care revealed by Mishnah, cannot be alleged even to have been intended to be handed on in memory only. The theory of a dual Torah by itself is not pertinent. The Essenes of Qumran, for one, had such a corpus of revealed materials external to Scriptures, and they wrote down at least part of those materials. But even if various sects had traditions and if those traditions were oral, it would not solve the problem, unless it can be shown that in behalf of such traditions was claimed not merely essential accuracy but exact verbal correspondence with what was originally stated by the authority standing behind them.

---

not of poets or other literary figures in the dim past, but of the tradents at Yavneh, Usha, and even later, who followed a simple form for the codification only of legal traditions.

Scholars of Buddhism take for granted that the earliest traditions of Buddha were shaped and transmitted orally. They have the support of Buddhist traditions, which refer to the calling of councils for the purpose of fixing orally the text of the sacred canon (Williams, 1970: 156–57). A carefully formulated oral canon was preserved for centuries, it is alleged. Modern scholars, while reluctant to accept the traditional Buddhist picture, nonetheless envisage a not-dissimilar process. Williams observes that Buddha certainly gave rules, and "there must have been many discourses known by heart to the disciples, and they may have been collected and recited in a . . . chanting together even during Buddha's lifetime." He clearly formulates the sort of claim made in behalf of rabbis, that they "must have" formulated teachings and given them to the disciples orally, and that the disciples then "must have" preserved and accurately handed on the very words of the master himself. Some have suggested that Buddha taught in a form with synonyms and repetitions so that the teaching could be easily learned by his disciples (Walpola Rahula, *What the Buddha Taught* [N.Y., 1962], cited by Williams, 158, n. 3). So, Williams continues, "After the death of the Buddha this collection and recitation must have become more important. . . . In oral transmission mnemonic conveniences play a large part. All sorts of aids to memory—set words, fixed phrases, familiar conventional descriptions in stereotyped terms and other *memoria technica*—became characteristic of the tradition." These materials were then organized into loose collections by form or content (Williams, 159). I take Williams' repeated use of *must have been* and *must have become* to mean that the evidence permits no more definitive conclusions. There can be no doubt that the Sutta discussed by Williams exhibits striking mnemonic patterns, formed of various short units and transmitted independently. The narrative framework is apt to be less reliable than the logia. One finds stock phrases and formulae, summaries arranged for easy memorization, serving merely as "key phrases intended to bring to mind the major teachings of the Buddha." At the end Williams concludes, "All of this gives evidence of the shaping of the material for ease in oral transmission. The verse form, the numerical sequences, repetitions, stock phrases and paragraphs and formalized encounters were probably shaped by the monks in the transmission, though it is possible that the Buddha's teaching methods included repetition and stylized formulae to aid memorization."

IV

Let us now turn to the sort of claim of oral tradition which does characterize diverse groups in ancient Judaism. At this point the inquiry of the folklorists into oral traditions may be brought into alignment with the argument, advanced to this point, that it is Mishnah, and Mishnah alone, in behalf of which are claimed oral formulation and oral transmission. For we shall now see that a second, and separate, claim is almost certainly valid. That is the claim that various groups possessed oral traditions, without reference of any sort to the verbal accuracy of those traditions in replicating exactly what was said by the people who are supposed to stand behind them. That is an entirely commonplace view. It is to be considered by itself and not in relationship to the widespread opinion that not merely oral traditions, but oral formulation and transmission of exactly what was said, characterize much of biblical literature as well.[5]

[5]Biblical scholarship on the oral composition and transmission of traditions is full of animadversions to the "Semitic mind" and similarly imprecise ideas. In general it rests on the assumption that when few people can read and write, oral recitation of traditions will be important—which says nothing about oral formulation and transmission, merely oral presentation. Carroll Stuhlmueller (1958) and Hans-Joachim Kraus (1956) provide useful summaries. Stuhlmueller claims that the "practical slant of Semitic mentality" (304) plays a role: "It was the present moment which preoccupied the Jewish mind. Surrounded by pressing hardships and urgent problems that left little or no leisure for cultural endeavors, the Israelites wanted to know the relevance of the past to their own day. . . . What does this passage really mean . . . right here and now?" (304). Oral tradition comes along to "rescue past events from the dusty book of history." While on the order of Gunkel's invitation to the fireside of the ancient Israelite to hear the old and beautiful stories of the tribe recited before eager listeners ("we enter and listen with them," etc.), Stuhlmueller's colorful fantasy is even more gross. What evidence is there to support his reification of "the Jewish mind"? If the "Jewish mind" at one period required orally recited materials, then why in that very same period, all the more so later on, did it also require written documents? How did that "Jewish mind" so change as to produce written materials?

Eduard Nielsen (1955) supplies another account of the biblical problem. He stresses that oral tradition is not merely a pre-literary stage (= tradition). The allegation rather is that, as Mowinckel said (Nielsen, 13), "The prophets were men of the spoken word and . . . their books were compositions based on oral tradition. We owe it to oral tradition, for instance, that the prophecies of Amos and Hosea were preserved until the exilic age, which was also the age when the prophecies were committed to writing." We note that no distinction is to be made between oral *tradition*—merely the pre-literary stage—and oral composition and oral transmission. All are one: the orator spoke; his words, it is claimed, were not written down but instantly memorized at the very outset. Only much later did anyone bother to write them down (presumably explained along the lines of a theory that the memorizers were thought to be dying out, as in the oral theory of the Avesta and the Babylonian Talmud). We may bypass arguments adduced from the extent of oral tradition in the ancient Near East, the contempt for oral tradition in modern Europe, the sociology of writing and schooling, and the importance of religious and epic texts in general. Nielsen himself observes that one cannot "give an answer that applies equally to the Old Nordic, the Hellenic, the Persian, the Indian, and the Semitic worlds." Of greater interest is the mode of argumentation undertaken in behalf of Nyberg's thesis that "The written Old Testament is a

Diverse forms of Judaism known to us from late antiquity invariably claim that there is a tradition, in addition to the written Torah, possessed uniquely by a particular group. The claim of tradition may be joined with the second claim that the truth held by the group was not even written down. For example, Qumranian scriptures occasionally refer to secret doctrines which were not written down but were transmitted with great care. Similarly, Jesus is alleged to have taught his disciples a secret tradition not to be publicly revealed until the proper time. But these are traditions and do not constitute the whole literature nor apparently a significant part of it. The main point, however, is that we do not find traces that such secret sayings were redacted for easy oral transmission—that would have defeated their original purpose. If Paul's allusions to Jesus came to him not by a "revelation of Jesus Christ" (Galatians 1:11), but in some sort of fixed oral formulation which was orally transmitted, he gives no hint of it. He alleges it is not man's gospel. He may have had traditions, but of *ipsissima verba* he gives no unambiguous testimony, except from his own visions. And Paul handed on his traditions in writing. The Gospels originally were written, according to the testimony of two of them, Luke and John. What traditions lie behind them, *if* originally composed and fixed *not* in writing but in the various forms of oral story-telling and in the disciplined formation of sayings, hardly gives significant evidence because of the poor state of their preservation. But even if *traditions* were handed on orally and not in writing, they would have been passed on in oral transmission for all of forty years. That hardly gives significant evidence for the institutionalization, in the Church, of an oral literature or for the availability of trained, suitably qualified, and officially certified memorizers, of whom we hear nothing. Obviously, one cannot draw on evidence for the existence of such an institution, for no such evidence exists. Perhaps the most striking evidence is the written Gospels themselves, not to mention Paul's letters: no one was prepared to rely for long upon any medium other than

---

creation of the post-exilic Jewish community; of what existed earlier undoubtedly only a small part was in fixed written form" (Nielsen, 39). Nielsen's important arguments are: first, writing was subordinated in a pre-exilic Israel; second, the Scriptures give direct evidence of oral transmission. The former is not pertinent to our problem since, as I said, it is difficult to argue that writing was subordinated to oral formulation and transmission of materials in the century or so before A.D. 70. Nielsen observes that while writing was institutionalized in scribes in Davidic times, these were not widespread. The culture as a whole did not tend "to a written fixation of its traditions" (49). The contrary was the case later on. Nielsen's "positive evidence for the existence of an oral tradition" is drawn in part from various references in Scriptures themselves, e.g., Deut. 1:5; 31:11. It is assumed that the father will orally teach his household: "The home is a miniature national community." Better proof derives from Psalms: "Since we are so fortunate as to possess parallel psalms in the book of Psalms, and these are not quite identical in their present textual form, we can by examining these variants establish *errors of hearing* [italics supplied] and thus prove that the oral tradition played its part in the composition of the Israelite psalms." That seems to me the most pertinent argument. That sort of argument and proof is nowhere undertaken by proponents of the oral theory of the rabbinic traditions before us.

writing for the formulation, preservation, and transmission of anything that really mattered. To be sure, Paul drew on tradition, even on oral tradition, e.g., 1 Cor 15:3-5, 1 Thess 4:1-8, etc. But Paul uses tradition very freely and the exact verbal formulation is not important to him. Early Christian tradition is quite fluid and variable, even when the content is of crucial importance.

We come now to the Pharisees who are generally supposed to stand as the immediate antecedents of the rabbinic Judaism which took shape after 70 ("Pharisaic-Rabbinic Judaism") and in behalf of whom are laid down the claims of oral formulation and oral transmission of *ipsissima verba*. Precisely what is alleged in the earliest sources which refer to the Pharisees? It is that the Pharisees possessed traditions *apart* from Scriptures. The testimonies of two independent sources, Josephus and the Gospels, as well as of the rabbinic traditions about the Pharisees, are clear on that point. If, for the moment, we make the unlikely assumption that the B. Shab 30b–31a story about Shammai and Hillel accurately reports what Shammai and Hillel actually said to the potential converts, we may grant that the theory of two Torahs, one in writing, the other oral, was held by both masters.

Josephus's evidence is more credible and quite unequivocal: the Pharisees did possess *traditions* apart from Scriptures. In *War* II, 162-3 (*Ant.* XIII, 171-3), the Pharisees are referred to as the most accurate interpreters of the laws. Here we find no reference to orally transmitted or other external traditions. But in his later story of John Hyrcanus and the Pharisees (*Ant.* XIII, 293ff.), Josephus adds a reference to traditions, although without specifying oral transmission let alone oral formulation, of *ipsissima verba*:

> For the present I wish merely to explain that the Pharisees had passed on to the people certain regulations handed down by former generations and not recorded in the Laws of Moses, for which reason they are rejected by the Sadducean group, who hold that only those regulations should be considered valid which were written down [Marcus adds: in Scripture], and that those which had been handed down by former generations need not be observed . . . (*Ant.* XIII, 297-8, trans. Ralph Marcus, 377).

If we had no preconception about oral tradition, this passage would not have led us to such an idea. It could as well pertain to a document like the Manual of Discipline as to *lay/not to lay* (M. Hag. 2:2). But even if Josephus meant to refer to traditions not written down at all, from his saying that the Sadducees did not observe the traditions of the fathers (*legon ekiena* [the Sadducees] *dein hegeisthai nomina ta gegrammena, ta d'ek paradoseōs tōn paterōn mē tērein*), one cannot forthwith derive the picture of formulation and transmission given by b. ᶜErub. and similar narratives.

It is one thing to allege that the fathers had handed on traditions external to Scriptures, even not writing them down at all. It is quite another to claim that the extra-Scriptural traditions of the Pharisees are in substance and also in form precisely the ones laid down by Moses, in the very language of Moses himself. This Josephus does not allege. But if he did, we should have to point out that he wrote *Antiquities* at, or shortly after, the very time that the Yavnean Pharisees were arranging and transmitting Mishnah in conformity with the picture he would have drawn. In *Ant.* XVIII, 12–15, we find no reference to a doctrine handed on orally, merely stress on belief in Pharisaic foresight, predestination, and the like. The Sadducees, he stresses (XVIII, 16), follow no observance outside of the laws. In *Life* 2, he refers to the Pharisees as having points of resemblance to the Stoic school; in *Life* 38 he speaks of the Pharisees as experts in "their country's laws." That is the whole picture.[6]

The references of the Synoptic Gospels to "the Pharisees' tradition of the elders" (Mark 7:4, Matt 15:2) are consistent with Josephus's picture. What characterized the Pharisees was firm belief in *paradosis tōn presbuterōn* (Mark 7:4); Josephus similarly refers to *nomima polla tine paradosan tō dēmō hoi Pharisaioi ek paterōn diadoxēs, haper ouk anagegraptai en tois Mōuseos nomois.*[7]

Josephus thus does *not* say the Pharisees have a non-literary tradition. They have a tradition, but this is *not* the law of Moses. It is beside the law of Moses. We not only do *not* have a reference to oral transmission, we do not *even* have an unequivocal Pharisaic reference to an oral Torah or to two Torahs. Guided by Josephus and the Gospels, we should have concluded the Pharisees claimed they possessed traditions from olden times. We should not have supposed such traditions were alleged to have been orally formulated and transmitted. We should not even have called such traditions the Oral Torah (*Torah shebeᶜal peh*).

V

This brings us back to Mishnah as the Oral Torah, that is, a Torah which has been formulated for oral transmission and then handed on not in writing but through the memory of the disciples. Saul Lieberman (1950:83–9) describes the process of formulating and transmitting the Mishnah. He asks: Was the Mishnah published? That is, did professional copyists hear it dictated and write it down? Or, did an authentic original take written form, and was it then deposited in an archive? Some Jewish books were published in the

---

[6]Compare Emil Schürer (1885: II, ii.2–5). It goes without saying that we eagerly look forward to the further formulation of this problem in the new Schürer, under preparation by Geza Vermes and Fergus Millar with Pamela Vermes. The first volume of the revised Schürer is a model of scholarly responsibility, the most up-to-date and reliable account of the subject.

[7]*Paradosis* in NT means tradition "only in the sense of what is transmitted, not of transmission," says F. Buchsel (Kittel, 1963: 172). I am not clear on what is being excluded by *not of transmission.* Buchsel seems to say that paradosis means the *content* of tradition without specific reference to the method of transmission. This would agree with the view that it was claimed that the Pharisees have a tradition in addition to Scripture, not that the tradition was transmitted in a peculiar way.

second way, that is, they were written and deposited. However, Lieberman notes, "Since in the entire Talmudic literature we do not find that a book of the Mishnah was ever consulted in case of controversies or doubt concerning a particular reading, we may safely conclude that the compilation was not published in writing." Rabbis did possess written *halakhot* and comments, but they were private notes without legal authority, with no more authority than an oral assertion. The Mishnah was published in a different way: "A regular oral . . . edition of the Mishnah was in existence, a fixed text recited by the Tannaim of the college. The Tanna (repeater, reciter) committed to memory the text of certain portions of the Mishnah, which he subsequently recited in the college in the presence of the great masters of the Law. . . . When the Mishnah was committed to memory and the Tannaim recited in the college, it was thereby published . . ." The authority of the college-Tanna ("a word apparently first used for college-reciter in the time of ᶜAqiba," [88, n. 39]) was that of a "published book" (89).

The procedure was as follows: "The Master taught the new Mishnah to the first Tanna; afterwards he taught it to the second Tanna"and so on. After the Mishnah was systematized and the Tannaim knew it thoroughly by heart, they repeated it in the college in the presence of the master, who supervised the recitation, corrected it, and gave it its final form (93). The disciples of ᶜAqiba continued the work, adding comments, and developed a larger number of different versions of the Mishnah. Judah the Patriarch then undertook a new edition. His Mishnah was virtually canonized; the rest were declared external with only secondary authority in comparison with the Mishnah of Judah.

Here we have the picture of the way in which a tradition was formulated orally.[8] Someone made up a sentence and dictated it to memorizers, who then

---

[8]We cannot leave the subject of the techniques of oral formulation and transmission of tradition without attention to the curious works of Jousse and Pautrel, contemporaries of Parry. These scholars aim at the isolation of "universal laws," by contrast to the very specific and concrete account of Lieberman. I refer to Marcel Jousse (1925: II, iv; 1930) and R. Pautrel (1934: 24.344–65; 1936: 26.1–45). Jousse's *Études* concentrate on the psychology of recitation, oral style, and similar issues. Jousse's theory is that universal laws permit us to detect originally oral materials. Whatever the text, wherever it is found, it will obey certain formal rules, some of them based upon the structure of the larynx and on various psychological responses to particular noises(!). Here we do not find the precision in metrical analysis of Parry, who formed his ideas in approximately the same time and setting, but concentration on the allegation of psychological foundations of oral style—a more general inquiry, but still, hermeneutically less deductive than the proponents of oral transmission of biblical materials. Remarks on the relationships between sound and meaning (44ff.) need not detain us. Nor are plays on words uniquely pertinent to oral formation of traditions (81ff.). Parallelism (95ff.) is not a trait unique either to the formation or to the transmission of oral materials. The presence of rhythm and rhyme-schemes may signify poetry, but it does not necessitate the hypothesis of an oral foundation. While one may grant that the power of memory is strengthened by each and every mnemonic characteristic adduced by Jousse, one still is not compelled to follow him to the starting point of his inquiry: mnemonic characteristics must signify beginnings in oral composition. To repeat what I have already said: they certainly may signify that a composition *would be* transmitted orally, but not necessarily that

mastered the tradition and constituted its testimonies. For that purpose, it was necessary to formulate matters in the mnemonic patterns we have isolated (among others), and we may account for such mnemonics as those of the Houses, possibly also (but this is far less clear) for the well-defined forms, within the theory herein presented. The picture of B. ᶜErub. 54b conforms to an isolable situation. We may draw on it for evidence of practices before the time of Judah b. Ilai.

VI

There is a final matter of interest to folklorists, namely, the dating of stories or traditions. It is claimed that we may do exactly that through the discovery of pertinent parallels. The matter is neatly formulated by Gerhardsson. One may verify as early some rabbinic traditions, attributed either to the Pharisees or to later rabbis, by parallel assertions in earlier literature:

> It is possible to grasp the fundamentals in the oldest "layers" of the Rabbinic tradition and to find correspondences in older literature, often in the Old Testament. We are able to fix dates—at least to some extent—by referring to Josephus, the Dead Sea Scrolls and the remaining "intertestamental" literature (1961:16).

We indeed find in rabbinic traditions about the Pharisees and, still more commonly, in later rabbinic and medieval traditions, sayings, ideas, themes, and stories similar to materials in earlier, but *not* (Pharisaic or) rabbinic, compilations. Hunters after parallels have come up with numerous examples of sayings and stories, Scriptural comments, and other sorts of traditions, which occur in Apocryphal, Pseudegraphical, and Qumranian writings, Philo, New Testament and Patristic literature, and the like, on the one side, and, in somewhat similar ways, in Targumim, or in rabbinic collections of *midrashim*, early, late, and medieval, on the other. The inference usually drawn from such parallels is that the late rabbinic materials are thereby

---

some sort of antecedent oral tradition lies at the foundations of the material. Allegations of oral style generally carry with them the assertion, or assumption, that the original composer (artist) never wrote down his ideas but dictated them for memorization (e.g., 195f.). That is alleged and not proved. Jousse's study of rabbinic maxims makes use of the result of his psychological and ethnic researches in the analysis of the oral style of ancient Palestine. He stresses the memorization of materials (xvff.), balanced parallels (xviiff.), cliché-parallels (e.g., poor, rich), parallel rhythmic schemes (xxi) and so on. Pautrel's NT texts are all quoted in Latin (!), and his stress is on images and parallels, rather than on internal characteristics of Greek, Aramaic, or Hebrew. His analysis of the canons of the rabbinic *mashal* stresses internal parallelisms, the construction of the *mashal*, the clearcut evidence of narrative techniques and forms, and other matters which do not settle the question of oral composition one way or the other. But the real point is that "oral materials were accurately preserved by oral means, and this must mean 'the *ipsissima verba* of Christ have been preserved'" (Streeter, quoted by Pautrel, 45), surely an adumbration of the argument of Gerhardsson.

"verified as early," as Gerhardsson states. And, indeed, that is the case. So we must concede that if a comment on a biblical figure occurs in the Testaments of the Twelve Patriarchs or Philo, on the one side, and in a late Talmudic or medieval compilation of rabbinic sayings, on the other, then the substance of that comment has already occurred to someone long before late Talmudic or medieval times. We must now ask: What conclusions are to be drawn?

One conclusion, routinely reached, is that congruence or similarity proves in this instance the antiquity of the rabbinic "tradition." That invariably is forthwith interpreted (whether articulately or otherwise) to mean that the ancient Pharisees, five or ten centuries earlier, had said such a thing, that the writer of the Patriarchal Testament, or Philo, heard it from Pharisees and, in writing it down, exhibited his affinity with, or even dependence upon, rabbinic authority or tradition.

Such an interpretation is possible because it is further assumed (but rarely made explicit) that everything in Pharisaic-rabbinic compilations, early and late, is quintessentially Pharisaic, then rabbinic; and nothing has been taken into that compilation and retroactively Pharisaized and rabbinized. The pan-Pharisaists hold that mere occurrence in a rabbinic document signifies the presence of Pharisaism-rabbinism, and this by definition. What is not defined, however, is what one means by "Pharisaic-rabbinic tradition," or what will characterize something as uniquely Pharisaic in origin or essence.

A second, closely related, and equally ubiquitous assumption is that similarities show parallels, parallels reveal sources, and sources demonstrate dependence. The source of all sources is Pharisaic-rabbinic tradition. Therefore if a saying appears early in Philo, and late in a medieval compilation of *midrashim* (whether attributed to an early master or anonymous, and pseudepigraphical considerations are rarely attended to), then Philo presumably has borrowed from Pharisaic-rabbinic tradition. Less defensible still, it is assumed that Christian exegetes, philosophers, and tradents always borrowed from Jewish ones, never contrariwise. One might readily suppose, for instance, that since Mark 10:2–10 looks much like a Pharisaic-rabbinic debate in form, the Christian tradent has borrowed a form from Pharisaic-rabbinic literary conventions; therefore, we have another instance of early Christian dependence upon rabbinic Judaism.

But a similarity is just that. Parallel lines do not meet. The fact of a parallel form or idea, standing by itself, may prove only that two men in the same country and social class reached a similar aesthetic or religious conclusion at much the same time, about much the same literary or theological problem, normally a difficulty provoked by the same Bible. That one borrowed from the other on the face of it is not a necessary and uncontingent conclusion. But if a late rabbinic compilation does contain an idea found in a pre-Christian sectarian document, one may more reasonably suppose that the compiler of that collection knew the pre-Christian sectarian document than that the pre-Christian sectarian writer knew the late rabbinic compilation. The implications of the oral theory of the formulation and transmission of Pharisaic-rabbinic traditions thus lead to the unnatural conclusions that everything was floating into the Pharisaic-rabbinic "air" and that appearance in a particular collection edited at a particular time implies nothing about the origins or provenance of that particular tradition. I think the opposite on the face of it is more congruent to probabilities.

VII

To summarize: The Pharisees certainly possessed traditions external to the written Scriptures. The evidence of Josephus and the New Testament is consistent on this point: Pharisees claimed to have *paradosis*, tradition. But Josephus's discussion lends little support for the theory that the Pharisees claimed to possess *the* Oral Torah dictated by Moses and handed on thereafter in the memories, but not in the writings, of prophets and sages. They have a tradition, but this is not described as part of the law of Moses. Josephus makes no reference to a Pharisaic claim that that tradition derives from Moses. He says it is from "the fathers." He makes no reference either to an oral Torah or two Torahs. And all the allegations about traditions from the fathers come only in *Antiquities*, written after the process of formulation in the Oral Torah had begun at Yavneh.

The evidence we do have points toward beginnings at Yavneh of the claim that people possessed verbatim traditions framed by ancient authorities and handed down orally from then on. While such traditions are assigned to Yoḥanan b. Zakkai, they seem in the end to belong not to his disciple Eliezer but to Eliezer's contemporaries. In the case of Joshua matters are not so clear. He refers simply to a decree, not to *ipsissima verba*. Nonetheless, important Yavnean masters have given evidence of a tendency to refer to oral teachings, of the discipline of oral transmission through mnemonic means to disciples, and, one need hardly add, of belief in the Oral Torah.

This suggests that both the forms of pericopae and the mnemonic elements in Mishnah come from Yavneh in the times of Eliezer, Joshua, Ṭarfon, and ᶜAqiba. We further find in Saul Lieberman's account of the publication of the Mishnah that the Mishnah begins with ᶜAqiba, that it was not published or even written down, but that it was to begin with dictated to disciples, thus orally formulated and then orally transmitted, primarily by professional memorizers present in the rabbinic schools, secondarily in unofficial notes. The picture drawn in B. ᶜErub. 54b therefore conforms to the realities described by Lieberman. The use of mnemonic patterns surely testifies to the intention of the redactors. No claim is made for ancient origins for the whole corpus of materials, still less for its present form. The present form derives from Yavneh.

Finally, we observe that the tendency of scholars is to find verifications for the antiquity of traditions first appearing on the rabbinic side in late

Talmudic and medieval compilations in the sectarian literature of Second Temple and later times, Josephus, Philo, or New Testament and Patristic literature. What is verified is only that someone, long before the medieval compiler, came to the same conclusion. It may further be alleged that that view is very old. But on that basis one cannot prove that pre-70 Pharisees held or did not hold the same opinion. One, moreover, cannot claim that the ancient writer who stated an opinion later on appearing in a rabbinic compilation learned it from a Pharisaic master or even that, when he said it, he viewed it as an opinion held by Pharisees. The opposite seems more likely. It may be more reasonable to suggest that some time after the first writing down of a tradition in, e.g., Qumranian writings or Apocrypha and Pseudepigrapha or Philo or Josephus, a rabbi heard the tradition from someone familiar with such literature (excluding the Qumranian instance) or learned it himself in its original location. But that sort of suggestion, while on the face of it is more reasonable than its opposite, is meant merely to propose a possible line of reflection and inquiry.

PART TWO

PROBLEMS OF MEANING IN THE STUDY OF EARLY RABBINIC JUDAISM
THE SECOND CENTURY

CHAPTER IV

Thematic or Systemic Description:
The Case of Mishnah's Division of Women

When we take up the study of an area defined by a common theme, rather than by a discipline or method, we first of all confront the problem of defining that which is to be studied. For a theme encompasses so wide a range of data that further definition, within the limits of the stated theme, becomes necessary. If, for example, our general topic is Jewish studies, black studies, Russian studies, American studies, or women's studies, our urgent task is to describe that part of the corpus of data relevant to Jews, blacks, Russians, Americans, or women; and we shall undertake to examine it. The second problem is locating useful issues worth investigating within the stated frame of data, that is, to interpret what we choose to describe. Description and interpretation, of course, form a dialectical system. For data which have been selected for description contain within themselves a core of issues or propositions (if only the self-validating, *self-evidently* interesting character of the data themselves) which define the task of interpretation. And when we attempt to interpret, to make sense of, the data, we find ourselves drawing upon disciplines and methods which themselves constitute results attained in the work of forming an intelligible picture of quite other data. Again to be more concrete: if we interpret through their own stated perspectives those data pertinent to Jews, blacks, Russians, Americans, or women, which have been chosen for description and interpretation, we learn nothing we did not know in selecting the data. But once we want to find out something the data do not contain and openly tell us, we step outside the frame of the area chosen for study. Then we draw upon those disciplinary considerations, those rigorous methods, which we reject when, to begin with, we choose to work in a thematic area rather than in accord with a stated discipline. The tension between defining our work through theme or topic, on the one side, and defining what we do through the requirements of a given discipline, on the other, is especially fructifying and engaging when we perceive the choices to be made.

My contribution to the exemplification of that proposition consists in the presentation of a particular case and its heuristic alternatives, namely, the problem of making sense of the treatment of women in a specific ancient Jewish document, the Mishnah. In so doing, I shall try to show the methodological choices to be made and to explain and spell out the ones I make in interpreting the way in which women are treated within the limits of that ancient document and its system. The problem is in two parts. We have first of all to account for the way in which the data are selected and laid forth, that is, the principle of selection and, it follows, the mode by which data are put forth as description. We must, second, apply that principle of selection and show how, in interpreting the data which have been laid forth, that principle leads to results of sense and worth, that is, how it yields meaning. The particular relevance of this exercise to the field of women's studies is in showing how that field, through its distinctive thematic and theoretical concerns, contributes to the interpretation of data totally unrelated to the topics and interests of the field itself. I shall suggest specifically that, from the way in which the ancient document before us treats women, we are able to make some sense of the way in which that same document selects and treats its other principal themes and topics. This I believe to be an important result.

The document to which reference is made is Mishnah, a six-part code of rules formed toward the end of the second century A.D. by a small number of Jewish sages and put forth as the constitution of Judaism under the sponsorship of Judah the Patriarch, the head of the Jewish community of Palestine at the end of that century. The reason the document is important is that Mishnah forms the definitive foundation for the Babylonian and Palestinian Talmuds. It therefore joins the Hebrew Bible as the document upon which the Judaism of the past nineteen hundred years is constructed. What makes the document urgent in this context is that, of the six principal divisions of which Mishnah is composed, one is devoted to women. While other ancient Jewish texts contain vast numbers of allusions to women,[1] it is only Mishnah which treats that topic as constitutive, fundamental to the whole. Here women appear not merely tangentially and in other contexts but as a distinct focus of discourse. To underline this point, I list the other five divisions: (1) agricultural rules, (2) laws governing appointed seasons, e.g., Sabbaths and festivals, (3) the system of civil and criminal law (corresponding to what we today should regard as "the legal system"), (4) laws for the conduct of the cult and the Temple, and (5) laws on the preservation of cultic purity both in the Temple and under domestic circumstances, with special reference to the table and bed. In fact, as we see, Mishnah's six divisions are meant to define the whole range and realm of reality. Beyond these frontiers, to Mishnah's sages' way of thinking, is nothing worthy of attention. To them the map is the territory. So when we observe that, to the framers of Mishnah, women form one of the six constitutive and definitive parts of reality, we realize that, in the circumstance of Mishnah, when we make sense of how women are treated, we find ourselves at the hermeneutical center of a much larger world-view.

[1]Compare Otwell (1977), who assembles 800 references to women and Swidler (1976), who gathers many allusions to women in "intertestamental" literature and in the Rabbinical writings as well. Swidler is discussed below.

Now the principal problem facing us is how to treat the data about women presented by Mishnah: how to describe and how to interpret them. In my view, there are two possibilities. First, we may lay out the Mishnah's data on women in discrete fashion and bring these data into relationship, e.g., for comparative purposes, with other discrete facts about women drawn from diverse Jewish and gentile sources. That is, we may work thematically. Second, we may view Mishnah's data on women as a system within a larger system. The choice I shall both propose and put into effect is the latter: systemic description and interpretation, as against thematic description and interpretation.

I

Facts by themselves mean little. It is when they are brought into relationship with other facts to form a *context* that they begin to make those statements of meaning which the system as a whole wants to express. Merely knowing, for example, that a woman receives a marriage-contract when she is betrothed and wed, and that she receives a writ of divorce when she is sent away, tells us very little. These are the sorts of things which, "common sense" tells us, women in general will have to receive in these circumstances. But what if we ask whether a principle of selection is to be discerned? Then, in seeking that principle, we ask fresh and fructifying questions. We want, for instance, to understand why it is that one given system wishes to talk, in particular, about the documentation of the transfer of women while some other system wants to speak about the prohibitions of consanguinity, the behavior of mothers in relationship to children, or the sexual activities of women when they are at diverse points in relationship to men. Then, I think, we begin to find something worth knowing. For what leads us into the center of a world-view, of a religious world-view in the case of an ancient Israelite document such as this one, is the capacity to discern and explain the principles of selection or inclusion, on the one side, and of disinterest or exclusion, on the other. Why this topic and not some other? These seem to me the questions of the most fundamental, and therefore most revealing, character. For the answers to them lay out before our eyes the principles of selection and permit us to understand, by contrasting one set of principles with some other, the taxonomy of systems, both within a given cultural framework and across frontiers of space and time.

I have now to explain the methodological choice before us in describing and explaining the Mishnaic system of women. There are, as I see it, two approaches to the description and explanation of data, thematic and systemic.[2] Thematic description takes a given topic and assembles data

---

[2] I apologize to the reader for my inability to present an objective account of a method I do not deem worthwhile. This is especially to be regretted because nearly everything else ever written on "women in Judaism" treats them topically, not systematically, as in the items listed in n. 1. So I

relevant to that topic from various contexts. The criterion of relevance is topical. Perforce one must ignore the boundaries of contexts, since material on the stated theme derives from many of them. The purposes of description, then, are accomplished by the thematic method when the pertinent data have been assembled into a construction which permits thematic questions to be framed and answered. The focus of interest is in the relationship of data drawn from one context to data drawn from some other. But this does not effect comparison. In the present instance one approach is to consider the theme of women in general and to bring into relationship data of all sorts and relevant to all matters of the present corpus of rules. The questions to be addressed to these bodies of facts, then, will emerge from the theme common to all of them, women: their status, role, activities, and similar subjects. A further, thematic inquiry would be into the legal facts of our seven tractates, e.g., marriage- and divorce-law—here, there, and everywhere.

Systemic description, by contrast, aims at making sense of facts by reference to the context in which they occur and only then, if then, asking about the relationship of one fully articulated system, in its context, to some other, in its setting. Once a context has been defined and its perimeters carefully delineated and justified, the work of description involves placing into that context all data, without regard to theme, drawn out of that context. That is to say, we have to make sense of the parts in the context of the whole, and of the whole (that is, facts about many themes and topics) by reference to the parts. The principal intellectual challenge is to find out how rules about one matter may express a viewpoint, a detail of a harmonious and comprehensive and cogent world view, shared and expressed in some other, indeed in many other, rules and details about other matters. But then the principal point of concern is not the data pertinent to a given theme but the systemic interrelationships of data on many themes.

Comparison, when it comes, is not among materials drawn from diverse contexts and relevant to a single theme, e.g., woman, or, more concretely, the character of divorce-documents and rules. Comparison is between one system and some other system. The appropriate task, in a taxonomy of systems compared to one another, will be to uncover the principles of selection, on the one side, and the relationships between those principles of selection and the encompassing ecological framework (using the word ecology in a social and historical sense) among the several systems under study, on the other.

External to its context, no fact bears on its own exegesis. But it is the context—and that alone—which supplies the exegesis. I do not conceive that within a given theme or topic is to be located a logic so compelling as to supply for thematic description and analysis the cogency and internal structure which context does for systemic description and analysis. I cannot imagine what it is

---

find myself unable to join in the presently-defined methods of discourse on "women in Judaism" and, it is clear, to frame the issues the way they conventionally are framed.

that the theme of "women" or of "the writ of divorce" tells me, so that, out of context, I may bring together, in the work of hermeneutics, diverse facts about that theme. There is no structure but in context. But context, too, is not structure. For mere definition of context also is insufficient for the work of interpretation. The meaning of what we find is to be perceived within the system located and constructed in context. Context is not *a priori*, but merely prior to the work of interpretation.

Having said so much about context, I clearly intend to justify the approach of systemic, as against thematic, description and interpretation. It follows, therefore, that the definition of what makes a system systemic becomes a critical problem. While diverse, subtle definitions of the drawing of lines of context may be attempted, I am inclined for the present purpose to choose the simplest. The boundaries of a system are drawn by the coincidence of the lines of a particular literary document with the lines of a particular, clearly defined social group. Obviously, I have drawn my definition from the document which, to begin with, I perceive as a system composed of systems: namely, Mishnah. That document is whole—by definition. It is complete since it knows its own subdivisions but, internal evidence indicates, depends upon no others for exegesis, let alone for application. It clearly proposes to describe a society and a social canopy for a world-view. We obviously do not know whether any of the law, at the time it was made up, was practical and applied.[3] That is why knowledge of a clearly defined social group, whose conceptions are contained within the document, is essential. The *Sitz im Leben* of Mishnah is the circle of authorities who made up Mishnah, the disciples and masters of the later first and second generation in what appears to be an intellectual continuum of nearly two centuries, but certainly a century and a half.

The systemic limits I have proposed are therefore literary and social. They are literary, so that we may be sure we have all the relevant data and no irrelevant ones. They are social, so that we may confidently claim to describe not merely a collection of facts but something addressed to a particular world by a particular group from its inner-facing perspective. This definition, of course, is narrow, as dictated by the circumstances and facts with which we must contend.

Systemic constructions need not be defined within the limits of documents. But then the lines and boundaries must be vividly drawn in some other way, for instance, by social walls so high as to be perceptible even long after the fact or by institutional boundaries crossed only through conversion

---

[3]Of Mishnah's six divisions at least two, on the Temple and cult and on cultic uncleanness, in no way could be relevant to the authorities who made up the document. For after A.D. 70 there was no Temple. But many other tractates are equally remote from everyday reality, e.g., the one which describes a court and government structure, Sanhedrin, which was in no way realized by the rabbis; and there are others as well. That is why the social parameters of the system are defined by the people who made it up, not by the world in which they lived.

or apostasy, depending on the direction of movement. But whether the facts derive from a book or from social realities related in many books and other sources of information (for instance, gravestones, broken pots, mosaic floors, and surviving walls of churches, temples, or synagogues), there must be a social referent. The facts must speak for someone and to someone, or we do not have a system, only a fantasy.

Mishnah speaks for the disciples and masters of the document. It addresses a world not fully realized, but not wholly imaginary. Its world view, therefore, constitutes a statement on how things are not but really are, that is to say, a judgment on how they are and also a design for a society expressive of the way things are meant by God to be. When, in time to come, there is a taxonomy of systems, this one will find its place on the list of those which hover somewhere between ideal and reality, within the division of systems made by intellectuals but meant for others, and in the subset of systems of man's (and only man's) power of sanctification of this life. But it is too soon to speak of taxonomies. As we shall see, in its own context, whether defined synchronically or delineated diachronically, Mishnah's system appears to be the sole extant systemic construction on its chosen theme. It is, alas, unique in that very taxonomic context which should prohibit our finding anything unique.

The stress on the hermeneutical priority of systemic description and analysis over thematic description and analysis, the description of how facts fit into their own context rather than relate to thematically relevant facts drawn out of some other context, surely does not begin here. For one example, Mary Boyce says precisely the same thing in connection with Zoroaster's eschatology:

> Zoroaster's eschatological teachings, with the individual judgment, the resurrection of the body, the Last Judgment, and life everlasting, became profoundly familiar, through borrowings, to Jews, Christians, and Muslims, and have exerted enormous influence on the lives and thoughts of men in many lands. *Yet it was in the framework of his own faith that they attained their fullest logical coherence* . . . (Neusner, 1977, XXII: 13).

At this point in the analysis of the Mishnah's whole system, we cannot make a similar statement of what it is that defines that systemic conviction, expressed equally in all the parts, which reveals the full, logical coherence of the whole and the meaning of these parts. Obviously, the fundamental message of the division of Women is that actions, including documents, having to do with the transfer of women both invoke the sacred and are subject to the oversight of Heaven. In a system which throughout its parts expresses the conception that man[4] is capable of effecting sanctification through his will and his works, it is

---

[4]In this system, it is man, not woman, who takes the active and definitive role. Whether in the theory of the document women also have the power to effect sanctification, I can not say. It does not matter. As we shall see at some length, Mishnah's system of women permits us to speak of *man*, not woman, in the present context.

no wonder that, as we shall see, what is written on a piece of paper is read in Heaven as it is on earth. Heaven responds to man's deeds on earth. Heaven shares that realm of the heart, governing will, intention, purpose, and plan, which is definitive of the weight and meaning of deeds.

II

Having explained why in my view the appropriate mode of description is systemic and not thematic, I have now to describe what I believe to be the principal intellectual components of the Mishnaic system of women, viewed both over all and with special reference to the seven Mishnaic tractates, defined by theme, which form Mishnah's division of Women and therefore constitute the system at hand. We begin with some generalizations and proceed to a brief account of the tractates themselves; and we shall end, later on, with a theory of the system's meaning.

The Mishnaic system of women defines the position of women in the social economy of Israel's supernatural and natural reality. That position acquires definition wholly in relationship to men, who impart form to the Israelite social economy. It is effected through both supernatural and natural, this-worldly action. What man and woman do on earth provokes a response in Heaven, and the correspondences are perfect. So the position of women is defined and secured both in Heaven and here on earth, and that position is always and invariably relative to men. The principal interest for Mishnah is the point at which a woman becomes, and ceases to be, *holy* to a particular man, that is, enters and leaves the marital union. These transfers of women are the dangerous and disorderly points in the relationship of woman to man, therefore, as I said, to society as well. Five of the seven tractates of this division are devoted to the formation and dissolution of the marital bond. Of them, three treat what by man is done here on earth, that is, formation of a marital bond through betrothal and marriage-contract and dissolution through divorce and its consequences: Qiddushin,[5] Ketubot,[6] and Gittin.[7] One of them is devoted to what by woman is done here on earth: Sotah.[8] And Yebamot,[9] greatest of the seven in size and in formal and substantive brilliance, deals with the corresponding Heavenly intervention into the formation and end of a marriage: the effect of death upon the marital bond and the dissolution, through death, of that bond. The other two tractates,

[5] Betrothals.

[6] Marriage-contracts and the settlement thereof; the transfer of property in connection with the transfer of a woman from the father's to the husband's domain.

[7] Writs of divorce.

[8] The wife suspected of adultery and the rite of drinking the bitter water described in Numbers 5.

[9] Levirate marriages, in accord with the rule of Deut 25:10–15.

Nedarim[10] and Nazir,[11] draw into one the two realms of reality, Heaven and earth, as they work out the effects of vows taken by women and subject to the confirmation or abrogation of the father or husband. These vows make a deep impact upon the marital life of the woman who has taken such a vow. So, in all, the division and its system delineate the natural and supernatural character of the woman's role in the social economy framed by man: the beginning, end, and middle of that relationship.

The Mishnaic system of women thus focuses upon the two crucial stages in the transfer of women and of property from one domain to another: the leaving of the father's house at its dissolution through divorce or through the husband's death. There is yet a third point of interest, though it is much less important than these first two stages: the duration of the marriage. Finally, included within the division and at a few points relevant to women in particular are rules of vows in general and of the special vow to be a Nazir, the former included because, in the Scriptural treatment of the theme, the rights of the father or husband to annul the vows of a daughter or wife form the central problematic, and the latter included for no very clear reason except that it is a species of which the vow is the genus.

To the message and the purpose of the Mishnaic system of women, woman is essential and central. But she is not critical. She sets the stage for the processes of the sacred. It is she who can be made sacred to man. It is she who ceases to stand within a man's sacred circle. But God, through supernature, and man, through the documentary expression of his will and intention, possess the active power of sanctification. Like the Holy Land of Mishnah's division of Agriculture, the Holy Temple of the division of Sacrifices, and the potentially holy realm of the clean of the division of Purities, women for the division of Women define a principal component of the Mishnah's orderly conception of reality. Women form a chief component of the six-part realm of the sacred. It is, as I said, their position in the social economy of the Israelite reality, natural and supernatural, which is the subject of the division and its tractates. But the whole—this six-part realm—is always important in *relationship* to man on earth and God in Heaven. Sanctification is effected through process and through relationship. The center of logical tension is critical relationship. The problematic of the subject is generated *at* the critical points of the relationship. The relationship, that is, *the process*, is what makes holy or marks as profane. God and man shape and effect that process. Earth, woman, cult, and the cult-like realm of the clean—these foci of the sacred form that inert matter made holy or marked as profane by the will and deed of God and of man, who is like God. This, I conceive, is the problematic so phrased as to elicit the desired response in our division. *The system shapes the problematic which defines how the topic will be explored and made*

[10]Vows.
[11]The vow of the Nazirite, as in Numbers 6.

consequential. Mishnah's is a system of sanctification through the word of God and through that which corresponds to God's word on earth, which is the will of man. If, as I have said, the division yields no propositions of encompassing and fundamental importance but merely legal facts about documents and relationships signified through documents, it still says a great deal both as a system and also in behalf of Mishnah's system as a whole.

Let us now consider the seven tractates and rapidly survey their principal topics.

Yebamot   The levirate connection is null in a case of consanguinity; *halisah* (Deut. 25:10ff.—the rite of removing the shoe) but no levirate marriage; a normal levirate connection, worked out through *halisah* or consummation of the marriage; marriage into the priesthood and the right to eat heave-offering; severing the marital bond; marital ties subject to doubt; the rite of *halisah*; the right of refusal; infirm marital bonds; the deaf-mute, the minor male; severing the marital bond through death of the husband; the woman's testimony; identifying a corpse.

Ketubot   The material rights of the parties to the marital union; the wife, the father, the husband; conflicting claims; fines paid to the father in the case of rape or seduction; the father's material rights; the husband's material rights; rules for the duration of the marriage; the wife's duties to the husband; the husband's marital rights and duties; the dowry; property rights of the wife while she is married; settlement of the marriage-contract in the event of the husband's death; multiple claims on an estate; the support of the widow.

Nedarim   The language of vows: euphemisms; language of no effect or of limited effect; the binding effects of vows, not to derive benefit in general, not to eat some specific kind of food in particular, and not to use certain objects; temporal application of vows; the absolution of vows; grounds for absolution; annulling the vows of a daughter and of a wife; the husband's power to annul the wife's vows; vows of a woman who is not subject to abrogation.

Nazir   Becoming a Nazir with special reference to the vow: the language of the vow, stipulations, the duration of the vow; annulling the Nazirite vow; the offerings required of the Nazir; designation and disposition; prohibitions on the Nazir; the grape, contracting corpse-uncleanness, cutting the hair.

Sotah   Invoking the ordeal of the bitter water, narrative of the ordeal and its conduct; rules of the ordeal: exemptions and applicability, testimony; rites conducted in Hebrew: the anointed for battle and the draft-exemptions, the rite of the heifer and the neglected corpse.

Gittin   Delivering a writ of divorce; preparing a writ of divorce; two irrelevant constructions: (I) confirming the prevailing supposition; (II) fifteen rulings made for the good order of society; the law of agency in writs of divorce; receiving the writ, appointing an agent to prepare and deliver a writ of divorce; stipulations in writs of divorce; invalid and impaired writs of divorce; improper delivery, improper preparation, improper stipulations, improper witnesses; grounds for divorce.

Qiddushin Rules of acquisition of a woman in betrothal; procedures of betrothal; agency, the token of betrothal, stipulations; impaired betrothals; stipulations; doubts in matters of betrothal; appropriate candidates for betrothal; castes and outcastes; the status of the offspring of impaired marriages; castes and marriage among castes; miscellanies and homilies.

We see in this detailed account of the division's repertoire of themes that we have an encompassing account of the formation, duration, and dissolution of marriages. The topic is worked out in a fairly systematic and orderly way. The Mishnaic system of women clearly does not pretend to deal with every topic pertinent to women. Indeed, it is what we do not find, as much as what we do, which permits us to claim we have a system. For when we can point to exclusions, we realize decisions have been made, within the potentialities of the *theme* of women, on what belongs and what does not belong to a distinctive *system* of women.

III

Efforts at thematic description and interpretation are inadequate not merely because they rest upon false epistemological foundations, wrenching out of context and depriving of all specific meaning the facts of the themes subject to description and interpretation. They are inadequate because the result produces exercises in confusion, triteness, and banality. Thematic approach to the data of our seven tractates, among a vast profusion of facts about "women in ancient Judaism," illustrates this proposition. To begin with, it is to be said that the topic of "woman" (or "woman in Judaism") is a snare and delusion. "The position of women" reduces even the great Evans-Pritchard to a series of banalities and trite remarks (1965). Lacking all purpose and definition, scholars in the fields of Old Testament (Bird in Reuther, 1974:41–88), Talmud (Hauptman in Reuther, 1974:184–212), and countless other fields are forced to substitute lists and catalogues for questions and insights. They have nothing to say. Lest I be thought to exaggerate, let us see how the descriptive and interpretive work is done by a scholar who has given us a sustained, complete picture of work defined along thematic lines, indeed, a whole book on *Women in Judaism.*

Leonard Swidler (1976:n.1) provides a stunningly apt illustration of the helplessness of thematic description in the face of the diverse data required by its program. In the end he can only set up two categories for interpretation, and they produce no interpretation at all. These are first, positive, and second, negative, sayings. He culls innumerable, diverse rabbinic sayings in favor of women and diverse sayings against them. He then concludes:

> On the basis of the evidence of both the positive and negative rabbinic statements about women thus far analyzed . . . it would be correct to conclude that quantitatively and qualitatively the negative attitude vastly outweighs the positive. It can be said, therefore, that the attitude of the ancient rabbis toward women was a continuation of the negative attitude toward women that evolved from the return from the Exile through the later Wisdom, apocryphal, and pseudepigraphical literature. In fact, it was in a way an intensification of it, in that the rabbis, through their great influence on the masses of Judaism, projected it most forcefully into the every day life of the observant Jew . . . (1976:82).

It follows that, for Swidler, masses of material have been suitably pigeonholed and utilized by his judgment; some are favorable, some unfavorable; and, in the balance, the overall effect is negative. What we learn from this judgment, how we better understand the data he has assembled, and the means by which we may interpret in a richer and fuller way than before the larger constructions out of which the data are drawn are questions he does not answer. He cannot. There is yet one more question I do not see answered. If it is so that "the negative attitude vastly outweighs the positive," then what do we learn which we want to know? That is, if we exclude acutely contemporary aspirations for reform, then—so what? It does not appear to a fair number of scholars that their task includes the making of such judgments in this context.

IV

In this setting of the analysis of "Women in Ancient Judaism," I point now to Isaksson (1965). For, while he does not show that there was an Essenic system of women (indeed, he shows there was none), he does make the effort to relate unsystematized *facts* about women in the Essene writings to the larger integrated system of the Essenes. His main point is that the details of the Essene writings take on meaning only within their own system (much as Boyce says of Zoroaster's teachings about eschatology) and cannot be properly interpreted when they stand apart from that system. I quote his summary and conclusions at great length in order to show how he both makes the point and demonstrates the correct methodology important for our study:

> In spite of their literal interpretation of the Pentateuch, the Qumran people came to maintain a view of marriage and a practice of marriage which differed greatly from the O.T. view and the view expressed in the rabbinical literature. This fact has proved to be entirely

due to the basically eschatological ideology of the Qumran community. They considered themselves to be engaged in a war in the eschatological period against the children of darkness. They therefore live in accordance with the laws relating to the holy war, even as regards marriage. The young man has a right to take a wife and live with her for a period of five years. After this period, the laws relating to the holy war stipulate that he is to refrain entirely from sexual cohabitation with his wife. Should his wife die during this five-year period, the man has nevertheless done his duty in propagating his race. He may not take another wife. Anyone who does so shows that he is not capable of living in accordance with the laws of the holy war but is addicted to fornication. The husband does not need to divorce his wife when he reaches the age of 25 but it is likely that such divorces occured, sometimes perhaps on the plea that the husband wished to avoid all suspicion that he had sexual intercourse with his wife even after the age of 25, when under the laws of the holy war he was no longer allowed to have it. The man who had reached the age of 25 was to live in sexual abstinence, in order to be able to do his part in the holy war against the children of darkness.

The men of Qumran were not monks governed by ascetic rules and refraining from marriage in order to combat the lust of the flesh or from aversion to women. They were soldiers mustered and sanctified to fight in the eschatological war against the children of darkness. The laws of this war allowed them to be married for a period in their youth and to live with their wives and beget children. But these laws also required them to live for the greater part of their lives in sexual abstinence. Every detail in the Qumran community's view of marriage and every detail in which its marriage *halakah* differs from those of other contemporary Jewish groups has proved to have originated in the basically eschatological ideology which dominated the life of the whole sect. This also means that the Qumran community's view of marriage must not be interpreted as an isolated detail in its ethical system. *Its moral principles on the subject of marriage are indissolubly linked with its eschatology* (1965:64–65).

Isaksson properly italicizes his concluding sentence. It would be difficult to improve upon his approach. We now very rapidly review other candidates, in the period in which Mishnah's system comes into being, for comparison, whether of minor details or of whole systems. The work will not detain us for very long.

V

Because we do not have literary evidence of systems such as Mishnah's does not mean that in ancient Judaism there were no systems encompassing women and in which, as in Mishnah, the topic of women filled an important place. But the absence of literary evidence does mean that we are not able to effect a comparison between Mishnah's system of women and some other system of the same time and place. So far as I am able to see, neither the Israelite nor the Greco-Roman world produces a document on women analogous to Mishnah's. Of the Israelite world we may be certain: among extant materials there is no system involving women as a principal component although all constructions we do have in hand include facts about, and references to, women—a very different thing. Obviously, the treatment of women, the role accorded to them in society, the place enjoyed by them in the imaginative and religious life of the diverse groups of late antiquity—all of these aspects of life required, and certainly received, attention. But how the facts about these matters fit into the larger context of which they were a part, and how these larger contexts may be described and so made available for comparison and systemic analysis I do not know. When, therefore, we state, as we must, that Mishnah is the only system of women known to us in late antiquity, the appropriate qualifications have been made. Let us now survey other Israelite writings of approximately the same time as Mishnah comes into being.

The Zadokite Document (CD) presents laws but "not a comprehensive handbook of *halakhah* [law]." Rather we have "a series of *halakhic* statements, roughly arranged by subjects" (Rabin, 1958:x). It follows that we cannot ask for the traits of CD's system as a whole, since we do not have access to the whole. We do have complete pericopae devoted to the oath, the order of the judges, purification with water, the Sabbath, the camp overseer, the meeting of all camps, preparing the requirements of the community, a woman's oath, and freewill gifts. The rule on the woman's oath (XVI, 10–13) simply observes that since the husband can annul the oath of the wife, he should not annul it unless he knows whether it ought to be carried out or annulled. If it is such as to lead to transgression of the covenant, let him annul it and not carry it out. Likewise is the rule for her father (Rabin, 1958: 76). It goes without saying that, so far as the presuppositions of Mishnah-tractate on vows, Nedarim, go, a vow contrary to what is written in the Torah is null to begin with and therefore will not require the husband's abrogation. An oath contrary to what is written in the Torah also is not binding. This hardly constitutes an ample "doctrine," let alone a system, of women or corpus of women's law. It is further forbidden to have sexual relations in Jerusalem (XII, 43), for reasons having to do with the theory of the character of the city, along the lines of Lev. 15:18 (Rabin, 1958: 58–59).

The relevant evidence in the Temple Scroll is summarized by Professor Baruch A. Levine as follows:

1) Col. 65:7–66:12 of the Scroll present a version of Deut. 22:13–23:1. There are lacunae in the Scroll, which can be reliably restored since, in other respects, the Scroll's version is faithful to the biblical original. The only variations are dialectical and orthographic.

2) Col. 66:12–17 take up the cue of Deut. 23:1, which is a statement on incest, prohibiting marriage with the wife of one's father, and link to what preceded a version of the incest code of Lev. 18 (cf. Lev. 20). The Scroll, as preserved, breaks off before this code is completed. Originally, it undoubtedly took up a part of the missing last column, col. 67. The listed incestuous unions are as follows: a) the wife of one's brother, including a half-brother, either by one's father or mother, b) one's sister, including one's half-sister, either by one's father or mother, c) the sister of one's father or the sister of one's mother (aunts), and d) one's niece, the daughter of one's brother or one's sister.

The significant addition here is, of course, the prohibition of marriage with nieces, not mentioned in Leviticus or elsewhere in Scripture (cf. *Zadokite Document* V:f.).

3) Col. 57:15–19 of the Scroll introduce into the code of conduct for Israelite kings two provisions, deriving from Deut. 17:17: a) the king must be monogamous, and b) the king is

not only forbidden to marry gentile women, but must marry a woman from his father's household, or family (cf. *Zadokite Document* IV:20, f. and Ezek. 36:16).

The prohibition of marriage with nieces, and the question of monogamy are discussed in: Baruch A. Levine, "The *Temple Scroll*: Aspects of its Historical Provenance and Literary Character," *BASOR*, no. 232 (due to appear January, 1979).

4) Col. 53:14–54:5 contain the *Scroll's* version of Num. 30:3 f. on the matter of vows (*nedarim*) and the respective roles of father and husband regarding vows pronounced by women. Except for the conversion of 3rd-person references to God into 1st-person references ("to Me," instead of "to the Lord,") the *Scroll's* version is essentially faithful to the biblical original.

5) Col. 63:10–15 of the *Scroll* present a version of the law governing marriage with captive women, Deut. 21:10 f. The statements regarding marriage are biblical, but the *Scroll* adds a stricture, which actually concerns purity, more than marriage, itself. The *Scroll* forbids the captive wife from partaking of *šĕlamim* offerings or what it calls *tohŏrah* "pure, sanctified food" for seven years.[12]

On the basis of this evidence it is not possible to maintain that the Temple Scroll presents anything like a system of women. Apart from a couple of Scriptural rules, the Temple Scroll and Mishnah's systemic construction have nothing in common. Two of the points at which the theme of women is important to the Temple Scroll and on which the author has something to say other than to cite Scripture—Levine's Nos. 2, 5—are not treated at all by Mishnah's division of Women. The third—Levine's No. 2—is shared, both in theme and detail, in Yebamot. For Yebamot, however, the list of incestuous unions forms a part of the factual substructure of the tractate. It scarcely forms a focus of inquiry or defines a critical problematic. So there is one point of intersection at the factual level, and none at that of generative conceptions, between Mishnah's division of Women and the Temple Scroll's allusions to women. Of greater consequence, the latter document in no way treats the theme of women systematically—e.g., within the program of Scripture's available allusions—nor does the theme play a major role in the Temple Scroll's system. What Mishnah and the Temple Scroll share is simply Scripture or, more accurately, a couple of facts supplied to both by Scripture.

If our problem were the position of women in general, then germane to our account would be the prominence assigned to women in all four Gospels. The women of Jesus' day and country seem to have had great liberty of movement and action (Donaldson, 1907:149). But there is no doctrine of women in the Gospels, nor can we find in the occasional remarks in Paul's letters even a remote equivalent to the Mishnaic system of women.

The Gospels' picture of women as a prominent and independent group in society is confirmed by the trove of legal documents belonging to a Jewish woman of the early second century. Among the Cave of Letters of the Bar Kokhba finds is the marriage-contract of a woman, among other legal

---

[12]Personal letter, September 10, 1978.

documents pertaining to her affairs (Yadin, 1971:222–53). The account of the affairs of this woman, Babata, leaves no doubt of her legal capacities. She received all the properties of her husband during his own lifetime and took possession of them when he died. She remarried and inherited another large property. She undertook and effected numerous important litigations and in general supervised what was hers. Any picture of the Israelte woman of the second century as chattel and a dumb animal hardly accords with the actualities revealed in the legal documents of Babata.

It is hardly necessary to observe that we have not accomplished a synchronic comparison between Mishnah's system of women and some other Israelite system(s) of women of approximately the same time and place. The reason is that we have not located an equivalent, nor partially equivalent, integrated and whole system of women other than Mishnah's. We have diverse rules on topics relevant to women. On their basis no progress toward the interpretation of Mishnah's system is possible.

VI

Mishnah's system may be brought into relationship with more than the systems of its own time and place, on one side, and of its distinct cultural continuum, on the other. It also may be usefully juxtaposed to systems of women worked out in other societies, in other times, and in other parts of the world. For there surely is a common continuum of humankind, a context of humanity, which will yield its contrasts and comparisons. But, to my knowledge, the work cannot yet be done. It is too soon. For while we may formulate a fruitful and well-constructed question, we do not, so far as I know, have a suitable formulation of data out of which to answer such a question. For example, if we ask, What is it that we learn about the traits of Israelite society, as envisaged by Mishnah, from Mishnah's system of women? we are unable to provide an answer. The reason is that, to my knowledge, we have no comparative studies of diverse possibilities of how women may be treated, the position which may be accorded to them or which they, for their own part, may define for themselves. Without taxonomies, we consequently do not know what sorts of societies will opt for which type of system among several possibilities and, still more interesting, what we learn about such societies from their choices in regard to women.

To spell this out: Mishnah's system of women deals with the transfer of women and of property associated with that transfer. It would be interesting to know the sorts of systems by which other societies (or the philosophers of other societies) arrange the same transaction. It would, further, be worth knowing what we learn about a society which does things in one way instead of some other. What do we learn about the world envisaged by Mishnah from the choices made by Mishnah in the matter of the transfer of women? Or, to state matters more accurately, what *else* do we learn? The answer to this type of question seems to me to lie in the future.

Still, anthropologists have not left us wholly without observations of a fructifying character. For example, Rosaldo observes:

> A woman's status will be lowest in those societies where there is a firm differentiation between domestic and public spheres of activity and where women are isolated from one another and placed under a single man's authority, in the home (1974:36).

It would appear at first glance that the present system accords to the woman a low status indeed for it conforms in its basic social and familial datum to Rosaldo's definition. Women not only are assigned tasks limited to the home, but they also are given few tasks in common and, outside of the home, are perceived merely to gossip in the moonlight.

But this is somewhat misleading. We observe, for one thing, that even while married, women may become property owners of substance, as their fathers leave them land. True, the husband enjoys the usufruct so long as the marriage continues. But the woman is ultimate owner. That means the husband has every material reason to want to preserve those conditions which will secure and perpetuate the marriage. Moreover, Mishnah makes provision for a husband's relinquishing his rights over his wife's property, even as a condition of marriage. This means that the world outside the linguistic frame of Mishnah looked much different from that inside, as the case of Babata suggests. Of greater importance than practical affairs, Mishnah within its theoretical frame does accord the woman rights of property. It does secure the marriage, through the marriage-contract and its settlement upon the occasion of divorce or death of the husband, so that in no way is the wife utterly and completely dependent upon the husband. That does not mean the woman enjoys a position, in her realm, equivalent to that of the man, in his. But it does mean that a woman's status in this system is not utterly lacking a measure of autonomy, dignity, and control of her own affairs. The measure, to be sure, is not overflowing.

Mishnah is produced within, and can only imagine, a patriarchal society. Its legislation on women to begin with expresses the values of that society. This is self-evident in that the critical points of the system—beginning, end of marriage—define what is important about woman. What requires close attention and regulation is important because the relationship of woman to man constitutes the criterion of significance. Women's relationships to other women never come under discussion, except as a realm from which a woman may not be wholly cut off at her husband's whim. But if there were activities used by women "as a basis for female solidarity and worth," Mishnah does not legislate about them. Since it is what Mishnah deems important that Mishnah chooses for its careful scrutiny, the point is obvious. Mishnah does not imagine that men live apart from women or that women exist outside of relationship with, and therefore control of, men. Mishnah is a man's document and imagines a man's world. Women have rights, protected by man and Heaven alike. But these rights pertain, specifically, to the relationship of women to men (and Heaven), and specified among them is none of consequence outside of male society. The reason, I think it is clear, is that relationship is derivative and dependent upon that to which relationship is formed. Man is at the center.

VII

The critical issue of the meaning of Mishnah's system of women brings us to the center of Mishnah's meaning, which the system of women, like all other Mishnaic systems, expresses in language particular to its topic. What Mishnah wishes to state it states systemically, as a whole. The parts and the details take on meaning only as part of that whole. At this point, therefore, while we may make some observations about what a subset of the Mishnaic system appears to wish to say, the full expression of that message must wait the completion of work on the whole.[13] For only when we understand why Mishnah chooses the six topics it chooses, and not some other set of six—or five, or nine or sixty-three—topics shall we make sense of what Mishnah says about, and through, each of those topics. To that inquiry, women mean no more, and no less, than albatrosses, rocks, trees, or study of Torah, on which we have neither tractates nor divisions, or torts, purities, or agricultural offerings to priests, on which we have both.

The first and most important point is that Mishnah's meaning is defined not only by, but also in behalf of, Mishnah's authorities. All we have in hand is a statement of how they imagine things should be. As I said, whole divisions (for instance, Holy Things and Purities) dwell upon matters which, at the moment at which the systems came into being and were worked out, simply did not exist. Others speak of matters which, at the time of discourse, lay wholly outside the practical power and authority of the participants to the discussion, for example, the organization of a government spelled out in Sanhedrin. Still others take for granted that only a small number of people will keep the law properly, as in the case of the larger part of Agricultural Rules. So Mishnah speaks for its authorities and tells us what is on their minds, that alone. Only in later times would the Israelite world come to approximate, and even to conform to, Mishnah's vision of reality. But the meaning of which we presently speak is in the minds of a handful of men.

[13]I lay out three of Mishnah's six divisions, with stress on the history and structure of the law (1974–77: I–XXII; 1978–80: I–VI; 1980f: I–V). My present work is on equivalent studies for *Appointed Times* and *Torts*, five volumes and four volumes, respectively. My students' project has already been outlined here.

From these men's perspective, second, women are abnormal; men are normal.[14] I am inclined to think that the reason they choose to work out a division on women flows from that fact. And, when we recall that the only other systems of women worthy of the name come to us under priestly auspices, in the Priestly Code (Lev 1–15) and in the Holiness Code (Lev 17ff.), we can hardly be surprised at the selection of women, for the men before us create Mishnah as a scribal-priestly document. Women in the priestly perspective on the holy life are excluded from the centers of holiness. They cannot enter the sensitive domain of the cult, cannot perform the cultic service, and cannot participate even in the cultic liturgy. Likewise, in time to come, when Rabbinic Judaism comes to full expression so that study of Torah comes to be seen as a cultic act, the Rabbi as equivalent to the priest, and the community of Israel assembled for study of Torah as equivalent to the holy Temple, it would be perfectly "natural" to continue the exclusion of women. Rabbinism is a Judaic system in which people who are neither priests nor scribes take up the method of the priests and the message of the scribes. To all of this, women form an anomaly and a threat, just as the priests concluded in Ezra's time when they produced Leviticus. That is why, as in other matters of anomaly or threat, Mishnah must devote a rather considerable measure of attention to forming a system of women—a system of law to regulate the irregular.

We shall now dwell on this matter of woman as anomaly because, as I have now indicated, I am inclined to see in it the core and key to the world-view laid out for us in the division of Women. I shall now try to show that, as I claimed at the outset, the treatment and selection of women constitute the exegetical fulcrum for the Mishnaic system as a whole. To repeat my main proposition: when we make sense of Mishnah's choice of the theme, Women, and what it wishes to say about that theme, we shall find ourselves at the heart of the Mishnaic system of reality-building.

To begin with, if we are going to be able to make sense of Mishnah's choices, its inclusions and exclusions in its discourse on women, it must, I think, be because of the basic conception of woman. They are abnormal and excluded, something out of the ordinary. That is why they form a focus of sanctification: restoration of the extraordinary to the ordinary and the normal.

Let me spell this out. Mishnah cannot declare a dead creeping thing clean. Mishnah cannot make women into men. It can provide for the purification of what is made unclean. It can provide for a world in which it is

[14]The notion of the woman as anomalous, which I first read in Beauvoir (1953) will now come to the fore as the hermeneutical fulcrum for the interpretation of the Mishnah's system of Women and, as I shall argue, of Mishnah's system as a whole. It is a commonplace in women's studies, but an exceptionally fresh and fructifying idea for the study of ancient Judaism. I underline this fact to indicate why I think women's studies as an academic field have the potential to make rich contributions to the unfolding of other areas of study.

normal for woman to be subject to man—father or husband—and a system which regularizes the transfer of women from the hand of the father to that of the husband. The regulation of the transfer of women is Mishnah's way of effecting the sanctification of what, for the moment, disturbs and disorders the orderly world. The work of sanctification *becomes* necessary in particular at the point of danger and disorder. An order of women must be devoted, therefore, to just these things, so as to preserve the normal modes of creation ("how these things really are") so that maleness, that is, normality, may encompass all, even and especially at the critical point of transfer.

In this sense the process outlined in the division of Purities for the restoration of normality, meaning cleanness, to what is abnormal, meaning uncleanness, is suggestive. What Mishnah proposes is to restore the equilibrium disturbed by the encounter with the disruptive, disorganizing, and abnormal sources of uncleanness specified in the priestly writings. So the division of Purities centers attention on the point of abnormality and its restoration to normality: sources of uncleanness, foci of uncleanness, modes of purification.[15] Now, when we reflect on the view of women contained in Mishnah, we observe a parallel interest in the point of abnormality and the restoration to normality of women: the moment at which a woman changes hands. So Rosaldo states:

> The fact that men, in contrast to women, can be said to be associated with culture reflects another aspect of cultural definitions of the female. Recent studies of symbolic culture have suggested that whatever violates a society's sense of order will be seen as threatening, nasty, disorderly, or wrong. . . . The idea of "order" depends, logically, on "disorder" as its opposite. . . . Now I would suggest that women in many societies will be seen as something "anomalous." Insofar as men, in their institutionalized relations of kinships, politics, and so on, define the public order, women are their opposite. Where men are classified in terms of ranked, institutional positions, women are simply women and their activities, interests, and differences receive only idiosyncratic note. Where male activities are justified and rationalized by a fine societal classification, by a system of norms acknowledging their different pursuits, women are classified together, and their particular goals are ignored. From the point of view of the larger social system, they are seen as deviants or manipulators; because systems of social classification rarely make room for their interests, they are not publicly understood. But women defy the ideal of the male order. They may be defined as virgins, yet be necessary to the group's regeneration. They may be excluded from authority, yet exercise all sorts of informal power. Their status may be derived from their male relations, yet they outlive their husbands and fathers. And insofar as the presence of women does introduce such contradictions, women will be seen as anomalous and defined as dangerous, dirty, and polluting, as something to be set apart (1974:31—32).

Rosaldo further states: "Women in conventional roles are not threatening. A woman who is a wife and a mother is benign" (1974). Now, as we have observed, it is the point at which a woman is perceived as threatening—when she has the capacity to become a wife and a mother but is not yet in a position

---

[15]This fact is spelled out at great length in my *Purities*, XXII (1977).

of realizing it, or when she ceases to be a wife—that her status requires the regulation, ordering, and protection of Mishnah's elaborate and reverent intellectual attention.

About woman as wife Mishnah has little to say; about woman as mother, I cannot think of ten relevant lines in Mishnah's division of Women[!]. For these are not the topics to which Mishnah will devote itself. The three systemically anomalous tractates from this perspective are not so far out of line. Sotah, of course, attends to the wife who is not a good wife. Nedarim, bearing Nazir in its wake, treats those moments specified by Scripture as especially important in the daughter's relationship to the father or the wife's to the husband. These are moments at which the father or the husband may intervene in the relationship of daughter or wife to God. In the present context, that relationship is unruly and dangerous, exactly like the relationship of daughter leaving father or of wife leaving husband, that is, at the critical moment of betrothal and consummation of the marriage, with attendant property settlement; or divorce or husband's death, at the critical moment of the dissolution of the marriage, with attendant property settlement.

Mishnah's system addresses and means to create an ordered and well-regulated world. Mishnah states that which is the order and regulation for such a world. The division of Purities spells out the balance and wholeness of the system of cleanness, defining what is a source of uncleanness, a focus affected by uncleanness, and a mode of effecting cleanness or restoring the balance and the wholeness of the system in stasis. It is the most complete statement of that wholeness and regulation which are at every point besought and realized. The division of Holy Things addresses a different sort of message, speaking, as the division of Purities does not, to a real world. But it is the message which is unreal, for in A.D. 200 there is no cult. Holy Things provides a map for a world which is both no more and not yet, for a Temple which was and will be. The stasis attained therein, it must follow, is to portray how things truly are, at a moment at which they are not that way at all. By contrast to Purities, which conceives of a sequence of states in a reality out there and tells the regulations for each of those states, Holy Things speaks of how things are in mind, at a moment at which mind is all there is. When we come to the division of Women, therefore, we find ourselves confronted by a familiar problem, expressed through (merely) unfamiliar facts. The familiar problem is an anomalous fact. An anomaly is for this system a situation requiring human intervention so that affairs may be brought into stasis, that is, made to conform with the Heavenly projections of the created world. That quest for stasis, order and regulation, which constitute wholeness and completeness, in the division of Women takes up yet another circumstance of uncertainty. This it confronts at its most uncertain. The system subjects the anomaly of woman to the capacity for ordering and regulating, which is the gift and skill of priests and scribes.

The anomaly of woman therefore is addressed at its most anomalous, that is, disorderly and dangerous, moment, the point at which women move from one setting and status to another. The very essence of the anomaly, woman's sexuality, is scarcely mentioned. But it always is just beneath the surface. For what defines the woman's status—what is rarely made explicit in the division of Women—is not whether or not she may have sexual relations, but with whom she may have them and with what consequence. It is assumed that, from long before the advent of puberty, a girl may be married and in any event is a candidate for sexuality. From puberty onward she will be married. But what is selected for intense and continuing concern is with whom she may legitimately do so, and with what economic and social effect. There is no sexual deed without public consequence; and only rarely will a sexual deed not yield economic results, in the aspect of the transfer of property from one hand to another. So, as I said, what is anomalous is the woman's sexuality, which is treated in a way wholly different from man's. And the goal and purpose of Mishnah's division of Women are to bring under control and force into stasis all of the wild and unruly potentialities of sexuality, with their dreadful threat of uncontrolled shifts in personal status and material possession alike.

Mishnah invokes Heaven's interest in this most critical moment for individual and society alike. Its conception is that what is rightly done on earth is confirmed in Heaven. A married woman who has sexual relations with any man but her husband has not merely committed a crime on earth. She has sinned against Heaven. It follows that when a married woman receives a writ of divorce and so is free to enter into relationships with any man of her choosing, the perceptions of that woman are affected in Heaven just as much as are those of man on earth. What was beforehand a crime and a sin afterward is holy, not subject to punishment at all. The woman may contract a new marriage on earth which Heaven, for its part, will oversee and sanctify. What is stated in these simple propositions is that those crucial and critical turnings at which a woman changes hands produce concern and response in Heaven above as much as on earth below. And the reason, as I suggested at the beginning, is that Heaven is invoked specifically at those times, and in those circumstances, in which Mishnah confronts a situation of anomaly or disorder and proposes to effect suitable regulation and besought order.

To conclude: It is to a situation which is so frought with danger as to threaten the order and regularity of the stable, sacred society in its perfection and at its point of stasis that Mishnah will devote its principal cognitive and legislative efforts. For that situation, Mishnah will invoke Heaven and express its most vivid concern for sanctification. What breaks established routine or what is broken out of established routine is what is subject to the fully articulated and extensive reflections of a whole division of Mishnah, or, in Hebrew, a *seder*, an order, of the whole. Mishnah, as usual, provides its own most reliable exegesis in calling each one of its six principal divisions a *seder*, an order. The anomaly of woman is worked out—that is, held in stasis—by assigning her to man's domain. It follows that the stasis is disturbed at the point when she changes hands. Then Mishnah's instincts for regulating and thereby restoring the balance and order of the world are aroused. So from the recognition of the anomalous character of women, we find ourselves moving toward the most profound and fundamental affirmations of Mishnah about the works of sanctification: the foci and the means. Women are sanctified through the deeds of men. So too are earth and time, the fruit of the herd and of the field, the bed,[16] chair, table, and hearth—but, in the nature of things, women most of all.

---

[16]I do not make reference to the menstrual taboo because Mishnah's *system* of Women does not deal with it. Menstrual laws are a subdivision, or tractate, of the system of Purities.

CHAPTER V

History and Structure:
The Case of Mishnah's
System of Purities

The history of the ideas of Mishnah, a compilation of rules formulated and redacted ca. A.D. 170–200 out of materials attributed to authorities who flourished in the preceding two centuries, works itself out on a grid of vertical and horizontal lines. The vertical is the line of thought, the sequence of ideas viewed from the generative principle at the outset to the last stages of the instantiation and refinement of that principle, at the end. The horizontal is the line of events of tremendous weight (for example, the destruction of the Temple of Jerusalem in A.D. 70, the catastrophe of Bar Kokhba's war in A.D. 132–135), events which should have had a profound effect upon the minds of the Jews of the Land of Israel and hence upon the unfolding of the ideas ultimately laid forth by the rabbis of Mishnah.

On the one hand, the tractates of Mishnah begin with some basic and generative notions, rich in unresolved logical tensions and incomplete conceptual potentialities. When we follow the history of these notions, we discover that their unfolding is to be described in a single and fairly straight line. What is attributed to an authority, for instance, of the period before 70 turns out in the main to lay out the problem of detail or of logic to be solved by a saying assigned to an authority of the period thereafter. The former's saying will be refined, revised, criticized, in some way subjected to logical refinement. On the other hand, the issues of Mishnah cannot have been investigated wholly without reference to events of the day. The changes in the socioreligious ecology of Judaism in this period are so profound and of such long lasting consequence that it is exceedingly difficult to think otherwise.

In so stating the problem before us, I have of course drawn close to a classic issue facing historians of ideas, namely, the interplay between events and ideas, the issues of whether people respond to what happens to them by reshaping ideas which, in the absence of such events, would have logically taken another course entirely and of whether the history of ideas is to be recovered principally through the unfolding of the inner potentialities of a conception. In the present chapter I offer a concrete example of how, in proposing an explanation for a problem in the history of ideas, we may mediate between two conflicting claims for the adequacy of explanation. The former makes reference to the completion and fulfillment of the logical potentialities of a proposition. The latter rests upon the adequacy of explanation by reference to events wholly outside of the logical and internal context.

The specific problem is this: Why is it that that sixth part of Mishnah, which is devoted to problems of ritual purity, is brought to conclusion at exactly the time that it is (i.e., the end of the second century) and why has that division ("Order") of Mishnah never enjoyed the sustained attention of the later thinkers of Rabbinic Judaism? At the outset I propose a criterion for determining whether or not a tractate of the division has fulfilled its logical potentialities, then exhaustively apply that criterion to the twelve tractates of the order. In the second part of the chapter, I take up a perspective entirely outside the issues of the inner tensions of conceptual and generative principles and turn to the larger historical setting in which our division, along with all of Mishnah, comes to completion and closure. In so doing, I am able to show that what the system of laws of purity proposes to state about the reality of second century Israelites reaches a closure at the moment of its conceptual perfection because the message had become implausible.

I

The various tractates of Mishnah supply more than facts about their respective topics. They also bring to bear upon these topics a distinctive problematic, asking a very particular set of questions about the themes under discussion. Accordingly, when we seek to define the deep structure of a topic of Mishnah, we inquire into the character of the core of its generative conception, not solely into details, or even the logical requirements of the subject matter subject to analysis. So far as a tractate fully and exhaustively works out the inherent requirements of its generative problematic, it may be said to have come to fulfillment and completion. To be sure, the subject under discussion may be investigated from diverse, further perspectives. But the tractate as we know it has done the work it set out to do. Ample instantiation of this proposition will be given in a moment.

The recognition that Mishnah tractates are formed not solely around the data of their subject matter but also in response to the inner requirements of their problematic is important for historical, not solely hermeneutical and phenomenological, inquiry. For one pressing problem in the history of the religious world of Mishnah, its literature and law, is the explanation of why the corpus comes to completion when it does. My *History of the Mishnaic Law of Purities* shows that by the last quarter of the second century the development of the laws of the several tractates of the Order of Purities stops.[1]

---

[1]This paper goes over the ground of Vol. XXII, *The Mishnaic System of Uncleanness: Its Context and History* (Neusner, 1974–77).

At that point, excluding a handful of sayings attributed to Judah the Patriarch (hereinafter, Rabbi) and his contemporaries, we find remarkably few conceptual initiatives in the unfolding of laws. While from the very beginnings to the middle of the second century the history of the several sets of laws is sequential, with a close correspondence between logical priority of laws and chronological priority of the authorities to whom laws are attributed, when the names of the principal figures (hereinafter, Ushans[2]) after the Bar Kokhba War (ca. 135) no longer are attached to sayings, virtually no further conceptual developments of the law are to be discerned. The work of the generation of Rabbi thus neglects the task of developing and further articulating the law. A survey in detail of the sayings in the names of Rabbi and his contemporaries merely yields a repertoire of unimportant contributions, almost all of them in the nature of glosses upon laws in the names of Ushans. It follows that the principal interest in the time of Rabbi, ca. 170 to 200, is in the work not of contributing new conceptions but of redaction and formulation of the ideas received from the earlier generations.[3] We have therefore to ask, How shall we account for the radical shift in interest, from developing the law to giving it its ultimate form and organization? Why does the redaction of the Order of Purities of Mishnah take place at just the time it did?[4] The recognition that tractates develop in line with the necessities of their generative problematic contributes to the definition of the situation confronted by Rabbi and his contemporaries though it does not satisfactorily answer the question.

We forthwith eliminate as sufficient cause the impact of a historical event or concatenation of events. History does not affect the formation of Mishnah's law. We discern remarkably little impact upon the law from external happenings of a world-shaking sort, e.g., after 70, the destruction of the Temple and Jerusalem, or after 140, the ultimate suppression of the messianic hopes roused by Bar Kokhba and the extermination of a vast portion of the Jewish population in the southern part of the Land of Israel. An examination of the history of the law of purities shows that the cataclysms of 70 and the Bar Kokhba War do not produce significant impact upon the

[2]Usha is the Palestinian town in which the principal gathering of sages is supposed to have taken place after the Bar Kokhba War, in the period from ca. 140 to ca. 170. Yavneh (hence: Yavneans) is the town generally assumed to have served as the equivalent location in the period from ca. 70 to ca. 130. Calling the two periods, the former from the destruction of the Temple to the Bar Kokhba War, the latter from the Bar Kokhba War to the time of Rabbi, by the place names, Yavneh and Usha, is simply a convenience.

[3]This work is described in Vol. XXI, *The Redaction and Formulation of the Order of Purities in Mishnah and Tosefta* (Neusner, 1974–77).

[4]The same question in due course will have to be addressed to the first five orders of Mishnah. All which is stated here, so far as Mishnah *as a whole* is concerned, is provisional and tentative. Much, moreover, will be seen to be particular to the Order of Purities. The first five orders will have to yield other sorts of answers entirely. But we are far from a notion of their history and development, let alone their principal foci and generative concerns.

formation, direction, and conceptual unfolding of the law. ~~The law is continuous, beginning to end, exhibiting much development of earlier ideas by later authorities, but few genuinely fresh ideas or unpredictable themes once the primary themes and lines of thought are laid down.~~ In any case, no events of equivalently far-reaching character and consequence are assigned to the period of Rabbi. So far as we know, for Israel[5] it was a time of peace and reconstruction, during which the Jews of the Land enjoyed good relationships with the Roman government and undertook no major political initiatives. True, Rabbi himself is supposed to have combined "learning and worldly power." It should follow that he had the opportunity, perhaps not available to his predecessors, to undertake ambitious literary work. But his part of the work clearly is not to continue the articulation of the law, to introduce new conceptions, or to revise and augment the governing problematic of a given tractate. He and his associates choose to do something wholly new, utterly without precedent in the system as we know it. And that fact requires explanation.

~~A system whose twists and turns through time exhibit little perceptible impact from external events, at this time given a character of completeness, general closure, and stylistic formalization, clearly is to be analyzed in its internal structure.~~ Specifically, we must ask: In a certain sense has the system become essentially "complete" by the end of the Ushan stage, so that the time had come to give it, in language and form, that permanence and ahistorical character which in logic and in inner structure it already had attained? Obviously, new rules, new matters of detail, will arise in the course of time. But, as I have said, a tractate takes shape around not only a theme or a topic, but a problem brought to bear upon the working out of said theme or topic. It is the problematic of a tractate which imparts conceptual shape and inner structure to the tractate, gives purpose to the exploration of its theme or topic. We therefore speculate on whether work had been left undone in the statement and development of a tractate's problematic or whether, in point of fact, the original requirements awaiting intellectual articulation and investigation had been met. If it should develop that by the end of Ushan times we find a complete working out of the logical requirements of the stated problematic of a tractate—without regard to whether new rules on the tractate's *theme* were to be forthcoming later on—then we shall have fair grounds on which to conclude that that tractate of Mishnah is brought to a close because, as I said, in a certain sense the system had become complete. It is the inquiry into the intrinsic structural character of the components of the system which lies before us.[6]

---

[5]In conformity with Mishnaic usage, I refer to the Jews as *Israel*.

[6]I owe my recognition of the question to Professors Noam Chomsky, Massachusetts Institute of Technology, and Dean Miller, University of Rochester.

II. THE PARTS

Our task is now to state the problematic of each of the dozen tractates of the Order of Purities and to speculate about the logical requirements of a complete and exhaustive working out of the implications of said problematic. We then shall ask whether, in point of fact, these requirements had been attained by the end of Ushan times. The statement of the problematic emerges from a reprise of the thematic structure of the tractate. That is, we work backward from the end product. Clearly, it is the character of the Ushan stratum that defines the range of both still open and completely closed questions. The assessment of the state of matters at that point, and not our subjective impression of how things should or might have been worked out, imposes the definitive criterion of the completion of the system. If Ushans raise truly fresh and suggestive questions on the one side, or leave open urgent issues on the other, then the system cannot be said to have become complete. But if Ushans occupy themselves with matters of completion of questions asked before their time and leave open no really major and unprecedented inquiries intrinsic to the character of the original problematic of a tractate, then we may conclude that no further work will have been required, and the time for closure and completion had come.

1. Kelim[7]

What Kelim wants to know about domestic utensils is when they become unclean, the status of their parts in relationship to the uncleanness of the whole utensil, when they cease to be unclean, and the status of their sherds and remnants in relationship to the uncleanness of the whole. The uncleanness of a utensil depends upon two criteria: the form of the utensils and the materials of which the utensil is composed. A utensil which forms, or has, a receptacle can contain uncleanness. A utensil which is fully processed and available for normal use is susceptible to uncleanness. Full processing must impose on the utensil a distinctive function. The criterion is the human conception of function. An object which is fully manufactured and routinely used for a fixed purpose by man is susceptible. Diverse materials to be sure exhibit different traits, but only within these criteria. The refinement of this view will deal with gray areas, e.g., imperfect receptacles, the status of parts or of subsidiary functions of a utensil, the distinction between the time at which a utensil serves man and the time at which it does not, and the revision of the distinctive purpose, e.g., by a change in the form of an object. The assessment of the

---

[7]Kelim deals with the susceptibility to uncleanness of domestic utensils, pots and pans. Relevant biblical verses are Lev 11:32–33. See Neusner, 1974–77: Vol. I, *Kelim. Chapters One through Eleven*; Vol. II, *Kelim. Chapters Twelve through Thirty*; Vol. III, *Kelim. Literary and Historical Problems*.

status of parts of a utensil or of things affixed to a utensil represents a further refinement. A part must be firmly affixed. Parts which are going to be removed because they interfere with the functioning of a utensil are not taken into account as susceptible to uncleanness. A part which is essential to the use of a utensil is deemed integral to it. Having completed the consideration of when a utensil is susceptible to uncleanness, we turn to the point at which it ceases to be susceptible. We simply state systematically the negative of the foregoing propositions. A utensil which is useless is insusceptible. One which is broken is useless. One which no longer serves its original function is no longer susceptible as it was before. When we assess uselessness, we again focus upon human intention in working with said utensil. Sherds and remnants are subject to the same criteria of uselessness. We determine whether or not the utensil's sherd continues to be useful on its own. At the end, we ask about the work of a skilled craftsman as against that of an ordinary person, the intention of the rich as against that of the poor, the actual accomplishment of a person's purpose, and the changing status of a utensil in respect to its form or in respect to its function.

When Kelim asks, When does a utensil become unclean? or When does a utensil become clean?, what the tractate really wants to know is, What is the relation of man—his purpose, intention, and convenience—to the susceptibility of the utensil or to the cessation of susceptibility? The tractate's supposition is that it is human intention which subjects an object to susceptibility, brings said object into the system of uncleanness, and removes it from the system. Its themes, utensils, and problems connected with its theme, catalogued above, therefore are worked out within the problematic of the capacity of man to introduce objects into, or remove them from, the process of contamination and purification. The Ushans' working out of quite secondary and derivative questions does not generate further exercises because such an inquiry, deriving from the Ushan answers to these questions, cannot advance matters in any significant way. A sign of that fact is the Ushans' inclusion of issues not particular to utensils, e.g., the distinction between rich man and poor man, between craftsman and ordinary person, and the like. Once the structure is complete, one can expand it only by moving outside the limits imposed by its intrinsic logic, the agendum defined at the outset.

The problematic of Kelim, therefore, is the point at which human intention and deliberate action introduce into, and remove from, the system of contamination and purification diverse sorts of utensils made from various materials. Its specific interest is in the role of man. Its point is that human intention and action govern the introduction of objects into the system of uncleanness. That point is fully and completely worked out within the multidimensional grid formed of lines emanating from (1) various materials and their traits, (2) various objects and their shapes, (3) the beginning of susceptibility, (4) the end of susceptibility, and other intersecting lines of

definition. ~~From the opening questions to the closing answers of Usha~~ the
~~system is whole and complete, indicated as I said by the fact that the Ushan~~
~~stratum is secondary, derivative, and, of greatest importance, generative of no~~
~~new and fundamental issues, themselves demanding further inquiry.~~

2. Ohalot[8]

This tractate is to be dealt with in two parts: its treatment of sources of
uncleanness and modes of their transfer and its interest in the theory of the
Tent.

The former segment cannot be said to exhibit a generative problematic. It
simply develops the notion that things which are like a principal source of
uncleanness (the corpse) impart uncleanness as does that to which they are
likened. ~~The definition of things which contaminate as do corpses leads~~
~~nowhere. It can go on indefinitely, to be sure, since the potentiality of analogy~~
~~is unlimited. The matter of modes of the transfer of uncleanness is curiously~~
~~undeveloped and does not take an important place in the tractate as a whole.~~
~~In point of fact the sole really interesting aspect of the problem is~~ ᶜAqiva's
~~inquiry into whether the tent is an active force, itself combining bits and pieces~~
~~of corpse-matter subject to its overshadowing into the requisite volume,~~ or
~~whether the tent is wholly a formal and passive thing.~~ The limits of
overshadowing—through a tent, not through a man or a utensil—likewise
lead nowhere. The one point of important expansion comes in the question of
whether modes of the transfer of uncleanness have the capacity to "join
together." This is secondary to the issue of combining sources of uncleanness.
The Ushans break little new ground in regard either to sources or to modes of
transfer of uncleanness. The structure of the system as a whole, while rich in
the definition of sources of uncleanness, contains little space for secondary
and tertiary movements out of primary allegations as to what is unclean and
how uncleanness of a given sort is transferred. I see no generative problematic
in this regard. ~~The formation of the tractate itself, which relegates these~~
~~questions to preliminary and concluding units while preserving the shank of~~
~~the tractate for a more important and consequential issue, confirms the view~~
~~that the definition and development of that which contaminates as does a~~
~~corpse are not principal concerns.~~

~~Once a tent is defined as something so small as a handbreadth squared,~~ by
~~contrast, we confront the generative problematic of the tractate.~~ The matter
begins in the notion that corpse-uncleanness flows through such a small space
or may be prevented from passing through such a small space. Conceived as a
kind of fluid, corpse-uncleanness then will be stopped up in such a way as to be

---

[8]Ohalot addresses itself to corpse-uncleanness. The first three and last three chapters discuss
materials deemed unclean just as a corpse is unclean. The shank of the tractate, from the end of
chaps. 3–15, concerns the effects of the tent referred to in Num 19:14–19. See Neusner, 1974–77:
Vol. IV, *Ohalot. Commentary*; Vol. V, *Ohalot. Literary and Historical Problems*.

forced to flow perpendicularly—that is, under pressure—or it will be so contained that it affects all the sides of its container—that is, not under pressure. These matters are not much developed, I think, because there is not much to be said about the physics of the flow of corpse-matter, once the comparison to the flow of liquid has been made.

But the conception of the tent as an enclosed area so small as a handbreadth absolutely requires the comparison of the tent to that other enclosed area of very small volume, an ordinary utensil. If a tent and a utensil are analogous, then we must ask, first, can man constitute a tent? Second, since a utensil is like a tent, how does a utensil function when it serves as a tent? Does it afford protection as does a tent? Third, since a utensil is like a tent, can a utensil join with a tent, participate in its work of preventing the spread of uncleanness or facilitating its flow? Fourth, since a utensil is like a tent, can a utensil form a tent? Does a utensil serve as part, e.g., a base, of a tent? How does an object serve sometimes as a utensil, sometimes as a tent (Ohalot, Chap. 9)? How does a utensil (a pot) serve, like a tent, to block up the egress of uncleanness (Ohalot, Chap. 10)? What is the role of the human body in the passage of corpse-uncleanness, which is to ask, if a utensil serves as a tent, does the body, which contains the belly, a kind of utensil, also serve as a tent?

The Ushan theorists carry to its logical conclusion the proposition that the squared handbreadth measures the space through which corpse uncleanness passes. When there is not adequate egress, then we have no tent. When there is adequate egress, then there is a domain separate and capable of containing uncleanness. The Ushans also develop the analogy of the tent and the conception of adequate egress. The entire structure begins in the standard measure, the squared handbreadth which itself expresses the generative problematic of the tractate, the notion that corpse-matter conforms to the stated dimension. Everything else flows from that notion. Once we reach Usha, we have come to the limits of the problematic. The Ushans ask, when is a utensil (a hive) a utensil and when is it a tent? They further wonder about the interrelationships between two tents, which is a closely correlated question. What is carefully omitted from the system of sources of uncleanness is human participation. Whether or not man can constitute a tent, man does nothing deliberately to create corpse-matter. But the tent as a human construction is central to the transmission of corpse-uncleanness. Things which man makes effect the transfer of that form of uncleanness, just as things which man makes are subject to uncleanness.

The problematic of Ohalot, therefore, is defined within the notion of the way in which corpse-uncleanness flows and the space through which it can pass. Within the stated problematic the range of issues is fully worked out by the end of Ushan times. Taking as our criterion the great constructions of Ohalot, Chaps. 9 and 10, we can hardly conclude other than that the structure is complete when the problem of the tent as utensil, sometimes and sometimes not, and as space, contained or enclosed within some larger space, has been investigated.

3. Negaim[9]

Negaim, Niddah, and the part of Zabin devoted to the uncleanness of the *Zab* and how that uncleanness is transferred, like the beginning and end of Ohalot, do not work out a problematic in connection with their respective themes, the uncleanness of the *nega^c*, menstruating woman, and the *Zab*. I am unable to discern any questions which serve to expand and deepen the logical inquiry, anything that people want to know *about* these sources of uncleanness other than rules for their definition and application. There is, therefore, no reason for Negaim to be brought to a conclusion at some specific time in its unfolding because there also is no reason for the tractate to commence its development. That is to say, since Negaim does not begin in a generative problematic, it therefore cannot be judged to draw to a conclusion when the implications of that problematic have been fully spelled out and entirely exhausted. A rapid restatement of the thematic structure of the tractate will satisfactorily show that all we have is a reprise and a logical expansion of biblical rules. We deal with the following subjects. First come rules applying to all plagues with special attention to the role of the priest, the process of inspection, the susceptibility of gentiles, the matter of doubts. Second are the issues of colors and their definition and interrelationship; third, the character of bright spots and the signification that they are unclean; fourth, the boil and the burning; fifth, baldspots; sixth, clothing; seventh, houses; and last, purification rites. Yavnean rulings are founded on the laws of Leviticus 13–14, and Ushan ones are built upon the Yavnean foundations. I therefore find it difficult to isolate a single important question brought to bear upon, and intrinsic to, the theme of Negaim, which asks other than about the details of the laws laid down in Scripture and how these laws are to be developed and refined. We never both stand outside of the theme and ask a question of the theme which has not been defined and generated within the theme. It follows that the tractate could have gone on and on, as further questions of fact are thought up. There is no point at which the generative problematic is fully worked out because, as I said, there is no problematic to be discovered within the theme or imposed upon it. Since we cannot maintain that Negaim answers all possible questions pertinent to its theme, we also cannot suggest that Negaim comes to an end because its structure is complete. On the contrary, because its structure is defined by theme and not by problematic, it cannot be claimed to have been brought to its logical fulfillment and conclusion, for there can ultimately be neither.

---

[9]Negaim concerns the uncleanness of the "leprosy (*sara^{c}at*)" or "spot (*nega^c*) of leprosy (*sara^{c}at*)" of Leviticus 13–14. Mishnah tractate Negaim distinguishes *nega^c* from *sara^{c}at* and treats the two as separate sources of uncleanness, focusing attention on the former. See Neusner, 1974–77: Vol. VI, *Negaim. Mishnah-Tosefta*; Vol. VII, *Negaim. Sifra*; Vol. VIII, *Negaim. Literary and Historical Problems.*

4. Parah[10]

The problematic of Parah shapes the tractate from beginning to end: the conduct of a sacrifice outside of the Temple in a place of uncleanness, its requirements and limitations. The deep structure of the tractate is readily discerned, for at each point the issue is how the requirements of the Temple determine the necessities of burning the cow and mixing its ashes with suitable water outside of the Temple. Do we do outside the Temple exactly what we do inside? Do we do the opposite? Do the Temple's requirements of cleanness define those of the burning of the red cow? Do they stand lower or higher in the progression of strictness? True, the tractate contains its share of rules required only by the theme, but not by the problematic, of the red cow. Defining the water, spelling out how the purification water is used, and other prescriptions hardly relate in detail to the overriding question before us. But the principal foci of the tractate—the principle that labor extraneous to the rite spoils the rite of the burning of the cow and spoils the drawn water, and the conception that cleanness-rules of unimagined strictness are to be observed—relate to that crucial point of interest which is the analogy to the Temple.

The tractate, moreover, centers upon the conception that human intervention in the process of preparing the purification water is absolutely essential. The utensil used for collecting the water and mixing the ashes must be a human construction. The act of drawing the water, by contrast to the act of forming an immersion pool, must be with full human deliberation. If at any point the human participant fails to devote his entire and complete attention to the work and so steps outside of the process, the whole process is spoiled. Once man is intruded, moreover, his attention is riveted to what he is doing by the omnipresent danger of contamination. If he touches any sort of object whatsoever—which is to say, if at any point he does anything at all which is not connected to the requirements of the rite—he automatically is made unclean. This is the rule for objects used for lying and sitting. The participant cannot cease from his labors in connection with the rite, for he cannot sit down on a chair. He cannot lie down on a bed. He must at all times be active, standing and alert, moving from the well from which he has drawn the water to the place at which he will mix it with the ash. It may also be the case that if he touches any sort of object which *can* become unclean, not only a bed or a chair, he is *eo ipse* unclean. Even though this is subject to dispute, the issue is secondary to the one on which all parties agree. Moreover, the assumption is that he will have burned the cow and only then have gone off to collect the

---

[10]Parah deals with the burning of the red cow and the mixing of its ashes with water for the preparation of purification water to remove corpse-uncleanness (Num 19:1-13, 20-22). The burning of the cow takes place outside the camp. See Neusner, 1974-77: Vol. IX, *Parah. Commentary*; Vol. X, *Parah. Literary and Historical Problems*.

necessary water. So the process is continuous, from selecting the cow and burning it—which the tractate places first in its sequence of themes—to the gathering of the water and the mixing of the water with the ash. Only then do we take up the use of the water in the purification process.

Accordingly, the tractate commences its development with the principle that man is the key figure in the preparation of purification water. It follows that man must remain forever alert and conscious throughout the process. Utensils must be prepared by man on the one side, and forever protected until used for their ultimate purpose on the other. Preparing the ash, then gathering the water, then mixing the two—these procedures require ultimate and complete devotion and attention. If the structure has been defined by the stated problematic—the essential role of man in the work—what questions await answer? It is difficult to imagine how the system has not been brought to its logical completion by the Ushans, who fully and completely work out the implications of the positions—the available metaphors—inherited by them and of the modes of thought by which those positions have been reached.

For it is not only the rules which have been brought to an end in accord with the generative problematic. It is also the modes of thought, based upon the inquiry into the appropriate analogy, which have been fully explored. The Ushans take up in turn each and every available analogy to the burning of the cow and the mixing of its ashes with the water: sacrifices carried on outside the Temple; Holy Things done in a state of perfect cleanness; the Passover, done outside the Temple, therefore in a locus of uncleanness; the heifer whose neck is broken, outside the Temple; even the *log* of oil of the leper and the blood of the guilt offering of the leper, which are utilized outside the main locus of the cult. At each point the issue is, How does the law before us respond to the analogy of other sacrifices done outside the Temple or outside the inner court of the Temple? The exhaustive inquiry into the generative capacity of the available analogies, therefore, is complete by Ushan times. No further analogies are even available for deeper inquiry than already have been accomplished. In the case of Parah we have no reason whatsoever to doubt that the tractate has come to conclusion because the logical potentialities of the generative problematic and modes of thought on said problematic have been exhausted.

It remains to observe that attention to the actual use of purification water is episodic and casual, just as Miqvaot has little to say about the practical use of the immersion pool but a great deal to contribute to thought on the making of the immersion pool and the character of water used therein. Accordingly, both of the tractates on the modes of purification from uncleanness focus attention upon the creation of materials for purification—the right kind of water—to the near exclusion of the utilization of said materials. The reason, it is clear, is that what is important to the two tractates is contained within the issue of purificatory substance, not purificatory procedures. Discussion of the latter is not spun out of the operative principles but tacked on at the end of

Miqvaot and Parah (not to mention Negaim). This is a highly suggestive fact, illustrative of the principal point of interest of the system as a whole. The system asks not about such practical matters as how one immerses or the sort of hyssop with which one sprinkles purification water (though these are attended to) but about a quite separate range of issues. Here we see how the generative problematic of a tractate defines the tractate's treatment of its theme or topic, to the neglect of the information people will have needed actually to carry out the law in practical ways. It follows that when the logical requirements of the problematic are exhausted, the tractate will draw to a close, even though the formation and definition of concrete laws on the tractate's topic may have to go on for many generations to come.

5. Tohorot[11]

The three paramount themes of Tohorot are to be treated separately. The first, the issue of removes of uncleanness and levels of sanctification, is fully worked out in the interplay between the one and the other. Once the levels of sanctification are defined, the structure demands completion through the specification of corresponding, and opposite, removes of uncleanness. It further will want to know how the two interrelate. At that point the system is complete. The secondary question of whether that which is unconsecrated may be raised, through appropriate deliberation and protection to the level of sanctification not only of heave offering but of Holy Things, is the only matter left open once the structure is complete. Ushans settle that question.

The second, the relationship between the ⁾am ha⁾areṣ and the ḥaber,[12] begins in two conflicting principles. The ⁾am ha⁾areṣ in general will act in such a way as to respect the cleanness of the property of the ḥaber. Or the ⁾am ha⁾areṣ is indifferent to the matter of cleanness. The problematic is to be stated in exactly those simple terms. It can be worked out in a myriad of cases, but no significant conceptual advance is possible or undertaken at Usha. Open to the generation of Rabbi is merely the proliferation of cases and illustrations of one or the other of the two conceptions. No essentially new problematic is to be constructed since people either respect or neglect the law. True, had there been a new conception of the range of choices, e.g., the ⁾am

---

[11]Tohorot concerns the cleanness of food and drink consumed in the home, not in the Temple cult or by priests in particular. Its interest is in the specification of the effects of contact with a source of uncleanness, e.g., a loaf of ordinary bread which touches a dead snake, then another loaf of ordinary bread which touches the first loaf, and so on; and of the effects of food's being deemed sanctified, e.g., as heave offering for priests, or as Holy Things of the cult. See Neusner, 1974–77: Vol. XI, *Tohorot. Commentary*; Vol. XII, *Tohorot. Literary and Historical Problems*.

[12]The *ḥaber* ("associate," "fellow") is one who eats his secular food—that is, food not set apart for priestly use or for the cult—in a state of cultic cleanness. The ⁾am ha⁾areṣ—*paganus*—is one who does not.

ha^ɔareṣ who keeps part of the law but not some other part, then a further and secondary level of inquiry would have been opened. Demai, another Ushan tractate, deals with exactly that matter. Demai therefore illustrates the nature of the Ushan work on the present subject, showing how the limits of the generative problematic had been reached by still another route.

The third, the resolution of doubts, is open-ended. Once we postulate that matters of doubt are to be worked out through the application of diverse principles, then the number of potential principles is scarcely limited. There is no reason to suppose that those specified in Tohorot exhaust the potential. But I perceive no generative problematic, e.g., an inquiry into the large-scale tendencies of doubts, into what at the bottom leads to doubt, or into an overall principle (for instance, leniency under all possible conditions as in Negaim) which is to be applied throughout. True, there are efforts in this direction. There is, for example, the excellent idea of Yosé that we confirm something in its established status and the principle of Meir that we take account of the remove of uncleanness which is at hand with a lenient decision in the case of a less virulent one. But it is difficult to discern a structure into which all of the essays on matters of doubt may be drawn together. Nor is the matter worked out in terms of a single underlying problematic. The problem is not the problematic.

Accordingly, it is difficult to claim that the system in this aspect has come, or even can come, to an end, though the character of the part of the tractate devoted to the matter—a mass of illustrations of a mass of diverse principles—hardly suggests that a great deal of fresh and original thinking has taken place. In this regard, Niddah (see 7, below) is a remarkable contrast. For by raising various sorts of doubt in connection with menstrual uncleanness, for example, the bloodstain, finding a drop of blood in such a setting that one woman may be held responsible and another not or determining whether an aborted object is a viable foetus and so protects the blood excreted therewith from being deemed menstrual blood, Niddah shows how a systematic definition of doubts within the range of the distinctive theme of a tractate can be worked out. But the contrast to Niddah in no way changes the picture. For Niddah, too, leads to no definitive conceptual conclusion, neither beginning in a generative problematic nor, it must follow, bringing to fulfillment and conclusion the logical requirements of its original proposition. The inquiry into matters of doubt can go on endlessly in response to the myriad of concrete circumstances which the workaday world can be relied upon to present for consideration. There is no tractate devoted to the principled resolution of doubt, though, as I said, Yosé and Meir (among others) are perfectly capable of shaping a conception suitable for the foundations of such a tractate. On the other hand, the resolution of doubt concerns many more matters than those of the Mishnaic system of uncleanness; and it is the bringing to completion of that system in particular which is under investigation.

6. Miqvaot[13]

What Miqvaot wants to know about the immersion pool is the sort of water which is to be used. This issue carries in its wake the question of the role of man in the process of purification. Man is rigidly excluded from the process of making the pool. Water drawn by man is not to be used in the pool. It will follow that we must answer these questions: What sort of water is to be used? How much of such water is needed? What is the rule if acceptable water is mixed with unacceptable water? Can the former purify the latter? If so, in what volume? Does the latter render the former irreparably unfit? This range of issues explores the deeper question of the *role* of suitable water in effecting purification. Once we say that a certain kind of water—specifically, that which man has not affected—is to be used, then we ask a range of questions dependent upon the workings of the suitable water, its relationship to unsuitable water, and its power to restore the suitability of unfit water. In asking these questions, moreover, we enter the inquiry into the actual workings of the immersion pool, for we want to know exactly what power the pool has even over its own constituent element, water, and, all the more so, over things which are different from its constituent element. The route to the analysis of the working of the pool, therefore, is the inquiry into the character of the water which is used in the pool and its power over all other things which enter therein. It follows that once we define the sort of water which is to be used, we must ask about its volume, the conditions of its collection, and the possibilities of its incapacitation. What is striking in Miqvaot is its focus upon exactly this range of issues, which are given full instantiation, and the right way in which these issues draw together their negative aspects (spoiling the pool, ruining water for use in the pool, and restoring the power of a spoiled pool or of spoiled water).

The tractate fully and exhaustively explores the issues defined, to begin with, by its problematic. It works out rules on the kinds of water suitable for purification, even showing that there are several sorts of such water, each with its own capacities in the larger structure. It then turns to water unsuitable for purification, showing under what conditions water has the effect of impairing a pool and, further, how these effects upon a formerly suitable pool may be mitigated. It follows that the problematic will have been fully explored once we have asked about restoring the suitability of unfit water. In all of these inquiries the determinative role of man is carefully delineated. There are things man must not do; and if he does them, he spoils the pool, the water of which, furthermore, itself then is held to impart uncleanness, an extreme

---

[13]The theme of Miqvaot is the provision of water for the immersion pool in which purification from uncleanness is effected. The pertinent Scripture is Lev 11:36. See Neusner, 1974–77: Vol. XIII, *Miqvaot. Commentary*; Vol XIV, *Miqvaot. Literary and Historical Problems.*

statement of the matter. There are things which man may do. And there are aspects of the matter which man must do—that is to say, making use of the pool for purification. But here the matter, as we noted earlier, is left curiously undeveloped. The rules on how to use the pool for purification are few and incomplete. The principal concern is for interposition; and the reason is that that matter, in the large framework of use of the pool, allows us to restate our interest in the role of man. Things which man cares about interpose, and those of no concern to man do not. Accordingly, the primary concern in the use of the pool is tied—though rather loosely—to the principal and generative problematic of the tractate as a whole. Within the problematic on the stated theme we find a complete and finished logical structure. No question generated by the problematic is left unattended to.

Miqvaot and Parah, moreover, complement and complete one another. The one describes an aspect of purification from which man is excluded, while the other deals with an aspect of purification to which human deliberation is absolutely necessary. The interplay with Parah is still closer when we recall that Parah treats a rite of sacrifice which takes place outside of the Temple and Miqvaot, it would seem, describes a rite of purification effective outside of the cult. The immersion pool lies beyond the imagination of the Priestly legislators who specify that things which are laundered, washed, or rinsed in ordinary water are unclean until the evening. Miqvaot and Parah together deal with sacrifice in the system's principal locus of uncleanness outside the cult and the mode of purification outside the cult. The profound issue to be worked out by both is the definition of the role of man. What is accomplished by the two together is the balancing of the essential participation of man in the deliberate formation of the worldly locus to be protected from uncleanness on the one side, and his rigid exclusion in the formation of the mode of worldly purification on the other. The system comes to completion in the tractates under discussion not only in its constituents but even in its principal parts. Parah without Miqvaot or Miqvaot without Parah can have been complete unto itself but open and unfinished in its context. The fulfillment of the complementary problematic of each tractate is in the completion of that of the other. Beyond lies the system's closure in fixed and formal language, but no questions generated at the outset by the end are left without consideration.

7. Niddah[14]

Niddah presents no problematic which defines the agendum of questions to be addressed to its theme. The tractate, like Negaim (= Leviticus 13–14),

---

[14]Niddah concerns the uncleanness of the woman in her menstrual period, Lev 15:19–24, the woman after childbirth, Lev 12:1–8, and the woman who has a discharge not during her menstrual period, Lev 15:25–30. See Neusner, 1974–77: Vol. XV, *Niddah. Commentary*; Vol. XVI, *Niddah. Literary and Historical Problems*.

constitutes merely an extended commentary, not in exegetical form, to be sure, upon the basic law of Scriptures, in particular Leviticus 12, 15. I see no important idea which does not derive directly or derivatively from Scripture. At no point does the tractate raise questions not provoked by Scripture or the extension, by analogy or contrast, of Scripture's definitions and conceptions. Nor is there an organizing problematic which unifies the tractate and outlines its conceptual foundations other than the statement of the rules of Scripture. These constitute no problematic; they are but mere facts augmented by Mishnah with more facts spun out by analogical or contrastive thinking.

The tractate is conceptually diffuse and lacks a logical center. The reason that there is no inner structure to the tractate is that facts, as distinct from logic and concept, are unable to do more than represent themselves and generate refinements. Accordingly, we cannot claim that by the end of Ushan times the generative problematic had been fully worked out and required no further amplification or extension. The criterion of an isolable problematic which stands at the core and the center of the tractate's structure is unmet. Even the outline of the tractate's contents is incapable of suggesting the presence of deep structure. What we have is a discourse on unclean body fluids and on doubts in reference to unclean body fluids, an exercise within the narrow conceptual framework of Negaim and the center of Tohorot, respectively. What we could not find in the aforenamed tractates we cannot find here either. It follows that the *Gemara* to the tractate does not help us in verifying or falsifying the claim that, by the end of Mishnah, the system had fully worked itself out; for, as I said, we discern neither system nor even structure in this mass of applied laws. The intellectual character of the following tractate, Makhshirin, underlines the contrast between the sort of tractate generated within a problematic and one formed merely by provision of rules on this and that aspect of a given theme.

8. Makhshirin[15]

The theme of Makhshirin is liquids which impart to dry produce susceptibility to uncleanness. The problematic is the role of human intention in the application of said liquids so that they function to render produce susceptible, and secondarily, the role of human intention in the definition of effective liquids. The working out of the problematic is in terms of the interplay between what a person wants to do and what he actually does. One possible position is that we interpret the effects of what is done in terms of what is intended. A second and opposite position is that we define what is

---

[15]Lev 11:34, 38 specify that if a dead creeping thing falls on food or upon seed and the food or seed is wet, then it is made unclean. It follows that if it is dry, it is not susceptible to uncleanness. Makhshirin then asks about the application of liquids to food to render said food susceptible to uncleanness. See Neusner, 1974–77: Vol. XVII, *Makhshirin*.

intended in terms of the ultimate result. A third is that we balance the one with the other, thus interpreting intention in terms of result, but also result in terms of prior intention. These are the three possible positions yielded by the logical requirements of the problematic. There are no others. These three, moreover, are fully worked out in the Ushan stratum of the tractate. The determinative problematic, whether or not liquids are applied intentionally, thus is itself redefined in terms of a still more profound and fundamental question.

The process begins in ᶜAqiva's position that we take account only of water which has actually conformed to a person's original intent, ignoring the presence of water which is peripheral to the accomplishment of one's purpose. The process then is completed by the Ushan inquiry into ᶜAqiva's position, specifically the meaning of intent: the limitations upon the capacity of water to impart susceptibility imposed by one's original intent in drawing the water. The structure is articulated in terms of the view that water intrinsic to one's purpose is detached with approval, while that which is not essential to one's original intent is not able to impart susceptibility. If water applied with approval can impart susceptibility, then, as I said, only that *part* of the water which is essential to one's accomplishment of his original intent imparts susceptibility. It is at this point that the question is raised about the relationship between intention and deed. First, intention to do something governs the effect of one's action, even though one's action had produced a different effect from his original intention. Or, second, one's consequent action revises the original definition, therefore the effects, of his prior intention. That is, what happens is retrospectively deemed to define what one wanted to happen. Or, third, as I noted above, what one wanted to make happen affects the assessment of what actually has happened. There are no other logical possibilities contained within the original problematic. The tractate concludes at the point at which its original inquiry is complete.

The place of Makhshirin at the inauguration of the system of intention underlines its close relationship to Kelim. Both tractates wish in essence to say the same thing. For liquids and for food as for utensils—that is, for all constituents of the system's entire realm of susceptibility to uncleanness—man must deliberately do something to bring the system into operation. He must complete an object, regard it as a utensil. He must deem food to be edible (not a major point in the Order), liquid to be drawn with approval or otherwise useful; he must take dry, insusceptible produce and wet it down, with an eye to making use of the produce. Accordingly, no component of the multi-dimensional locus of uncleanness—utensils, food (produce), and drink—is exempt from the requirement that human deliberation play the principal and definitive role. It is man who creates the entire locus of uncleanness by introducing into that locus—rendering susceptible to uncleanness—the several materials which form its components. While Kelim, Makhshirin, and the relevant units of Tohorot fully work out their respective problematic, each one, moreover, finds completion and fulfillment in the provision of the corresponding and reciprocally pertinent tractate. Each says concerning its own topic what all of them say in common about the shared theme.

9. Zabim[16]

Zabim is to be considered in two parts: first, its definitions of how a man becomes unclean as a *Zab* and modes of transfer of his uncleanness in general and, second, how a *Zab* imparts uncleanness through pressure in particular. The former, like Niddah and Negaim, is not characterized by a fundamental and generative problematic, being little more than a series of refinements and amplifications of Scripture's basic definition of the *Zab*.

But the latter, in Chaps. 3–4, does turn around a single, organizing problematic, which is the nature of pressure. The matter of pressure begins with Joshua's view that pressure need not be formal in the sense that the *Zab* exerts physical pressure upon a bed. If the *Zab*'s weight is *indirectly* transferred to something which *might* be used for lying or sitting, even though that object is not utilized at present for that purpose, then the uncleanness has been transferred. Having defined the problem of pressure in general, we find in the Ushan materials a full working out of the logical possibilities. Either (1) we hold that any pressure, even of both a *Zab* and a clean person on one side of an object, involves the transfer of uncleanness. Or (2) only if the *Zab* presses against a clean person or object is there such a transfer. That is to say, only if the clean person certainly has borne the weight of the unclean one are the person and his clothing unclean. For both positions at Usha we require the qualifications that, first, only if the object is capable of submitting to pressure, being infirm, is pressure-uncleanness transferred; and only if the pressure is exerted equally throughout the object is the transfer effected; and only if the greater part of the *Zab*'s weight is pressed against the object is the object unclean.

Judah's view is that the only situation in which there is a transfer of uncleanness is when the clean person bears the weight of the unclean. But if the unclean bears the weight of the clean, then there is no carrying, no pressure. Meir maintains that the *Zab* imparts *midras*-uncleanness if he exerts pressure on something, and also the person who exerts pressure on the *Zab* is equivalently unclean. Simeon, too, wants the unclean person to exert weight on the clean. We require, Simeon adds, the greater part of the weight of the *Zab*'s body. All will concur that mere vibration, not direct pressure, does not accomplish the transfer of uncleanness. So far, therefore, as Zabim deals with the source of uncleanness, it exhibits the same conceptual traits as Niddah,

---

[16]The *Zab* is the man who has a discharge from his body, Lev 15:1–5. Scripture is clear that any bed upon which he sits is unclean, hence the conception of pressure uncleanness (*midras*). See Neusner, 1974–77: Vol. XVIII, *Zabim*.

Negaim, and the opening and closing units of Ohalot. So far as it takes up the problematic of the definition of the pressure of the *Zab*, it exhausts the logical possibilities inherent in the question. The former matter can be subjected to a great deal more inquiry, I suppose, but the latter permits none.

10. Tebul Yom[17]

The theme of Tebul Yom is drastically limited by the problematic around which the tractate takes shape. Its first element is whether a person in the status of Tebul Yom is essentially clean or essentially unclean. If he is essentially unclean, then the matter is concluded. He functions to impart uncleanness as does any other source. But if he is essentially clean, then the next stage unfolds. We distinguish between what is primary and what is secondary in a mixture. If what is primary is affected, then what is secondary likewise is unclean. But if what is secondary is affected, what is primary remains clean. Now this distinction is distinctively related to the Tebul Yom who, because of his own ambiguous status, is able to illuminate the ambiguities presented by the stated distinction as to connection. If the Tebul Yom touches what is secondary in a mixture, what is primary is unaffected and vice versa. This completes the statement of the problematic of the tractate, and it also incorporates the whole of the Ushan stratum of the tractate. There are no unanswered questions, no undeveloped aspects of the problematic. Every possible position inherent in the twin-problematic—the ambiguous status of the Tebul Yom, the ambivalent aspect of connection—is stated. The theme of the Tebul Yom, of course, is hardly exhausted or even fully spelled out in the necessary detailed rules. But the tractate is complete and comes to conclusion because there is nothing more to say about the issue to which the tractate, for its part, chooses to address itself. This is the best example of the larger thesis of the present inquiry.

11. Yadayim[18]

Yadayim cannot be said to have fulfilled the limits of its problematic. The theme itself is spelled out in diverse rules; provision of further rules is entirely possible. The problematic, by contrast, has to do with cleaning hands in a way different from the way in which other parts of the body and other unclean things are cleaned, which is in an immersion pool. Once we determine that

[17]Tebul Yom deals with the person or object which has been immersed in an immersion pool. Scripture specifies, e.g., Lev 15:17, that what is immersed in water is unclean until evening. The Tebul Yom then is that which has been immersed during the remainder of the day on which immersion has taken place. See Neusner, 1974–77: Vol. XIX, *Tebul Yom and Yadayim*.

[18]The subject of Yadayim is the uncleanness of hands and how they may be made clean *not* through immersion in an immersion pool but through a different process of purification, pouring water out on the hands. See Neusner, 1974–77: Vol. XIX, *Tebul Yom and Yadayim*.

hands are unclean when the rest of the body remains unaffected, then we have
to find an appropriate analogy for the mode of purification herein under
discussion. It is in the law not of Miqvaot,[19] which concerns undifferentiated
purification, but of Parah. The result is the strict requirement of the use of a
utensil and of water drawn by man in a utensil, as against the conception of
Miqvaot that we do not use water drawn in a utensil at all. What can have been
done, once this conclusion is reached, is difficult to imagine. The bulk of the
tractate in any event is unsustained and episodic—a sequence of rules on this
and that, filled out at the end with entirely irrelevant materials. Since the
materials herein assembled scarcely can be regarded as a tractate at all, it is
hardly surprising that we cannot point to an organizing principle, let alone a
generative problematic, through which to account for the inner structure of
the tractate as a whole. There is no whole.

12. Uqsin[20]

Uqsin by contrast to Yadayim is coherent and exhibits traits of
sophisticated formulary and redactional work. It is not difficult to specify its
generative and unifying problematic. The problematic is, first, the status of
inedible parts of food, whether they are susceptible because they are
connected to edible parts or insusceptible because they are inedible. The
second aspect of the problematic is joined to the first: How do we treat these
inedible parts when we estimate the bulk or the volume of food? Accordingly,
the generative problematic is the status of what is joined to food but is not to
be eaten. The logical possibilities, that these inedible parts are deemed (1)
wholly part of the produce to which they are connected, (2) wholly separate
from said produce, or (3) under some circumstances part and under some
circumstances not part of the edible part of the food, are fully worked out. The
tractate therefore completes the analysis of its subject, leaving no logical
possibility outside of its structure.

III.   THE WHOLE

We need not repeat the points already made about the complementarity
of conceptions applied to tractates within the same component of the system
as a whole, e.g., Kelim and Tohorot, for loci of uncleanness; Parah and
Miqvaot, for modes of purification. The system begins as a whole and ends as
a whole. It makes provision for each of the principal aspects of its problem:

---

[19]For using the analogy of Miqvaot will bring in its wake the issue of the uncleanness of the
hands in the status of Tebul Yom. Since things in that status impart uncleanness to heave offering,
it will hardly serve the system to make no provision at all for cleanness of hands in one moment,
and not only through the double process of immersion in an immersion pool and sunset.

[20]‘Uqsin—‘stalks’—is another tractate, along with Tohorot, on cleanness of foods. See
Neusner, 1974–77: Vol. XX, *Uqsin. Cumulative Index, Parts I–XX.*

the beginning, middle, and end of uncleanness; the sources, loci, and removal thereof. The logical unfolding of the system's fundamental and generative conceptions, that uncleanness is important outside the cult, in particular in respect to food, drink, and domestic utensils, that what imparts uncleanness in the cult does so outside as well, that man inaugurates the system, and that nature both constitutes its datum and brings it to a conclusion—these and similar conceptions by the end of Ushan times not only are fully spelled out and provided with a rich corpus of legal detail, they also are exhaustively completed in their structural-logical potentialities. If the system exhibits no clearcut problematic in treating sources of uncleanness—corpse-matter, the $nega^c$, the Zab, the menstruating woman—it is because the system has nothing it wishes to say about the subject beyond Scripture's designation of these as sources of uncleanness. Its generative tensions emerge form consideration of loci of uncleanness—the table, not only cult—and modes of purification for life outside, not only inside, the sanctuary.

We now return to the question, Why has Mishnah been brought into being at one particular time and not some other? Mishnah comes into being just when it does because the successors of the Ushans, with little to contribute to the formation of the conceptual heritage and ideational structure distinctive to Mishnah (that is, exclusive of sources of uncleanness), undertake its formulation and redaction, a work which itself exhibits remarkably profound reflection. Shall we then conclude that Mishnah is a document wholly exempt from historical circumstance or that the existence of Mishnah is explicable solely in terms of the inner inertial force of its own logical unfolding? It seems to me an unlikely conclusion for two reasons.

First of all, we have the fact of Mishnah itself, a creation which, in its long career after ca. 200, produced definitive results for the history of Judaism.[21] We have, moreover, the fact that Mishnah's inner conceptual structure does come into existence over a period of some 250 or more years before ca. 200[22] and that the main outlines of that structure do conform to those revealed in at least one comparable system (the Essene as shown in CD and 1QS). It follows that if Mishnah is deemed a work spun out of its own inner tensions, it nonetheless was made by a particular group of people over a specific period of

[21]Mishnah is the principal foundation of the Talmuds of Babylonia and the Land of Israel, which in the main are organized around, and in part serve as commentaries upon, Mishnah. The Babylonian Talmud, for its part, then served as the primary legal authority of Judaism from its conclusion at the end of the sixth century to the present day.

[22]That is, the earliest conceptions of the Order of Purities are taken for granted by the named authorities who flourish before the turn of the first century A.D. These conceptions moreover comprise the fundamental and generative notions of Kelim, Ohalot, Niddah, Zabim, and Miqvaot. It is by no means certain that Parah does not originate in the same period. Accordingly, the principal and generative ideas of the system as a whole are to be located at its very beginnings, some time before the turn of the first century. The Mishnaic system of that time and the system revealed, without rich detail to be sure, in the Damascus rule (CD) and in the Manual of Discipline (1QS) are wholly congruent in their principal parts.

years. It therefore is to be seen whole—if not in the unfolding of its parts—as a work of a given period; and, consequently, in some ways it is a work deemed important to people who lived in a given sociopolitical circumstance, not solely in a given logico-conceptual context. Even if, as I said above, we cannot adduce as sufficient cause for shifts in the law after 70 and after 140 the calamities of those years, nonetheless, the law does shift and those calamities did take place.

There is yet a second consideration, by no means excluded by the first. Mishnah is assigned to a particular personality, Judah the Patriarch. The attribution to Judah the Patriarch of responsibility for the completion of the document is *post facto*. Our Order contains virtually no internal evidence that named redactors, let alone Judah the Patriarch in particular, are responsible for the work. The notion that Judah the Patriarch promulgated Mishnah, nonetheless, is attributed to successive generations of Amoraim and is a powerful tradition from the time of Mishnah onward. There are, moreover, diverse stories which attribute to Judah support from the Roman government and, while we cannot know whether these stores report things actually said and done, they do make a *prima facie* case for Judah's position of dominance in the Jewish community of the Land of Israel. If that is so, then he will have had a considerable motive for putting Mishnah together for use in his administration.[23] There is no doubt that Mishnah served from the time of Samuel and Rab as a kind of legal canon for the Babylonian Jewish courts run by rabbis.[24]

But it does not necessarily follow that Mishnah was purposefully created in order to meet the political and administrative needs of the Palestinian patriarchate and the Babylonian exilarchate, the two Jewish regimes of the time, for we cannot commit the error of arguing *post hoc, ergo propter hoc.* Even though the centrality of Mishnah in the Jewish legal system under rabbinical rule is an established fact from the promulgation of Mishnah, we cannot derive from that fact the motive of these who to begin with brought Mishnah into being. That also may be the case. But it is only on the basis of the internal evidence of Mishnah itself that the intention of the people who made it is to be adduced. Mishnah in our Order certainly is scarcely relevant to the administrative, let alone judicial, tasks of a Jewish government. The one really important tractate for common practice is Niddah. That is hardly a tractate which seems to have been brought to closure because the systemic structure had become complete, for there is none. It might be argued that Niddah represents the sort of tractate which is created to serve the needs of rabbis consulted about the application of its laws. But Niddah fits tightly within the

---

[23]I owe this point to Professor John Strugnell, Harvard University.

[24]See my *History of the Jews in Babylonia* (1965–70). This of course does not exclude an equivalent role in the rabbinical administration of the Land of Israel, but we have as yet no history of the Jews in Palestine which takes up the agendum worked out in my *History.*

framework of the Order as a whole; and I find it difficult to imagine that diverse motives, intellectual and practical, have produced the redaction of the several tractates.

The upshot is that internal evidence is only partially sufficient to produce a definitive answer to the question, Why did Mishnah come to completion at just the point that it did? The character of the ideational structure of the document, specifically the fulfillment of the logical requirements of the underlying problematic in the bulk of the tractates, is suggestive but by itself hardly probative.

IV.   STRUCTURE AND MEANING

The entire world view of Mishnah is to be described only when the inner structure of all tractates of the six divisions of the law is fully revealed and the interrelationships of the divisions spelled out.[25] Our Order, however, presents sufficient evidence for us to raise, though not wholly to respond to, the question: What do we learn about people from what they say?

The Order of Purities forms its meanings upon a two-dimensional grid. One is laid out so that the Temple stands in the middle, the world roundabout, with the sanctity of the Temple definitive of the potential sanctification of table and bed, the profane and unclean world outside. The other, superimposed upon the former, places man at one pole, nature at the other, each reciprocally complementing and completing the place and role of the other. Nature produces uncleanness and removes uncleanness. Man subjects food and utensils to uncleanness and, through his action, also imparts significance to the system as a whole.

In the end the question is, What can a man do? And the answer is, Man stands at the center of this world's locus of sanctification and uncleanness. The sustenance of his life and his reproductive activity form the focus of intense concentration. The life of man which is systemically central, the rhythm of his eating, drinking, and sexual activity, defines the working of the system; and the intention and deliberation of man provide the key to the system. Without human will the system is inert. Utensils not useful to man are not susceptible. Vegetable matter and liquids not subject to human utilization are not going to be made unclean. Things which are dry are permanently clean. Only produce wet down deliberately and purposefully by man to serve his needs, is susceptible to uncleanness. What man does not do is equally decisive in the process of forming the principal means of purification. He does not intervene in nature's processes at the end of the system, just as he must

---

[25]My students and former students are now at work on *A History of the Mishnaic Law of Agriculture*, the first division. I now work on *A History of the Mishnaic Law of Holy Things*, the fifth division. The earliest results suggest a totally different situation from that described here, requiring quite new questions, see pp. 133–153, below.

determine purposefully to inaugurate the forces of uncleanness by deciding to use a utensil or to wet down and use wheat. He cannot stimulate the bodily sources of uncleanness, e.g., in the case of the *Zab*, all the more so in the case of *Zab* and the *nega^c*, or, under normal circumstances, in the case of the corpse. But he must impart purpose and significance to the things affected by those bodily sources of uncleanness. These facts have repeatedly come to the fore as we moved from one component of the system to the next.

When we describe the formation of the system, its comprehensive structure, we discover at its very foundations the conception of the definitive role of man and mind. What the system proposes is to locate a place of critical importance for activity expressive of human purpose in the unseen world of uncleanness and holiness, in the material and metaphysical processes of the sanctification of this profane world in the model of the holy Temple's sanctity. Man is not helpless in the work of sanctification but, on the contrary, is the responsible, decisive figure, both in what he does deliberately and in what he sedulously refrains from doing. He is not a passive object of an *independent* process of material, absolute sanctification, begun and effected by Heaven working solely through nature, but the principal subject of the *contingent* process of immaterial, relative sanctification. And the arena for his activity is his own basic life's processes, eating food and so sustaining life, engaging in sexual relations and so maintaining life's continuity. Let us reflect on the meaning of that particular and distinctive definition of the locus of sanctification.

The system of uncleanness forms part of a larger structure of order and wholeness. As Professor Mary Douglas says, "Each tribe actively construes its particular universe in the course of an internal dialogue about law and order" (1975:26). Within the range of human possibility, the Israelite system selects for its particular interest those aspects of life through which life is reproduced and sustained. And for our Order of Mishnah, it is food which is the principal interest. Again Douglas: "Pollution rules can thus be seen as an extension of the perceptual process: insofar as they impose order on experience, they support clarification of forms and thus reduce dissonance" (1975:53). That part of experience selected by Mishnah for principal attention is the act of eating. The point at which systematization—ordering imposed on dissonant reality—is to be imposed is the table, a remarkably limited focus, excluding a virtually unlimited range of loci and activities which in this context can have come under consideration but in fact do not receive attention. To be sure, Mishnah as a whole deems as susceptible to sanctification the whole structure of social life: the economy, the family, the ordering of time, the resolution of societal conflict, not to mention the cult. But so far as the language of clean and unclean is extensively used in Mishnah, it is principally, though not exclusively, in reference to food and to the cult.

Since the bodily function upon which emphasis is laid is nourishment, we must attempt to understand the principle of selection. Here the Scriptural heritage of the Priestly Code seems to me decisive: God is served meals of meat and meal, wine and oil, not holocausts of jewelry, not flowers or logs of wood, not perpetual fires, not mounds of ore, not fish or insects, and not ejaculations of semen. What sustains God nourishes man. God is perceived to be isomorphic with man. In God's image is man made, and all of the circles of creation are concentric with the inner circle formed of man's creation. If, as Douglas says, "The grain of millet in its husk, the human foetus in the uterus, the world in its atmospheric envelope are each analogues of the others" (1975:125), then the Israelite structure of the holy, in Scripture and in Mishnah alike, begins in the conception of the Priestly analogy of Genesis. Of all creation, man is most like God. Man alone is truly like God. Man therefore generates this world's analogical and contrastive meanings, being the mythopoeic simile of similes. Again Douglas: "No man eats flesh with blood in it. Blood belongs to God alone, for life is in the blood" (1975:270). What she says of the Levitical food classification applies with still greater force to Mishnah's correlative but somewhat different system:

> But if the unity of Godhead is to be related to the unity of Israel and made into a rule of life, the difficulties start.
>
> First, there are creatures whose behavior defies the rigid classification. It is relatively easy to deal with them by rejection and avoidance.
>
> Second, there are the difficulties that arise from our biological condition. It is all very well to worship the holiness of God in the perfection of his creation. But the Israelites must be nourished and must reproduce. It is impossible for a pastoral people to eat their flocks and herds without damaging the bodily completeness they respect. It is impossible to renew Israel without emission of blood and sexual fluids. These problems are met sometimes by avoidance and sometimes by consecration to the Temple. The draining of blood from meat is a ritual act which figures the bloody sacrifice at the altar. Meat is thus transformed from a living creature into a food item. (1975:270-71)

Man when dead, moreover, is a grand source of uncleanness; when alive, is at the center of the system.

What sustains man is what the system proposes to sanctify. The purpose is that man, renewing life as God perpetually lives in the cult, may be formed and nourished by sustenance which is like God's, and so in nature become like supernature. To state matters simply: *By eating like God, man becomes like God.* And this "eating like God" is done naturally and routinely, in the context and course of ordinary life, with utensils available for any purpose, with food and drink, bed and chair, commonly used in the workaday world. Man at his most domestic and in his most natural context is susceptible to uncleanness and therefore potentially capable also of sanctification. What is unclean can be holy. What is most susceptible to uncleanness also is most available for sanctification.

For what does man do within the system? In a profound sense, he does perfectly routine, natural actions. The system is remarkably lacking in specific cultic rituals or ties. The food is not subjected to blessing in order to become susceptible. The utensil is not made to pass through a rite, but is susceptible without prayer. The corpus of law lacks all mythic expression. The laws are wholly descriptive of how ordinary things are, speaking of the natural course of workaday events. Eating takes place all the time. Utensils are always available for use. All things are neutral except for human intervention. What the man does is merely use things, not muttering incantations, blessings, prayers, or other sacred formulas or doing gestures analogous to those of the priests in the cult. He immerses in any suitable pond—so far as Miqvaot is concerned—without a word or deed of ritual concerning the pond or immersion therein. When the cow is burned and the ashes are collected and mixed with suitable water, not a word or unnecessary action is prescribed. When the hands are rinsed two times, the name of Heaven is not invoked, so far as Yadayim is concerned. Kelim speaks of the creation of ordinary objects for domestic use, Tohorot of ordinary olives and grapes for the table. Ohalot, which proposes to describe how the economy of nature is restored when the body, which contained that which is emitted by the body at death, breaks that economy in death, is remarkably reticent on the subject of funeral rites, of which it knows nothing. The several sources of uncleanness to which tractates are devoted (Negaim, Niddah, Zabim, Tebul Yom, the fore and aft sections of Ohalot) all speak of the perfectly natural workings of the body in life or in death. Nothing man does brings uncleanness on himself. Constraint, intention, accident are explicitly excluded from effective causes of the bodily flows which contaminate. The natural character of the sources of uncleanness and the modes of its removal on the one side, and the highly deliberate and conscious action of man required to subject food and drink, domestic utensils and objects, to the effect of the system on the other, are complementary. The structure is formed of these two opposite elements: the availability of inert nature, the deliberation of man who forms intention and acts to effect it.

If we stand back from the system of uncleanness and look at the structure of which it is a principal part, we observe a set of balanced circles: Israel at the center, the nations at the periphery; the Land at the center, the lands at the periphery; the Temple at the center, the profane world at the periphery. To these circles the system merely adds the *haber* at the center, the ᶜ*am* ha⁵*ares* at the periphery, a late and unimportant conception generated by societal, not metaphysical, considerations. Accordingly, when we enter the system of purity, we come to the pivot of the world: Temple, the holiest place of the holy Land of the holy people, Israel. *We bring the life-sustaining processes of the people into conformity with the world-sustaining processes of the Temple* (Douglas, 1973:139). Life outside is lived in accord with the rules observed at the center. Dangers and threats to the center bode ill also for the life at periphery. Yet in so describing the structure, which places into relationship land, cult, and people and, with the Mishnaic layer, further introduces into the state of sacred equilibrium the individual's bed, table, chair, plate and spoon, and all food, we ignore an important fact. From the time of the Maccabees the

Temple itself was repeatedly violated and contaminated. The Essenes of Qumran most certainly conceived that the Temple not only had been contaminated one time only, but remained in a state of perpetual disgrace. Herod's political priests cannot have found favor with pietists whether of priestly or common origin. For the Essenes the catastrophe of 70 took place much more than a century before 70. The systemic stability of Mishnah consequent upon the destruction of the Temple strongly suggests that for the system ultimately contained in Mishnah the destruction meant little because it already had taken place in some, to us unknown, way—an event, a personality, a critical disaster. The issues consequent upon whether or not human intention matters and, if it does matter, how it affects nature—these issues clearly are inherent in the earliest strata of the Mishnaic system and are dealt with in a clear-cut way at the very outset.

Imitation of the cult in the home therefore bespeaks something more than the effort to *extend* the realm of the sacred, even though viewed ahistorically the system says just that. While as Mary Douglas observes, "The table, the marriage bed, and the altar match each others' rules, as do the farmer, the husband, and the priest match each others' roles in the total pattern",[26] something has happened to shatter the original boundaries of the Priestly Code's definition of the structure. The Priestly conception of a neatly divided world, clean made distinct from unclean, with separation marked between clean and unclean animals as between cult and world, is not only fulfilled by the extension of the lines of division outward to the table, the treatment of the domestic table in accord with the analogy of the cultic altar. It also is treated with a measure of irony: Temple rules and sex rules and food rules form a *single* system of analogies "and do not converge on any one point but sustain the whole moral and physical universe simultaneously in their systematic interrelatedness" (Douglas, 1973:140). So the Temple is not the only locus of cleanness or sanctification. But if that is so, then what now defines the *pivot* of the single system of multivalent analogies?

The answer is clear once the question is phrased in this way. It now is either the sect, as at the Essene community at Qumran, or the people as a whole, as in the mind of the second century rabbis, who do not ignore the ʿam haʿareṣ or leave him out of the system. The Temple, now secondary, is made itself to signify the godly community, which is analogically generative, therefore primary. The system is made to depend upon the intention of ordinary people living commonplace lives. The Mishnaic laws of purity show beyond doubt that uncleanness derives from intention and not *ex opere operato* from the faulty association of material things (Douglas, 1973:142). Breach of the rules has afflicted the people as a whole—that is the very heart of the rabbinic theodicy of the second century—and the people as a whole is the locus of that detail of the Israelite structure, defined by the rabbis, in which the

---

[26]Critique of my *Idea of Purity in Ancient Judaism. The Haskell Lectures for 1972-73.*

system of uncleanness finds it capacious niche. Accordingly, *ab initio*, not only *post facto*, the Mishnaic system no less than that of the Essene community at Qumran testifies to a shift at the foundation of the deepest levels of the symbolic structure. The Temple, once that to which all things are deemed analogous, now itself is likened to something else. The community— whether commune as with the Essenes, or church as with the Christians of Jerusalem, or the people as a whole as with the second century rabbis— generates the metaphor and lays forth the lines of structure defined by the unclean and the clean. So far as the structure stands upon a pivot, it is the people of Israel, not the Temple, which is pivotal.

In the context of Israelite life from ca. 100–50 B.C. to ca. A.D. 200, the approximately three centuries or so in which the system's principal, distinctive ideas take shape and come to fulfillment in Mishnah itself, to keep clean among ordinary folk means to prepare for a pilgrimage to the Temple and to participate in the rites thereof. Accordingly, the system of uncleanness imposes the pretense that people forever live en route to the holy place and as if they already found themselves within its precincts. If life is lived as pilgrims and as priests, yet, as we have said many times, the pilgrimage and altar are to, and at, the domestic table. (So far as the bed itself enters our Order, it is in respect to the woman's uncleanness, with the effect of uncleanness being her exclusion as much from the table as the bed.) What one does because he is clean is eat his ordinary meals as if he were a priest, and what he cannot do because he is unclean is join with those who eat like priests. In the history of the unfolding of the system the presence of the Temple and its removal come to be remarkably unimportant. The system takes shape while the Temple stands. It gathers force and comes to completion after the Temple has fallen. Indeed, it is not the Temple's destruction which marks the system's fulfillment but, at the designated, innovative points, the structural completion of the system itself.

Yet we should not ignore the fact that within a few generations of the completion of Mishnah the system of uncleanness falls out of the Israelite system as defined by the rabbis of the Talmud. People observe the taboo in respect to the menstrual period, but they do so principally in connection with sexual relations. Apart from Niddah, no tractates of our Order are subjected to systematic investigation in the Talmuds; and, of still greater importance, evidence that people after 200 ate their meals in a state of cultic cleanness is sparse indeed. The system thus not only is complete with Mishnah but collapses in the aftermath of Mishnah. What the destruction of the Temple did not, and (evidently) could not, effect is accomplished in a very brief moment after the promulgation of Mishnah: the abandonment of the system as a whole at its climactic hour.

We must now speculate on why the system of uncleanness ends. Perhaps it falls of its own weight. Since the system of uncleanness expresses in so radical a way the fundamental priestly ontology, it may be that with the rise to prominence of the quite distinct and distinctive rabbinic ontology, shaped in the late first and second centuries and centered upon a different set of analogies and a different conception of heaven, the system of uncleanness at the end falls from prominence because it has been replaced by another. To be sure, "dietary" laws persist. But the priestly-Pharisaic conception of the table as analogous to the cult, embedded in and enshrined by the Order of Purities, no longer finds for itself the central position of earlier centuries. But I think there is another reason than the conflict of ontologies and of the institutions which embodied them. I think the system of cultic cleanness at the domestic table becomes implausible and deeply ironic.

Let us for a moment dwell on the history of Israel, the people, the limits of whose history mark out the boundaries of the Mishnaic structure as a whole. It is a history the ecological framework of which inevitably generates resentment and dissonance. For at the outset, after 586, the Scriptural heritage spoke of promises made and kept, exile and restoration, a weak people and frail society which form the very heart of human history. For many centuries after the restoration the promises, once kept, continue to be kept. The Temple stood inviolable, the land loosely gathered into the borders of one or another distant empire, the people left pretty much to its own devices. But from Hasmonean times forward something seems to have gone wrong. More and more people perceived a dissonant note in their collective fate. For the Temple now was violated, not once but many times, by the Syrians, by contentious Hasmoneans, by Pompey and the Romans, by Herod in his way. When, moreover, we pass the watershed of 70, we come at 140 to the recognition of a deep flaw: the failure of restoration after the divine punishment. At 70 the rod and staff of God smote once, but healed not at all three generations thereafter. To the rabbis and folk after Bar Kokhba it surely was clear that the three generations of biblical prophecy had passed, but all had not been made right as in the past. And that called into question the continuing reliability of the hoary paradigm of Israel's sin, God's punishment, Israel's suffering and expiation of sin thereby, and God's reconciliation.

So far as the Temple had formed the pivot of the structure, the foundations may have been shaken long before 70, whether deep within Israelite society or by blows delivered from without. But they were wholly and irreparably shattered by the sequence of events begun in 70 and brought to conclusion by the Bar Kokhba calamity. Where were the ancient promises now, the dignities assured of old? The people which stood in the center of history found its worst fears confirmed. So far as the Christians found a hearing, what was feared within the old community of Israel was heard proclaimed to be vindication of the faith of the new one. How deep the resentment, how blatant the dissonance!

It is in this setting that still another element is to be discerned in the context in which the system of uncleanness comes to fulfillment and completion. Neither the Temple nor its temporary absence could have called the system into question. But the recognition of misplaced and implausible metaphor could and did. For life could scarcely be organized around the cultic metaphor and realized in the domestic analogy to cultic cleanness, once the metaphor itself produced not meaning but the vivid cognition of nonmeaning. So long as the Temple stood or people hoped it would soon be restored, keeping clean at home brought into a single continuum the sustenance of domestic life and the maintenance of both the social and the cosmic order. But at the moment at which the system was coming to its richest and most dense affirmations of the relativity of all things to Israelite man's intentions, at the hour of its most stout affirmation that man and his mind impose meaning on inert nature, which always is present but never effective without human deliberation—at that same time—the dissonance of the symbolic system comes to acute crisis.

Each meal now reminds people of the Temple they had lost and, in the aftermath of Bar Kokhba's calamity, knew they could not regain—or even enter—through their own deliberate action. The sustenance of life is now accomplished in such wise as to underline the incapacity of the Israelites so to behave as to replicate and regain the very center, the point from which lines of structure and meaning radiated. The bed and the table, sexual activity and eating, now turn out to run counter to the besought, but unavailable, meanings of Israelite society as a whole. This is another side of that irony to which I alluded a moment ago: the making of the processes of the sustenance of life into a kind of joke upon the living.

True, the system comes to completion. But in its fullness it also imposes unbearable burdens upon the people who make it work, who find the meaning of their ordinary activities within its referential structure. Douglas says, "Being holy means being set apart. The Israelites cherish their boundaries and want nothing better than to keep them strong and high" (1975:304). When we contemplate the history of the people of Israel in the last century B.C. and the first two thereafter, however, we find nothing more ubiquitous than violated boundaries. It is one thing to live under the supervision of distant empires. It is quite another to discover Syrians sacrificing pigs within the Temple precincts, contentious Hasmoneans shedding Israelite blood upon the Lord's altar, Romans pacing through the sanctuary, Herod making the Temple into a vehicle of political patronage, Romans burning the Temple and three generations later making certain that it would not ever be rebuilt. Not only were the sacred bounds polluted but, as I said, Israelites after Bar Kokhba could not even enter into them again. Was nothing then sacred? Are all boundaries always to be violated? Surely there must be a way to construct boundaries which never again will be transgressed, because none but an Israelite can cross them and enter into the inviolable realm of the sacred marked out by them. The marking out of those new frontiers, inviolable because they are transcendent and ineffable, is the task of the second century rabbis. The cultic analogy proves not only useless to them, but offensive and destructive.

Israelite life at the end of the first century after 70 must find some other path than the pilgrim's, some new direction at every meal than toward the Temple, some less painful metaphor of the sacred than the priestly mode of sanctification. If this Order, a principal part of Mishnah, is brought to completion, it also comes to its natural conclusion because it imposes a burden of unnatural irony ultimately too heavy to bear. Mishnah finds ample space for the matter of cleanness. But the heirs and continuators of Mishnah turn their minds to other things. For hope defines the criterion of meaning, and a structure held together by despair cannot stand. The Orders of Nashim (women, family), Neziqin (civil torts), Moed (seasons), even Qodoshim (Holy Things)—the affairs of the family and of the social polity, the passage of time and the expectation of the ultimate restoration of the cult—these aspects of being constitute a viable definition of, and boundary for, Israelite ontology. They shape a world worth man's deliberation and continuing, acute reflection. With the ultimate statement of Mishnah, by contrast, the Order of Purities comes to an end. Other Orders go forward, gaining strength in the passage of time. Each one but ours is heavy with the promise of the sanctification of the ordinary life, the promise kept but also not kept in the system of uncleanness. Ordinary doings of common folk indeed are susceptible of sanctification. Commonplaces are to be shaped into a sacred structure held together by hope, unweighed down by irony, unblighted by despair. The house of Israel endures in time, built in the inner relationships of the Israelite life in society, in time, at home. And the hope refused to die (compare Schürer: 557).

CHAPTER VI

Map Without Territory:
Mishnah's System of Sacrifice
and Sanctuary

I

The proper mode of comparison of religions, as I argue in the fourth chapter, is through the juxtaposition and contrast of complete systems, not of mere details. But for that purpose, the work of systemic description and interpretation must be completed. What is crucial in the work of description and interpretation is discovering how a given system addresses itself to its concrete social and historical context, that is, the history of a system is essential to its explanation. This task of description of context, to be sure, cannot be deemed to complete the hermeneutical enterprise. But it also is clear, comparison of systems without a firm historical context for each produces results which are either trivial and obvious (part V below) or farfetched and meaningless. In this chapter I propose briefly to describe one of the six fundamental components of the Mishnaic version of Judaism, the subsystem of sacrifice and sanctuary, which, along with the other five subsystems, defines Mishnah's world-view. Systemic description completed, we then turn to the question of how Mishnah in this topic addresses itself to the world of the late first and second centuries A.D., in which the document as a whole comes into being. Finally, we attempt to locate Mishnah, its world-view and intellectual structure, in the larger context both of Judaism and of the history of religions of late antiquity. It is at this point that the methodological statement, on the interplay of history of religions and history of Judaism, with which I opened, will have been fully illustrated; and further efforts of a comparative character may be undertaken.

The task for us, therefore, is to recover a clear picture of the history of Judaism and of its principal constituent structures, not to leap from some text or rite of Judaism, viewed out of context, to some text or rite, whether of another version of Judaism or of some other religion—it hardly matters—also viewed anticontextually. In this regard, we recall the wise comment of Morton Smith:

Historical method enables us to produce the individual histories of the individual religions which have arisen, flourished, and declined among the civilized peoples of the world. These individual histories are not, of course, the history of religion. That, I suppose, if we use the terms strictly, would be an enormous, unknowable thing, an account of all religious activities all over the world, from year to year, throughout the whole course of history. This . . . has never been attempted, and the term "history of religion" is usually misused for what should be called "the science of religion"; that is, the attempt to classify religions by types, to describe the patterns of development and decline which are followed by the various types, to determine the causes which produce these patterns and the methods which might be used to alter them (1968:9–10).

The work of describing and interpreting the history of Judaism, carried forward in the research whose results are presented here, is shaped and defined, however, by issues brought to bear in describing and interpreting the histories of other religions as well. There are generative questions to be addressed uniformly to each. Through the results we gain a better understanding not only of the histories of religions but also of the history of religions.[1]

At the outset I describe the system of sacrifice and sanctuary laid forth by Mishnah's Order of Holy Things (part II). It is that system, and only that system, which here requires interpretation in its own historical—that is, social and intellectual—context: Israelite society of first and second centuries. There are two *historical* facts which are paramount: first, the destruction of the Temple in A.D. 70; second, the defeat of Bar Kokhba and the permanent 'paganization' of Jerusalem in the aftermath of the war of ca. 135. In the former time, the cult ceased to operate; in the later, it became permanently unavailable, and Jerusalem, inaccessible.

There is a third fact, which defines the *intellectual* context of our division: the availability of Scripture, upon which our system lays out its foundations and builds its constructions. Just as the two disasters define the temporal and historical framework for description and interpretation, so the availability of Scripture, with its facts and lessons, defines the intellectual setting.[2] Having

[1] I leave it to philosophers of religion to decide whether what is accomplished here is history of Judaism, history of religions (of the late antique world), comparative religions, or whatever. Just now a philosopher of religion declares that my undertaking does not fall within history of religions because I do not compare different religions. History of religions, he claims, is the same as comparative religions. I find the question arid and boring. But I think it is nothing short of ignorant to declare that, in the study of Judaism, what is attempted here is more or less equivalent to what, in the study of Christianity, is called "Church History." I cannot think of anything which the approach to the history of Judaism laid out here (and in parallel studies) has in common with Church History.

[2] On the relationship of Scripture and Mishnah for the Order of Purities, see my "From Scripture to Mishnah: The Case of Niddah," (1978) which summarizes the diverse relationships to Scripture of each of the twelve of the Order of Purities; "From Scripture to Mishnah: The Exegetical Origins of *Maddaf*," in *Fiftieth Anniversary Festschrift of the American Academy for Jewish Research*, in press (papers written by Fellows of the Academy); "From Scripture to Mishnah: The Origins of Mishnah's Fifth Division," (1979) and the more theoretical statement, "The Meaning of Torah Shebeᶜal Peh," (1977).

described these contexts—historical (part III), intellectual (part IV)—we turn to explore three perspectives of interpretation of our division. The first is supplied by anthropological theory of sacrifice (part V); the second, by the Israelite historical context (part VI); and the third, by the larger historical situation of religions in late antiquity (part VII).

II

Our first task is to describe Mishnah's system. Even those entirely familiar with the several tractates of Mishnah-Tosefta may be glad to follow this brief survey of the contents of the whole,[3] meant to describe, for the purposes of contextual interpretation, the complete system, not merely to point up one or another interesting detail. As Morton Smith says, "Those who have memorized the Babylonian Talmud can never know it all at once—they can only recall it part by part" (1968:8). Hence, it is not superfluous, even for learned scholarly readers, to provide a rapid and simple review of the system as a whole.

When Mishnah speaks of Holy Things (*Qodoshim*), it means to refer in particular to sacrifice and sanctuary: matters concerning the praxis of the altar and maintenance of the sanctuary. The praxis of the altar, specifically, involves sacrifice and things set aside for sacrifice and so deemed consecrated. The topic covers these among the eleven tractates of our division: Zebahim and part of Hullin, Menahot, Temurah, Keritot, part of Meilah, Tamid, and Qinnim. The maintenance of the sanctuary (inclusive of the personnel) is dealt with in Bekhorot, Arakhin, part of Meilah, Middot, and part of Hullin. That is why we call the Mishnaic corpus of holy things a *system of sacrifice and sanctuary*.

Yet, from the perspective of Mishnah as a whole, the system of our division by itself is grossly incomplete. More important rules on the maintenance of the priesthood are excluded from our division than included in it. These are, specifically, those which pertain to the income in produce accruing to the priesthood outside of the cultic fees, e.g., Demai, Terumot, Maaserot, Hallah.[4] Equally central rules on the praxis of the sacrificial cult are dealt with elsewhere; specifically, those offerings tied up to specific points in the sacred calendar: Pesahim, Yoma, Hagigah. Sheqalim, for its part, treats a major source of Temple income and is not located in our division. The accused wife's meal-offering is not described here but in tractate Sotah, in the third division, on women. Unacceptable forms of worship are treated in the fourth division, Abodah Zarah in Neziqin, and the sacrifice of the red cow and the purification-rite of the *meṣora* ("leper") are described in the sixth, Parah

---

[3]But if not, they should skip directly to section III.

[4]As noted above, my former students are in the process of publishing their dissertations on the division of agriculture.

and Negaim in Tohorot. Clearly, therefore, what is excluded is at least as important as what is included.

Furthermore, a broad construction of Qodoshim would require the inclusion of tractates which specify in a recurrent apodosis liability for particular offerings or explain such liability, e.g., Shabuot for one, Shabbat for another (HYYB = liable for a sin-offering). If we were to interpret in generic terms Mishnah's definition of the frame of reference of the fifth division, it would be difficult to find grounds for the exclusion of a fair number of tractates in the other five divisions. For the world referred to by Mishnah as a whole rests upon foundations formed by the priesthood, the sacrificial system correlated to the lunar calendar, the Temple, and the holy city. Upon those realities Mishnah forms its conceptions for the bulk of at least four of its six divisions: Zeraim, Moed, Qodoshim, and Tohorot. It requires the data of the cult for a full picture of the other two, Nashim and Neziqin, as well.

What requires explanation is not exclusions, which will have to be dealt with in their several contexts, but inclusions. What is it that Mishnah wishes to say by its choices of the eleven tractates before us? We begin by specifying the tractates and their principal points:

Zebahim   The effect of attitude or intention upon the act of killing a designated (sanctified) beast or bird; rules for the offering up of the slaughtered beast or bird; the conduct of the altar.

Menahot   The effect of attitude or intention upon the taking of a handful of meal-offering and offering it up; rules for the offering up of meal-offerings; vows and meal-offerings.

Hullin   Rules of slaughter of animals for use in the cult or at home—how an animal is killed; whether or not an animal is fit for Israelite consumption and for the altar; application of Scriptural rules about gifts to the priest—first fleece, priestly gifts of shoulder, two cheeks, and maw of animals slaughtered for secular purposes; application of rules about preparation of food at home or in the cult—milk, meat, covering up the blood, prohibition of the sinew of the hip; application of rules about what may be suitably eaten or offered—prohibition of taking the dam and the eggs, prohibition of slaughtering on the same day the dam and the young.

Bekhorot   Firstborn of animals which are either offered up or redeemed, with the priest receiving the benefit of the animal either way; slaughtering a blemished firstling for the benefit of the priest, definition of blemishes, examination thereof; firstborn sons, redeemed through gift of five *selas* to the priest; tithe of cattle.

Arakhin   Valuations and vows for the benefit of the Temple and the altar (Lev. 27:1–8); the dedication and redemption of a field received as an inheritance; the devoted thing.

Temurah   A beast designated as a substitute for one already consecrated enters the status of that consecrated beast, but the latter remains holy (Lev. 27:9–10)—the rules of substitution; the status of the offspring of substitutes; the language used in effecting an act of substitution.

Keritot   Liability to sin-offerings; liability to guilt-offerings (Lev. 5:17–19); the possibility of liability to more than a single sin- or guilt-offering in the commission of a single act; a single sin-offering and multiple sins.

Meilah   The definition of the sacrilege to which Scripture (Lev. 5:14–16) refers, with specific reference to what itself is consecrated for the altar and what in its value is consecrated; when laws of sacrilege cease to apply, but other taboos commence to apply; sacrilege against Temple-property in general.

Tamid   The daily burnt-offering and how it is offered up, a narrative.

Middot   The layout of the Temple, a descriptive-narrative.

Qinnim   A set of fantastic conundrums on procedure at the altar when diverse sets of bird-offerings are confused with one another.

Viewed from a distance, therefore, our division's tractates divide themselves up into the following groups (in parentheses are names of tractates containing relevant materials):

1. *rules for the altar and the praxis of the cult*: Zebahim, Menahot, Hullin, Keritot, Tamid, Qinnim (Bekhorot, Meilah);
2. *rules for the altar and animals set aside for the cult*: Arakhin, Temurah, Meilah (Bekhorot);
3. *rules for the upkeep of the altar and support of the Temple staff and buildings*: Bekhorot, Middot (Arakhin, Meilah, Tamid).

In a word, our division speaks of the sacrificial cult and the sanctuary in which the cult is conducted. The law pays special attention to the matter of the status of the property of the altar and of the sanctuary, both materials to be utilized in the actual sacrificial rites, and property, the value of which supports the cult and sanctuary in general. Both are deemed to be sanctified, that is: *qodoshim*, Holy Things.

Our division prefers not to deal with the special offerings, e.g., those designated for particular days of the week or seasons of the year, which are going to be treated in Moed; with other than animal-fees for the priesthood, specifically omitting reference to agricultural dues paid over in their support, dealt with in Zeraim; or with that matrix of cleanness in which the cult is to be carried on, expounded in Tohorot. At best, allusions to those other three areas of the law pertinent to the cult will occur here.

The interests of Qodoshim, upon closer examination, prove to be clearcut and carefully defined. The matter consists of much less than everything relevant to "cult." There are decisive and pointed choices. By *Holy Things* we refer specifically to the altar and animals and cereals offered on the altar or belonging to the altar, and to property and goods belonging to the altar or to the sanctuary. Within these two categories we find a place for the whole of the thematic repertoire of the fifth division or, at the very least, account for the inclusion of each and every one of its significant topics. If, therefore, our division is contented to leave over for use in other divisions materials pertinent to the altar and the sanctuary, the reason is twofold.

First, it is absolutely self-evident that the division of Holy Things takes for granted the existence of other divisions. Thus, our division knows that it is to be located in Mishnah as a whole. The conceptual redaction of (or: topical plan for) the document Mishnah, therefore, precedes the conceptual (let alone literary) redaction of its divisions and tractates. It follows that Mishnah as such is systemically complete only in its penultimate stages.

Second, and in consequence, our division has its clear and sufficient reasons for wanting to talk only about the things it does talk about and to omit the things it bypasses in silence. What it wants to speak of is the altar in general, the cult and its praxis, and, as a secondary but important theme, the general support of the altar and the maintenance, through the altar and Temple, of the priesthood and of the cult. These two things, as I said, define the parameters of Holy Things—but not, our division hastens to emphasize, of holiness.

The system of Qodoshim centers upon the everyday rules always applicable to the cult: the daily whole-offering, the sin-offering and guilt-offering which one may bring any time under ordinary circumstances; the right sequence of diverse offerings; the way in which the rites of the whole-offering, sin-, and guilt-offering are carried out; the sorts of animals which are acceptable; the accompanying cereal-offerings; the support and provision of animals for the cult and of meat for the priesthood; the support and material maintenance of the cult and its building. We have a system before us: the system of the cult of the Jerusalem Temple, seen as an ordinary and everyday affair, a continuing and routine operation.

Special rules for the cult, both in respect to the altar and in regard to the maintenance of the buildings, personnel, and even the holy city, will be elsewhere, in Moed and Zeraim. Whether or not those divisions form their own systems we cannot say. But from the perspective of Qodoshim, they intersect by supplying special rules and raising extraordinary considerations for that theme which Qodoshim claims to set forth in its most general and unexceptional way: the cult as something permanent and everyday. But, as we shall now observe, in the time in which our division, along with the rest of Mishnah, is coming to closure and completion, the cult is anything but routine, permanent, and everyday. In the first stage of the formation of Mishnah's system, the cult lies in ruins. In the second, the cult's locus, the Holy City (the Temple mount), is not even accessible to Israelites. So our division creates a map for a fictitious territory. It describes, with remarkable precision and concrete detail, a perfect fantasy.

III

The Order of Things in a concrete way maps out the cosmology of the sanctuary and its sacrificial system, that is, the world of the Temple, which had been the cosmic center of Israelite life. A later saying states matters as follows:

> Just as the navel is found at the center of a human being, so the land of Israel is found at the center of the world . . . and it is the foundation of the world. Jerusalem is at the center of the land of Israel, the Temple is at the center of Jerusalem, the Holy of Holies is at the center of the Temple, the Ark is at the center of the Holy of Holies, and the Foundation Stone is in front of the Ark, which spot is the foundation of the world [*Tanhuma Qedoshim* 10 (Harlow, 1963:143)].

When the Temple was destroyed in 70, therefore, the center of a national life shaped around a cosmic metaphor was in ruins. When Jerusalem became Aelia in 140, with the Temple-site ploughed over, the ruins were made permanent. The problem confronting all Israelites in the ten decades from 70 to 170—the period of the formation of our tractates[5]—is to work out a way of viewing the world, of making sense of a cosmos which, having lost its center, is nonsense.

To state the problem of interpretation which must now occupy our attention: Mishnah maps out nonsense.[6] It speaks in ultimate seriousness about a never-never-land, giving endless, concrete, and intimate detail about a utopian cosmos—things which are not and, for now, also cannot be. Surely we must ask: Why do sages say these things? To whom do they matter? True, moving out of the locative world of Temple, sanctuary and sacrifice alike, and into a frame focused upon community and upon activity possible anywhere (among people of a certain sort), Mishnah by no means presents maps of a

[5]This is shown in *Holy Things*, VI, Chapters Two through Ten.

[6]I allude here to the (in)famous introduction, supplied to Professor Gershom Scholem by Professor Saul Lieberman, at Jewish Theological Seminary of America in spring, 1957, when Scholem gave the lectures ultimately printed as *Jewish Gnosticism, Merkabah Mysticism, and Talmud Tradition. Based on the Israel Goldstein Lectures, Delivered at the Jewish Theological Seminary of America, New York* (1960/1965). In presenting Scholem, Lieberman said, "Nonsense is nonsense. But the *history* of nonsense is scholarship." That is so of Mishnah, as much as of Qabbalah.

world of nonsense. From one perspective, it outlines the terrain and the route from cult to community, from cosmology to anthropology.[7] But on the surface it should speak of things other than sacrifice and sanctuary. Giving us, instead, a detailed account of things no one needs to know is wholly dissonant with the world to which Mishnah speaks: the map ignores the *territory*.

Our work now is to examine this one component—Holy Things—of Mishnah's six-frame map of the world, its definition of one of the six things it proposes Israelites should have in mind. We study the world-view religion of those first and second century Jews who speak through Mishnah. At the outset, therefore, we have to define what it is that we mean by studying about a religion. We define our frame of reference through Smith's words:

> What we study when we study religion is one mode of constructing worlds of meaning, worlds within which men find themselves and in which they choose to dwell. What we study is the passion and drama of man discovering the truth of what it is to be human. History is the framework within whose perimeter those human expressions, activities and intentionalities that we call "religious" occur. Religion is the quest, within the grounds of the human, historical condition, for the power to manipulate and negotiate one's "situation" so as to have "space" in which to meaningfully dwell. It is the power to relate one's domain to the plurality of environmental and social spheres in such a way as to guarantee the conviction that one's existence "matters." Religion is a distinctive mode of human creativity, a creativity which both discovers limits and creates limits for human existence. What we study when we study religion is the variety of attempts to map, construct and inhabit such positions of power through the use of myths, rituals and experiences of transformation (1978: xii–xiii).[8]

As we have noted, the world-view of our division is dissonant, clashing with the reality of the environment supposed to receive the document. Our division is incongruous to its world, wholly out of joint with the reality of the people who made it, irrelevant to the everyday alternatives facing those to whom it speaks. So far as Mishnah's fifth division proposes to map out the cult, sacrificial system, and sanctuary of the Israelite world, it speaks not only of what is no more, but also of what for the foreseeable future cannot be. Mishnah maps out a territory wholly of the imagination, a realm of the unreal: *Not only is map not territory; map also is all one has, for now there is no territory*. I here allude to Smith's concluding lines:

---

[7] The entire theoretical framework of this paper, from this point to the end, forms a detailed concurring response to the brilliant essays of Jonathan Z. Smith (1978). I *do* claim that when I answer questions raised by historians of religions, and when I do so in the framework of interpretive issues set forth in history of religions, then (even though I address said questions and speak in said framework only in the context of the data of a small part of a single, itself kaleidoscopic, religious tradition) I commit history of religions. In any case, the movement in late antiquity from *cosmos* to *anthropos* as the formative metaphors of religious imagination is (to my knowledge, first) worked out by Smith. The present phrase, therefore, really belongs to Smith and is used by me in the framework of his thinking.

[8] Scholars of Jewish history and even history of Judaism tend to identify the study of *religions* with the study of religious *thought*. But history of religions, including Judaism, encompasses a wider range of issues than solely history of Judaic ideas as, I believe, is illustrated in this paper.

We need to reflect on and play with the necessary incongruity of our maps before we set out
on a voyage of discovery to chart the worlds of other men. For the dictum of Alfred
Korzybski is inescapable: "Map is not territory"—but maps are all we possess (1978:309).

Our task now is to ask what it means to make maps of a forbidden city, to
reflect upon an unattainable sanctuary, and to make rules on a sacrificial
system none can carry out.

IV

In trying to understand the sort of map we have, we turn first to its
relationship to that other important map, the one of Scripture, to which
Mishnah scarcely alludes but upon which in fact our division is drawn (see n.
2). In what sense does our division serve as an exegesis of the equivalent
materials of Scripture? Holy Things complements Scripture's rules or moves
forward from them in supplementary, but essentially predictable, patterns.[9] It
follows that the principal exegesis effected by the division is to point to those
(limited) areas in which Scripture requires some further amplification and to
underline, through blatant and tedious repetition (e.g., in Menahot, Hullin,
and Keritot), those (many) areas in which Scripture is complete.[10]

It is one thing to speak of the system of sanctuary and sacrifice described
by Leviticus and Numbers, together with the whole of Mishnah. It is quite
another to address that much more limited system contained within the eleven
tractates of our division. In the former, we have an adequate description of the
social process of sacrifice: what we do on all sorts of occasions of crisis, sin,
suffering, or disturbance of the sacred.[11] In the latter we find only a partial
description of the process, specifically, that part which is done day by day
through undifferentiated time. These are the components of Mishnah's
distinct system: the cult as it normally is on weekdays, with its sin-offerings
and guilt-offerings and daily whole-offerings; the cult as it is in its great
buildings; the cult as recipient of ordinary objects rendered sacred by devotion
to its upkeep. If we want to understand this cult, however, we must turn to the
meanings imputed to it in Scripture since Mishnah adds nothing to the
Scripture's meanings and changes nothing in them. So it would waste our time
to ask, in the context of Mishnah, those questions of sacrifice and atonement
which are properly addressed only to the priestly authors of Leviticus and

[9]We need not review the survey of the division as a whole, at which this point is made
perfectly obvious.

[10]The really interesting question, which requires analysis in its own terms, is why anyone
should have wanted merely to repeat what already is explicitly stated in Scriptures. What sort of
document is intended by people who do not hesitate to draw upon Scripture's facts but to state
them—in a quite unoriginal way—in their own words? I approach this problem in my "Learning
and Transcendence in Judaism" (1978). But I do not claim to be able to solve it.

[11]Compare Baruch A. Levine (1974).

Numbers, or of those cultic Psalms which raise the profound issues of meaning associated with the Temple experience.[12]

So far as there is a ritual process of sacrifice, therefore, it is not described in Mishnah, but in Scripture. The ritual of Mishnah must be isolated in some way other than by asking questions relevant to *what* it says, its substance and subject-matter. The consequent, ineluctable problematic, then, is *why* we have the document at all since the document says little more than it learns from an already-available Scripture. Why someone made it, what he meant to say thereby—these are the sole right questions to address to our division.

If, therefore, any of our tractates has, or conforms to, a "theory of sacrifice," I cannot specify what that theory is, except for Scripture's. I see no important point at which a profound and fundamental conviction of Scripture is reversed or even examined. Time and again all we find in our division is an amplification of secondary implications of Scripture, never a confrontation with the primary assertions or fundamental ideas thereof. The absence of explicit theorizing on questions of meaning is clearly seen when we refer to the Christian writers on sacrifice, whether in Letter to the Hebrews or Irenaeus or the Pseudo-Clementines. They refer not to details only, but to the total phenomena of sacrifice and cult and their meaning. If our authorities fail to do so, it is because their principal message is expressed in their formal-topical work, the things they say and do not say, and how they say them. It must follow that, so far as they wish to say something about sacrifice in the abstract, its meaning and significance in the life of Israel here and in the heavens, it is not only that Scripture's message remains valid but also that it is exhaustive: *All there said is right, and all that is right is said there.* And in the context of second century Israelite history, that message is hardly trivial or banal, but defiant and triumphant.

V

If we turn to anthropology to supply questions to be addressed to any sacrificial system, we are best advised[13] to take up the theoretical program laid out by Hubert and Mauss (1964:10–18). We ask whether or not we are able to identify the various components of our system along the lines of the theory by

---

[12]The results of my *History of the Mishnaic Law of Purities* (1974–1977: I–XXII) are precisely the opposite, which is why we must find these obvious conclusions so remarkable. We never need to ask why someone made up a Mishnaic Order of Purities, because nearly the whole of the corpus of that division, exclusive of sources of uncleanness, is fresh and new, unimagined within the conceptual framework of the priestly legislators of the sixth or fifth centuries who give us Leviticus and the rest of P. The response in Holy Things to the corpus of these very same legislators then is wholly different.

[13]I regret to report that I was unable to find theoretical issues of suggestive and fructifying effect in either Victor Turner (1977) or Adolf E. Jensen (1963). The former seemed to me rather private and intellectually self-indulgent, and the latter, not terribly relevant to the data which I am

which any system must be constructed. The answer is affirmative. We know, for example, who is the sacrifier—the subject to whom the benefits of sacrifice accrue or who undergoes its effects (1964:10), namely, the community, in the case of the Tamid, of the individual, in the case of the offerings of Keritot. We are able to address the matter of the objects of sacrifice, namely, the kinds of things for whose sake the sacrifice takes place. We are familiar with oblations of various kinds; we know what has been sacrificed, the victim. If then we attempt a definition of sacrifice within the system of Holy Things, we may find ourselves quite at home in the following:

> Sacrifice is a religious act which, through the consecration of a victim, modifies the condition of the moral person who [we must add: or *community which*] accomplishes it or that of certain objects with which he [or it] is concerned (1964:13).

Since important to Hubert and Mauss is the notion of the generic unity of sacrifices, therefore, we may affirm that in no way does Mishnah's division of Holy Things, or the Scripture upon which it is constructed, contradict their fundamental conception. However various the forms of sacrifice, all of them may fall within the taxonomy provided by Hubert and Mauss. To be sure, the reason may well be the compendiousness of the definition, not the inner, universal structure of sacrifice hither and yon. But that is to be said to all successful taxonomists; and, indeed, it is the condition of success. Generic unities yield notions too general to be definitive in the analysis of specific phenomena until what is assigned to the generic says something of consequence. But first let me show how our division may respond to Hubert and Mauss's concrete allegation.

It would be difficult to find a better example than Meilah for their propositions of sacralization and desacralization. Hubert and Mauss state:

> Of all the procedures of sacrifice, the most general, the least rich in particular elements . . . are some of sacralization and desacralization. Now actually in any sacrifice of desacralization, however pure it may be, we always find a sacralization of the victim. Conversely, in any sacrifice of sacralization, even the most clearly marked, a desacralization is necessarily implied, for otherwise the remains of the victim could not be used. The two elements are thus so closely interdependent that the one cannot exist without the other (1964:95).

Joshua's conceptions at M. Meilah 1:1–3, which lay the foundations for Meilah, will accord entirely with those propositions. The laws of sacrilege are invoked as soon as the animal is designated as a sacrifice. They are lifted as

---

responsible to interpret. The contrast between anthropological work on pollution, which proved so remarkably enriching for my *Purities* XXII, and that on sacrifice, which helped so little for *Holy Things* VI, is to be noted. There is no equivalent known to me to *Purity and Danger* (1966) by the inestimable Mary Douglas.

soon as the blood-rite has been carried out. That, sum and substance, is the sequence of sacralization (we should have said, sanctification) and desacralization known to Mishnah. Here, therefore, our system falls wholly within the parameters outlined by the great French philosophers. It is all the more striking, therefore, that we cannot locate a "philosophy" of Holy Things. We neither confirm, nor reject, Hubert and Mauss's conclusion:

> But if sacrifice is so complex, whence comes its unity? It is because, fundamentally, beneath the diverse forms it takes, it always consists in one same procedure, which may be used for the most widely differing purposes. This procedure consists in establishing a means of communication between the sacred and the profane world through the mediation of a victim, that is, of a thing that in the course of the ceremony is destroyed (1964:97).

This I find too general to be very helpful or even interesting. They further state:

> There is no need to explain at length why the profane thus enters into a relationship with the divine: it is because it sees in it the very source of life. It therefore has every interest in drawing closer to it, since it is there that the very conditions for its existence are to be found (1964:98).

Hubert and Mauss then posit that the victim takes the place of the sacrificer; the victim dies and so protects the sacrificer: "The gods take the victim instead of him. *The victim redeems him.*"[14] Now if we look in our division of Mishnah-Tosefta for materials even relevant to these so fundamental propositions, by contrast to the one cited just now, we find nothing. Perhaps it is self-evident to our authorities that through the sacrifice and in the sanctuary we establish "communication between the sacred and the profane world through the mediation of a victim." And Mishnah's masters rarely say banal things, even though they do not always say interesting ones.

But perhaps it is because the direction of the argument ("the victim redeems him") is counter to the thrust of our tractates, which do not raise the question of what God ("the gods") has in mind in establishing the cult. The author of the Letter to the Hebrews, to be sure, readily will concur about the

---

[14]It is not for us to speculate on cultural causes for the astonishing agreement, as to the ultimate generic meaning of all sacrifice, between Hubert and Mauss, on the one side, and the corpus of Christian thought on the sacrifice of the Mass, on the other side: "the victim redeems him." Nor are we able to show that the imaginative powers of the philosophers have been shaped, to begin with, by the culturally-embedded data of Christian conceptions of sacrifice. We only point to the fact that the author of Hebrews will have found much satisfaction in the allegation that the generic unity of sacrifice, in diverse forms and settings, consists in the very concrete and specific conception advanced in Hebrews (and other first and second century Christian writings). In a few moments (note 15, below) we shall notice an equally remarkable concurrence between first and second century Christian thinkers on the subject of the meaning, for the history of Judaism, of the destruction of the Temple in A.D. 70 and a contemporary scholar's ("secular") conclusion about the same event's impact upon the history of Judaism.

redemptive power of the victim. But the author of that Letter is not profoundly concerned with the details—Scriptural or otherwise—of sacrifice and sanctuary as they are framed in our division. In point of fact he has as his problem to explain away through "spiritualization" precisely those bloody this-worldly facts restated and confirmed in our division. That is, the appeal of the this-worldly cult of Jerusalem, of its sanctuary and of its blood-rite, is the problem to be worked out by the author of the Letter to the Hebrews. Then the restatement of the realities of the sanctuary and the sacrifice *re-present* once again that same reality. If we could demonstrate that our authorities, from 70 to 170, knew Hebrews and its conceptions, we could advance a powerful case that our division forms an eloquent Israelite reply to Hebrews. But, of course, we cannot show ᶜAqiba or Judah and Meir have read Hebrews or even heard about the people addressed in it, and we therefore do not know it.

Having gladly conceded the fact that Mishnah's system of sacrifice and sanctuary falls comfortably into the taxonomic structure of Hubert and Mauss, we therefore have gained little; and they, nothing. For the analysis of those exegetical processes by which our division (and Mishnah as a whole) may be unpacked is not thereby facilitated. It is not only that our division speaks wholly about details. It is that, beneath the details, we have not been able to state any important and distinctive general notions, along the lines of those many general and distinctive principles expressed in later glosses to be sure, in the context of *Purities*. Mishnah seems to me to have very little which it wants to say *about* Holy Things, once it has taken up the topic. Its selections for inclusion and exclusion clearly are important, in that they limit Holy Things to animals used for normal and regular offerings. But they do not exclude from the category special or extraordinary offerings; these are dealt with elsewhere and are no less holy. It follows that the division contributes some facts, repeats a great many facts already available, and organizes the whole into compendious and well-laid-forth tractates. What is important in all this, therefore, is *that* the work is done, just as we saw above: *Here the form is all we have for meaning.* I need not hasten to apologize and claim that we do not deal with a system of outward and empty forms. That is not quite to the point in a construction resting, to begin with, upon no material base in actual fact, but upon imagination and hope. It might then be said that Holy Things forms an elaborate construction with no content: a design of an imaginary system which, if it were realized, would be all formalism and no meaning. Perhaps so; but all we have, for purposes of interpretation, is the work of imagination, the making of the document itself.

VI

Just as ancient Christian thinkers from the framer of Matthew 24:1–2 onward maintain that the destruction of the Temple marks the definitive end of the "Judaism of the Old Testament" and the confirmation of the "Christianity of the New," so modern Christian scholars repeat the same view. For example, S. G. F. Brandon states:

> [The destruction] had a paralyzing effect on the life of the Jewish people, and from it they only slowly recovered and settled to an essentially maimed existence, with their cherished religion bereft of much of its *raison d'être* (1951:167).[15]

Brandon's judgment of the world framed by Mishnah to begin with hardly exhibits understanding (or even knowledge) of those ways in which the destruction of the Temple turned out to inaugurate not a time of decay and dissolution, but a remarkable age of reconstruction and creativity in the history of Judaism. The working out of Mishnah, that vast and difficult document (so much larger than the whole of the New Testament, inclusive of the bulk of its apocrypha), surely is not the accomplishment of people who are "paralyzed" and who have settled to "an essentially maimed existence."

If we now ask our document how it proposes to rebuild the world, it must answer, "By changing everything while pretending nothing has changed." Mishnah's system of Holy Things defies its own context. It unfolds as if there were some prospect, near at hand, for the utilization of its materials. But there is none. With its severe and unnuanced descriptive statements about what is to be done in a Temple, Mishnah instructs a world in fact beyond recovery. But the division also makes certain a Temple will not be brought into existence, since it insists upon Jerusalem alone, when there is no Jerusalem.[16] That is the really powerful, anticontextual datum of our division. Then again, we recall, when we place our division up against Scripture, we find an easy and comfortable fit, with few ideas or facts not provided by Scripture itself. So it is as if our division chooses not only to ignore its world and the potentialities for the exegesis of contemporary times, but also to turn itself backward toward Leviticus and other relevant passages in Scripture. Perhaps it means to look forward (the text never says so) toward the eschaton.[17]

[15]A survey of the writings of second and third-century Christian thinkers turns up innumerable statements of exactly the same position. Justin, for instance, repeats this view when the topic of sacrifice and atonement is raised. Brandon shows how even historians of religion may turn out to restate theological dogma in the very center of what they would claim to be mere history. For a demonstration of how difficult it is for scholars of Christian origins to do creditable scholarly work on Judaism, see George F. Moore (1921). But Moore's own *Judaism* (1927) also demonstrates how great an achievement is possible, for his is by far the best dogmatic theology of early rabbinic Judaism ever produced, by Christian or Jew, New Testament scholar or Talmudist, down to the present time.

[16]This point is repeatedly made in our division, that, outside of Jerusalem, there is no legitimate Temple and no permissible cult. It is stated by implication at M. Zebahim, Chapter Fourteen, and explicitly at M. Menahot, Chapter Thirteen, among many other places in the *Order of Holy Things*.

[17]Among many, I share that view, made explicit in later strata of Rabbinic writings, that by studying the sacrificial rules, it is as if one has made a sacrifice. But, it must be pointed out, that

The peculiarity of this perspective emerges when we call to mind how contemporaries of Mishnah at its several periods, first and second century (for instance, the author of the Letter to the Hebrews), reshaped exactly the same themes and topics into important polemics in behalf of Christian faith. Mishnah's refusal to reinterpret in any detail and in any aspect a single rule of Scripture, its dogmatic insistence upon the literal meaning of such Scriptures as it does resort to, and, more important, its extensive access to all those facts and conceptions of Scripture which generate Mishnah's own rules—these facts in context cannot be taken as routine and unexceptional. The pretense that nothing has changed in five hundred years (and, since the rabbis of Mishnah believe Moses revealed the Torah, closer to fourteen hundred years) and that the ancient system goes forward unaffected by change and by time is the most eloquent apologetic. To gain some notion of the meaning of Mishnah's powerful affirmation of Temple, sacrifice, and all the rich detail of law focusing upon both, we have to recall that Mishnah comes forth in an age in which Christians, for one, had long since given up on animal sacrifice. We need hardly review the judgments of Justin, Irenaeus, and the Pseudo-Clementine writers on that matter.

Why is it that Mishnah's rabbis insist upon saying something old, when others of their own day, inheriting the same Scriptures, so radically revise their meaning? Obviously, there is the element of the restabilization of a society which has been profoundly upset by the loss of its Temple, then of the city, and finally of all hope of access to the Temple-site. Clearly, the rabbis of Mishnah do not wish to admit the possibility of reestablishing the cult somewhere else. At the same time they assuredly do not propose to remove the cult from the focus of Israelite consciousness. On the contrary, as we noted earlier, seen as a whole, Mishnah is surely the most profoundly priestly document we could imagine. Four of its six divisions center upon peculiarly priestly conceptions. These are not reinterpreted or given new meaning or even much new nuance. They are restated pretty much as priests of P would have stated them to begin with. In four of the six divisions Mishnah wants the Israelites of its day to know about careful separation of heave-offerings and tithes, about the synchronization of calendar and cult, about the conduct of sanctuary and sacrifice, and about the purity laws. If Mishnah turns, also, to matters of home, family, and society—well—so, too, did the priests of the Temple govern Israelite life and judge the country. P is quite interested in who marries whom.

So Mishnah is a priestly document. But it is without priestly sponsorship. Everything in Mishnah points towards a group of people who take over the whole of the priestly legacy but the priesthood itself. It follows that, from its

---

conception is not made explicit in our division nor, to my knowledge, in any other Rabbinic document redacted before the mid-third century. We may find it a plausible view of what the sages of Mishnah meant to accomplish; but, unfortunately, they do not say so themselves.

beginnings, long before 70 for Tohorot, and sometime after 70 for Qodoshim,[18] Mishnah reaffirms its conviction that God is served through the sacrifice in the Temple by the priesthood. The holy days and festivals (e.g., Yoma, Pesahim) are marked through sacrifice in the Temple by the priesthood. It is the duty of Israelites at home to imitate the cleanness of the priesthood in the Temple. It is the duty of the Israelites to support the priesthood. In the stresses of second century disasters, Mishnah emerges with a message amazingly irrelevant, not only to its own day, but also to its own sponsorship. For, we need hardly point out, sages are not priests. And Mishnah does not try to look like a book composed along the lines of ancient Scripture. It does not attempt to imitate—for instance, in form or language—Leviticus, Numbers, or Deuteronomy (see n. 10).

Having argued at some length for the proposition that our division and much of Mishnah beyond it speak from and about the world of priests, Temple, and cult, I have now to point out that the authorities of Mishnah speak like scribes. That is, Mishnah for our division above all is a work of making lists, *Listenwissenschaft*, as Smith says:

> The essence of scribal knowledge was its character as *Listenwissenschaft*. . . . It depends upon catalogues and classification; it progresses by establishing precedents, by observing patterns, similarities and conjunctions, and by noting their repetitions. As such their basic faith was in the relevance of a limited number of paradigms to every new situation. Their goal . . . was nothing less than absolute perfection, the inclusion of everything within their categories. In the quest of this perfection, they developed complex hermeneutic and exegetical techniques to bridge the gap between paradigm and particular instance, between past and present (1978:70).

I cannot think of a more telling instantiation of Smith's remarks than our division. Here the aristocracy of learning has taken over the works of the aristocracy of priesthood: *Talking like scribes about priestly matters, the sages have come up with the Order of Holy Things.*

It remains to ask whether the Temple's greatest service to the people of Israel was not its destruction, then definitive prohibition to the Jews. Smith states this proposition as follows:

> I should want to go so far as to argue that if the Temple had not been destroyed, it would have had to be neglected. For it represented a locative type of religious activity no longer perceived as effective in a new, utopian religious situation with a concomitant shift from a cosmological to an anthropological view-point (1978:128).

Clearly, the position of the rabbis of Mishnah on this matter is ambiguous.

[18]These propositions are demonstrated in my *History of the Mishnaic Law of Purities* XXII, and *History of the Mishnaic Law of Holy Things* VI. So far as I can see, the whole system of purities is adumbrated *in complete form(!)* even before the turn of the first century A.D., see *Purities* (1977, XXII: 50–109).

For they do not permit the rebuilding of a cult. But they do everything they can to preserve concrete facts—not merely a generalized memory—about the one which has been destroyed. That must mean they wanted the Temple rebuilt and the cult restored.

Now, on the one hand, Mishnah may be studied anywhere. It is utopian. Self-evidently, it hardly requires carrying out, in concrete practice, the bulk of its laws, or even expects most of them to be kept. That, after all, is the datum of our division. On the other hand, Mishnah does choose to organize the world around the themes and topics of the Temple. It is locative. What, thereby, does Mishnah say to a world which cannot have a Temple?

I am not certain that Mishnah's position is accurately stated when we claim that, in Mishnah's view, by studying about the offerings, it is as if we made those offerings (see n. 17). True, that is a viewpoint flowing from Mishnah and a commonplace in Rabbinism later on. But Mishnah does not say it. On the contrary, the loci of most intense interest for Mishnah are cases and problems of the cult, many of them phrased in casuistic language (not Tamid but Zebahim-Menahot). So Mishnah is a kind of case-book, in the context of most of Zebahim. And whom would Mishnah serve, with its easily-memorized formal constructions on which offerings are brought near and waved, which are brought near but not waved, and so on? And who should learn the list of thirty-six sins punishable by extirpation? Surely these are not "Torah-study"-pericopae, addressing a society of schoolmen. They are *priestly* pericopae, facing the cult. If Mishnah plans to have its materials studied, its intention therefore is to turn whoever studies the document into someone who knows what priests know and, excluding only the matter of proper pedigree, *can* do pretty much what priests can do. But only priests *may* do these things. Now it is in this paradox that we must respond to Smith's fruitful conception. For Mishnah's Temple-tractates are not locative. But, in substance, cult and Temple still must be in one place. Mishnah thematically and conceptually does not open outward toward a new, utopian religious situation. Mishnah in substance turns backward and inward, to an old, this-worldly, situation.

Mishnah appears in the present context as a mediating document. It stands between the old and the new. It refers backward. But, in the very nature of its accessibility to a broad world of Jews, it also opens out toward the community. Now the focus will be upon people, not place; anywhere, not somewhere. Mishnah, in function, appropriates human models of society and not heavenly models of cosmology.

To conclude our view of Mishnah seen in the context of the rabbis behind it, we turn again to Smith who says:

> Social change is symbol change . . . society or culture is preeminently the construction of significance and order through symbolic activity. Social change may then be specified as the discovery or creation of modes of significance and order (1978:144).

If we ask our division whether social change has taken place, it must answer in the negative.

"Nothing has changed. The old world of Temple is what is to be studied."

"For our part," the authorities must then add, "we have nothing new to say, merely repeating what is in the Scriptures."

But both allegations are false on this face: "If there is nothing new to say, then why have you given us Mishnah?"

"If nothing has changed, then where is the priesthood? Nor do we see a real Temple or even its surrogate."

In truth the profound shift in Israelite symbols, effected by our document (at least) for those who make and memorize it, is a movement toward a society where, as I said, all know what priests know. But in this society all know it in the form and language given by sages, accessible only among their circles. To put matters simply: In the world of disaster and cataclysmic change, Mishnah stands as a statement of how the old is to be retained. It defines and effects the permanence amid change.

VII

At the end let us place our problem into the context of the world of late antiquity. The description of that larger setting is conveniently and reliably done for us by Jonathan Z. Smith whom we cite at length to conclude this discussion:

> Almost every religion in Late Antiquity occurred in both its homeland and in diasporic centers. With few exceptions, each of these religions, originally tied to a specific geographical area and people, had thousand year old traditions. In their homeland, they were inextricably tied to local loyalties and ambitions. Each persisted in its native land throughout Late Antiquity, frequently becoming linked to nationalistic movements seeking to overthrow Greco-Roman or Christian political and cultural domination. Indeed, many of these religions underwent a conscious archaicization during their period. Old texts in native languages were recopied (especially those which were related to such resistance themes as sacred kingship), national temples were restored and old, mythic traditions revived (especially those which contained such resistance themes as the creation battle of the national deity against the forces of chaos—now reinterpreted as the foreign dominators). From Palestine to Persia one may trace the rise of Wisdom, Messianic and Apocalyptic traditions which reinterpret and maintain these central themes: the importance of the ancient, traditional lore; the saving power of kingship and the revival of myth.
>
> Each of these native traditions likewise underwent, in their homeland, what might properly be called hellenization. This was frequently related to the establishment of a Hellenistic *polis*. Here, while the old, native religion continued uninterrupted in its traditional shrines (in some cases exhibiting a revival), the authority of the native priests remained unchallenged and the native language persisted (although in some instances being reduced to a learned or liturgical tongue), new religious practices and sensibilities were introduced. Sometimes the native and native-hellenistic forms remained apart; other times they mutually influenced one another, occasionally resulting in the discovery of genuinely new forms of an archaic deity. . . .
>
> Each native tradition also had diasporic centers which exhibited marked change during the Late Antique period. There was a noticeable lessening of concern on the part of those in

the diaspora for the destiny and fortunes of the native land and a relative severing of the archaic ties between religion and the land. Certain cult centers remained sites of pilgrimage or sentimental attachment, but the old beliefs in national deities and the inextricable relationship of the deity to particular places was weakened. Rather than a god who dwelt in his temple or would regularly manifest himself in a cult house, the diaspora evolved complicated techniques for achieving visions, epiphanies or heavenly journeys. That is to say, they evolved modes of access to the deity which transcended any particular place. Some traditions gave renewed emphasis to Protean deities, divinities who were interstitial in the older locative system, figures of uncertain form and habits subject only to their own inscrutable initiative.

Within diasporic religion, the chief religious figures were no longer priests or kings but rather god-men, saviors or religious entrepreneurs. The chief mode of religious activity shifted from celebration to initiation. Rather than being born into a divinely established and protected land whose glories one celebrated, one was initiated (reborn) into a divine protector who was tied to no land.

For the native religionist, homeplace, the place to which one belongs, was *the* central religious category. One's self-definition, one's reality was the place into which one had been born—understood as both geographical and social place. To the new immigrant in the diaspora, nostalgia for homeplace and cultic substitutes for the old, sacred center were central religious values. For the thoroughly diasporic member, who may not have belonged to the deity's original ethnic group, freedom from place became *the* central religious category. Projecting the group's diasporic existence into the cosmos, he discovered himself to be in exile from his true home (a world beyond this world), he found his fulfillment in serving the god beyond the god of this world and true freedom in stripping off his body which belonged to this world and in awakening that aspect of himself which was from the Beyond. *Diasporic religion, in contrast to native, locative religion, was utopian in the strictest sense of the word, a religion of "nowhere," of transcendence* [italics mine] (1978:xiii–xv, pass.).

The links between the larger context described by Smith and the details of our division have to be specified, for they are hardly self-evident. Some points are immediately relevant, and all of them ultimately are so.

One of the saliant traits of our laws is their disinterest in the diaspora and their rejection of the notion that sacrifice takes place there.[19] This may yet be generalized: Mishnah's cultic divisions, Agriculture, Holy Things, and Purities, as well as important tractates of Seasons, scarcely relate to the life of Jews outside of the country, who could not keep the laws if they wanted to. So far as Mishnah addresses a world in which the cult is tied inextricably to Jerusalem and Holy Land, it not only ignores its own context; it also pays no attention, in its repertoire of topics deemed important, to communities outside of the Holy Land. If Mishnah provides access to a diety which transcends a particular place, it is not through clearcut references. On the contrary, part of its remarkably conservative character consists in its pretense of the very opposite. Mishnah creates a world of specific place—Jerusalem, Temple—and rejects the utopianism represented in pictures of a cult which is other than the concrete, here-and-now Temple of the ruined, earthly Jerusalem. But Mishnah at the same time is radical, for in its existence, if not

[19]I first noticed this in the context of the rabbinical redefinition of the conception of *nega^c-sara^{c}at*, see *The Idea of Purity in Ancient Judaism* (1973: 72–107).

in its topical and thematic message, it embodies an effort to break out of the cosmic conception of order, embodied, as we have seen, in the cult itself and to break into that anthropological order in which society—Israelite society—forms the mythopoeic center and the model.

That former, cosmic analogy, expressed through the Temple and its cult, is described as follows by Cornelius Loew:

> ... the conviction that the meaning of life is rooted in an encompassing cosmic order, in which man, society, and the Gods all participate (J. Z. Smith, 1978:160).

There are five facets to this conviction:

> (1) There is a cosmic order that permeates every level of reality; (2) this cosmic order is the divine society of the gods; (3) the structure and dynamics of this society can be discerned in the movements and patterned juxtapositions of the heavenly bodies; (4) human society should be a microcosm of the divine society; and (5) the chief responsibility of priests and kings is to attune human order to the divine order (1978:160).

The cosmological conviction shifts, in Hellenistic times, so that "man is no longer defined by the degree to which he harmonizes himself and his society to the cosmic patterns of order, but rather by the degree to which he can escape the patterns" (1978:162). The world is perceived as a prison, its limits awaiting transcendence. "And each culture," Smith goes on, "rebelled against these archaic traditions, developed a complex series of techniques for escaping destiny and for 'righting' the world, discovered a new set of myths which described the origins of the sort of world in which they now found themselves living" (1978:163).

The extraordinary events of the century from 70 to 170 profoundly shake faith "in the good order of the cosmos and its ability to confer reality" (1978:170). The very locus at which the center is to be found is first ruined, then rendered inaccessible. It is difficult to imagine a more shattering event, a more complete way utterly to wipe out that "cosmological conviction" symbolized and realized in the cult, the center of the world. What Mishnah does by representing this cult, laying out its measurements, describing its rite, and specifying its rules, is to permit Israel in the words of Mishnah to experience anywhere and anytime that cosmic center of the world described by Mishnah: *Cosmic center in words is made utopia.* Mishnah permits the people, Israel, to carry that world along through time until the center once more will be regained. Mishnah transforms Israel into the bearer. So Israel here (to shift metaphors) is made into the pivot, in lieu of cult: Temurah is the operative tractate. Obviously, Mishnah is mobile. Memorizing its words is the guarantee of ubiquity. The priests who effect the sacrifice, the Temple as locus of revelation, the picture of building and daily rites—all these are preserved in the amber of language, to be defined and governed and carried everywhere by the masters of Mishnah themselves.

Citing Peter Brown's statement, "The emergence of the holy man at the expense of the Temple marks the end of the classical world" (1971:102), Jonathan Smith states the following:

> One way of stating this shift is to note that the cosmos has become anthropologized. The old, imperial cosmological language that was the major mode of religious expression of the archaic temple and court cultus has been transformed. Rather than a city wall, the new enclave protecting man against external, hostile powers will be a human group, a religious association or secret society. Rather than a return to chaos or the threat of decreation, the enemy will be described as other men or demons, the threat as evil or death. Rather than a sacred place, the new center and chief means of access to divinity will be a divine man, a magician, who will function, by and large, as an entrepreneur without fixed office and will be, by and large, related to "protean deities" of relatively unfixed form whose major characteristic is their sudden and dramatic autophanies. Rather than celebration, purification and pilgrimage, the new rituals will be those of conversion, of initiation into the secret society or identification with the divine man (1978:170).

By including in Mishnah a division on sacrifice and sanctuary, the sages address Israelite society with the message that cosmic order is not now to be replicated. But it can at least be studied in sages' words. The Temple cannot be regained. It can at least be remembered in vivid detail supplied by sages. If there is no access to the holy place, there is at least, therefore, the persistent engagement with the ubiquitous master of the rules of the holy place (to be sure, not a magician [that will come later] but at least an "entrepreneur without fixed office"). It is with the sage who knows "them and their names"—the rules of the cult—that one who wants to know the cult must identify. Here, as in so many other foci of the law, at the heart and center is the one thing which endures amid holocaust and calamity: the people of Israel. That people constitutes the society which forms the enclave to protect and sustain an orderly world. In the long centuries after Mishnah (complete with its useless map of the inaccessible cosmos, its rules of the cult) comes into being, learning Mishnah would describe a remarkably apt mode of cartography of that unattainable sacred city, the city constructed only in the consciousness of the Jewish people. This, then, is the map of the city of Israel, in which, in mind only, now are joined heaven and earth. In the metaphor of Temurah, that city is the substitute for Jerusalem and Temple and sacrifice. It therefore enters the sanctity of Jerusalem and Temple and sacrifice, but Jerusalem and Temple and sacrifice remain sanctified: *And if he makes any exchange . . . then both it and that for which it is exchanged shall be holy* (Lev 27:10).

CHAPTER VII

Form and Meaning:
Mishnah's System and Mishnah's Language

I

Mishnah, a corpus of laws redacted at ca. A.D. 200, serves as one of the two principal documents of that form of Judaism which has been predominant and normative from the third century to the present, Rabbinic Judaism. The other is the Old Testament (in Judaism: Tanakh) and, therein, the Torah, the Five Books of Moses. It is the claim of Rabbinic Judaism that two Torahs together, revealed at Sinai, constitute the one "whole Torah of Moses, our Rabbi." Mishnah, it is further claimed, was transmitted through processes of memorization and, therefore, is called "The Oral Torah," while the Pentateuch is "The Written Torah." Accordingly, the document under discussion stands at the very center of Judaism.

Our interest is in the social analysis of Mishnah's linguistic character, Specifically, we ask: What do we learn about people from the way in which they say things? It, therefore, is necessary briefly to summarize the paramount literary and redactional traits of Mishnah.[1] Mishnah to the Order of Purities is divided into twelve tractates. The criterion of division, internal to the document and not merely imposed by copyists and printers, is thematic. The twelve tractates are readily distinguishable from one another since each treats a distinct topic. If, moreover, Mishnah were to be copied out in a long scroll without the signification of lines of demarcation among the several tractates, the opening pericope of each tractate would leave no doubt that one topic had been completed and a new one undertaken. The same is so within the tractates, in that intermediate divisions of these same principal divisions are to be discerned on the basis of internal evidence, through the confluence of theme and form. That is to say, a given intermediate division of a principal one will be marked by a particular, recurrent, formal pattern in accord with which

---

[1]The following discussion is based upon the evidence of the sixth of Mishnah's six divisions, the Order of Purities, which comprises nearly 24% of Mishnah as a whole, 126 out of 531 chapters (43% larger than average). In my *History of the Mishnaic Law of Purities* (1974–1977), I present a complete translation and commentary on the entire Order in Mishnah and Tosefta, as well as studies on the literary traits and of the history of ideas of the Order of Purities.

155

sentences are constructed and also by a particular and distinct theme to which said sentences are addressed. When a new theme commences, a fresh formal pattern will be used. Within the intermediate divisions, we are able to recognize the components, or smallest whole units of thought (hereinafter, cognitive units), because there will be a recurrent pattern of sentence-structure repeated time and again within the unit and a shifting at the commencement of the next theme. Each point at which the recurrent pattern commences marks the beginning of a new cognitive unit. In general, an intermediate division will contain a carefully enumerated sequence of exempla of cognitive units, in the established formal pattern, in groups of three or five or multiples of three or five (90% of all intermediate units in our Order are built in such sequences of three's and five's).

The cognitive units resort to a remarkably limited repertoire of formulary patterns. Mishnah manages to say whatever it wants in one of the following: 1. the simple declarative sentence, in which the subject, verb, and predicate are syntactically tightly joined to one another, e.g., *he who does so and so is such and such*; 2. the duplicated subject, in which the subject of the sentence is stated twice, e.g., *He who does so and so, lo, he is such and such*; 3. mild apocopation, in which the subject of the sentence is cut off from the verb, which refers to its own subject, and not the one with which the sentence commences, e.g., *He who does so and so . . . , it* [the thing he has done] *is such and such*; 4. extreme apocopation, in which a series of clauses is presented, none of them tightly joined to what precedes or follows, and all of them cut off from the predicate of the sentence, e.g., *he who does so and so . . . , it* [the thing he has done] *is such and such . . . , it is a matter of doubt whether . . . or whether . . . , lo, it* [referring to nothing in the antecedent, apocopated clauses of the subject of the sentence] *is so and so. . . .* In addition to these formulary patterns, in which the distinctive formulary traits are effected through variations in the relationship between the subject and the predicate of the sentence, or in which he subject itself is given a distinctive development, there is yet a fifth. In this last one we have a contrastive complex predicate, in which case we may have two sentences, independent of one another, yet clearly formulated so as to stand in acute balance with one another in the predicate, thus, *He who does . . . is unclean, and he who does not . . . is clean.*

It naturally will be objected: Is it possible that a simple declarative sentence may be asked to serve as a formulary pattern, alongside the rather distinctive and unusual constructions which follow? The answer is that while, by itself, a tightly constructed sentence consisting of subject, verb, and complement in which the verb refers to the subject, and the complement to the verb, hardly exhibits traits of particular formal interest, yet a sequence of such sentences, built along the same gross grammatical lines, may well exhibit a clearcut and distinctive pattern. The contrastive predicate is one such example, and Mishnah contains many more. The important point of differentiation, particularly for the simple declarative sentence, appears in the intermediate unit. It is there that we see a single pattern recurring in a long sequence of sentences, e.g., *the X which has lost its Y is unclean because of its Z. The Z which has lost its Y is unclean because of its X.* Another example will be a long sequence of highly developed sentences, laden with relative clauses and other explanatory matter, in which a single syntactical pattern will govern the articulation of three or six or nine exempla. That sequence will be followed by one repeated terse sentence pattern, e.g., *X is so and so, Y is such and such, Z is thus and so.* The former group will treat one principle or theme, the latter some other. There can be no doubt, therefore, that the declarative sentence in recurrent patterns is, in its way, just as carefully formalized as a sequence of severely apocopated sentences or of contrastive predicates or duplicated subjects.[2]

In order to appreciate the highly formal character of Mishnah, we rapidly turn to its correlative document, Tosefta, a corpus of supplementary materials serving to augment, amplify, and expand Mishnah in various ways, brought to redaction between ca. A.D. 200 and 400. Tosefta's tractates follow those of Mishnah, which is hardly surprising. When, however, we examine the ways in which Tosefta's tractates are then subdivided, we do not see the slightest effort to group materials in accord with a confluence of common theme and form nor to redact intermediate divisions in accord with a single fixed number of exempla, e.g., three's or five's. Furthermore, Tosefta's units of thought are not highly patterned and exhibit none of the traits of carefully stylized formulation which we find in Mishnah—except in those pericopae in which Mishnah itself is cited and then glossed (and they are very many). Accordingly, Tosefta, a document dependent on Mishnah, in no way exhibits the careful traits of structured redaction, formal correspondence between formulary patterns and distinctive themes, for the internal demarcation of an intermediate division, or highly formalized formulation of individual units of thought. Mishnah's traits emerge most clearly in the contrast established by its supplementary document. The mode of grouping cognitive units in Tosefta is in accord with one of three fixed relationships to Mishnah. Pericopae which cite Mishnah verbatim will stand together. There commonly will follow units which do not cite Mishnah but which clearly complement the principal document, augmenting its materials in some obvious way. And, at the end, will be grouped together still other groups which supplement Mishnah but which in no clear way depend upon Mishnah for full and exhaustive exegesis. Accordingly, Tosefta's arrangement of its materials clearly relates to Mishnah; and the contrast in the ways in which Mishnah's own groups of cognitive units are set forth could not be more blatant.

---

[2] The distribution in the Order of Purities of the principal types of formulary patterns is as follows: simple declarative sentences (all types), 276 cognitive units; duplicated subject, 69; contrastive complex predicate, 77; *he who . . . it is . . .*-apocopation, 110; extreme apocopation, 103. Simple sentences are evenly distributed among the tractates; the other patterns are not.

This brief survey of the literary traits of Mishnah now permits us to turn to the question at hand, which is: What is to be learned about the authorities who bear responsibility for the peculiar way in which Mishnah is formulated and redacted from the way in which they have done their work? We speak, in particular, of the final generation represented in Mishnah itself, the authorities of the period ca. A.D. 200 who in fact gave the document its present literary character.[3]

II

The dominant stylistic trait of Mishnah is the acute formalization of its syntactical structure, and its carefully framed sequences of formalized language, specifically, its intermediate divisions, so organized that the limits of a theme correspond to those of a formulary pattern. The balance and order of Mishnah are particular to Mishnah. It now must be asked to testify to the intentions of the people who so made it. About whom does it speak? And why, in particular, have its authorities distinctively shaped language, which in Tosefta does not speak, in rhymes and balanced, matched, declarative sentences, imposing upon the conceptual, factual prose of the law to be expressed a peculiar kind of poetry? Why do they create rhythmic order, grammatically balanced sentences containing discrete law, laid out in what seem to be carefully enumerated sequences, and the like? Language not only contains culture, which could not exist without it; language—in our case, linguistic and syntactical style and stylization—expresses a world-view and ethos. Whose world-view is contained and expressed in Mishnah's formalized rhetoric?

There is no reason to doubt that if we asked the tradental-redactional authorities behind Mishnah the immediate purpose of their formalization, their answer would be to facilitate memorization. For that is the proximate effect of the acute formalization of their document. Much in its character can be seen as mnemonic. Mishnah was not published in writing, Lieberman maintains: "Since in the entire Talmudic literature we do not find that a book of the Mishnah was ever consulted in the case of controversies or doubt concerning a particular reading, we may safely conclude that the compilation was not published in writing, that a written *ekdosis* [edition] of the Mishnah did not exist" (1950:87). Mishnah was published in a different way:

---

[3]In my *History* XXI. *The Formulation and Redaction of the Order of Purities in Mishnah and Tosefta*, I have shown that the world of formalized formulation takes place in the intermediate divisions of a tractate and, further, that the layout of intermediate divisions accords with the logical requirements of sequence imposed by the large-scale topical arrangement of the tractate as a whole. This means that the tradental work of formulation is part and parcel of the redactional process and that there is no significant and recoverable literary history both behind the document as we know it and still revealed within it. That is why we can ask Mishnah's formal character to testify only about the traits of mind of its ultimate redactional generation.

A regular oral *ekdosis*, edition, of the Mishnah was in existence, a fixed text recited by the Tannaim of the college. The *Tanna* (repeater, reciter) committed to memory the text of certain portions of the Mishnah which he subsequently recited in the college in the presence of the great masters of the Law. Those Tannaim were pupils chosen for their extraordinary memory, although they were not always endowed with due intelligence. . . . When the Mishnah was committed to memory and the Tannaim recited it in the college, it was thereby published and possessed all the traits and features of a written *ekdosis*. . . . Once the Mishnah was accepted among the college Tannaim (reciters) it was difficult to cancel it (87).

Lieberman's evidence for these conclusions is drawn from two sources: first, sayings within the Rabbinical corpus and stories about how diverse problems of transmission of materials were worked out; second, parallels, some of them germane but none of them probative, drawn from Greco-Roman procedures of literary transmission.

Considerably more compelling evidence of the same proposition derives from the internal character of Mishnah itself. But if the evidence of stylization and formalization testifies to a mnemonic program, then absence of the same evidence must imply that some materials were not intended to be memorized; and that means that Mishnah, and Mishnah alone, was the object to be formulated for memorization and transmitted through "living books," Tannaim, to the coming generations. Tosefta cannot have been formulated along the same lines. Accordingly, Mishnah is given a special place and role by those who stand behind it.

III

It follows that the system of grammar and syntax distinctive to Mishnah expresses rules and conventions intelligible to members of a particular community, that which stands behind Mishnah. It certainly is a peculiar kind of formalized language. So far as it is formed to facilitate a principal function, memorization and transmission of special rules, the language of Mishnah does not relate those who made and used it, in particular in ordinary affairs, to one another or to the world in which they lived. It is not a functional instrument of neutral communication. Rather, it distinguishes its users from that ordinary world and sets apart one aspect of their interrelationships, the one defined in Mishnah, from such other aspects as did not require speech in a few patterns and in a kind of poetry. Accordingly, while the language, Middle Hebrew, represented in part by Mishnah, may or may not have been used for other purposes than those defined by Mishnah, the way in which that language *is* used in Mishnah bespeaks a limited and circumscribed circumstance. How things were said can have been grasped primarily by the people instructed in saying and hearing things in just that way. In this sense formalized language sets Mishnah apart from its larger linguistic context, for Middle Hebrew was a language utilized outside of Rabbinical circles.

Mishnah's is a language for an occasion. The occasion is particular: formation and transmission of special sorts of conceptions in a special way. The predominant, referential function of language, giving verbal structure to the message itself, is secondary in our document. The expressive function, conveying the speaker's attitude toward what he is talking about, the conative function, focusing upon *who* is being addressed, and other ritualized functions of language come to the fore. Mishnah's language, therefore, as I said, is special, meant as an expression of a non-referential function (Farb, 1974: 23–24). So far as Mishnah was meant to be memorized by a distinctive group of people for an extraordinary purpose, it is language which includes few and excludes many, unites those who use it, and sets them apart from others who do not.

The formal aspects of Mishnaic rhetoric are empty of content, which is proved by the fact that pretty much all themes and conceptions can be reduced to these same few formal patterns. These patterns, I have shown, are established by syntactical recurrences, as distinct from recurrence of sounds.[4] The same words do not recur. Long sequences of patterned and disciplined sentences fail to repeat the same words—that is, syllabic balance, rhythm, or sound—yet they do establish a powerful claim to order and formulary sophistication and perfection. That is why we could name a pattern, *he who ... it is ...*-apocopation: the arrangement of the words, as a grammatical pattern, not their substance, is indicative of pattern. Accordingly, while we have a document composed along what clearly are mnemonic lines, *Mishnah's susceptibility to memorization rests principally upon the utter abstraction of recurrent syntactical patterns, rather than on the concrete repetition of particular words, rhythms, syllabic counts, or sounds.*

It therefore appears that a sense for the deep, inner logic of word-patterns, of grammar and syntax, rather than for their external similarities, governs the Mishnaic mnemonic. And that means that, even though Mishnah is to be memorized and handed on orally, it expresses a mode of thought attuned to abstract relationships, rather than concrete and substantive forms. The formulaic, not the formal, character of Mishnaic rhetoric yields a picture of a subculture which speaks of immaterial and not material things. In this subculture the relationship, rather than the thing or person which is related, is

---

[4]I have not alluded to the probability that Mishnah was intended to be sung. The musical line evidently was meant to serve any sequence of words, determined rather by the structure and position of phrases. Bayer (1972: 735) states, "The transmission of an unwritten text depends on constant repetition . . . , and the more formal such a text becomes, the more its rendition will tend to develop into a formal—and soon also formulaic—sequence of quasi-melodic phrases." T. Oh. 16:8 has ᶜAqiba tell his students to sing, and b. Meg. 32b is more explicit still, "He who repeats [Mishnah-traditions] without a tune . . ." Accordingly, we have every reason to suppose there was some sort of "melodic (or rather melodized) rendition," but we do not know the nature or structure of these melodies for Mishnah. In any event the repetition of a melodic line for diverse materials will have constituted still one more formal pattern.

primary and constitutes the principle of reality. The thing in itself is less than the thing in cathexis with other things, so too the person. The repetition of form creates form. But what here is repeated is not external or superficial form, but formulary patterns, effected through persistent grammatical or syntactical relationships and affecting an infinite range of diverse objects and topics. Form and structure emerge not from concrete, formal things but from abstract and unstated, but ubiquitous and powerful relationships.

This fact—the creation of pattern through grammatical relationship of syntactical elements, more than through concrete sounds[5]—tells us that the people who memorized conceptions reduced to these particular forms were capable of extraordinarily abstract perception. Hearing peculiarities of word-order in diverse cognitive contexts, their ears and minds perceived regularities of grammatical arrangement, repeated functional variations of utilization of diverse words, and grasped from such subtleties syntactical patterns not expressed by recurrent external phenomena and autonomous of particular meanings. What they heard, it is clear, were not only abstract relationships but also *principles* conveyed along with and through these relationships. For what was memorized was a recurrent and fundamental notion, expressed in diverse examples but in recurrent rhetorical-syntactical patterns. Accordingly, what they could and did hear was what lay far beneath the surface of the rule: the unstated principle, the unsounded pattern. This means that their mode of thought was attuned to what lay beneath the surface; their minds and their ears perceived what was *not* said behind what *was* said and how it was said. They besought that ineffable and metaphysical reality concealed within, but conveyed through spoken and palpable material reality. Social interrelationships within the community of Israel are left behind in the ritual speech of Mishnah, just as, within the laws, natural realities are made to give form and expression to supernatural or metaphysical regularities. Mishnah speaks of Israel, but the speakers are a group apart. Mishnah talks of this-worldly things, but the things stand for and speak of another world entirely.

Who is the personna serving as Mishnah's voice? Mishnah is remarkably indifferent to the identification and establishment of the character of the person who speaks. It not only is formally anonymous, in that it does not bear a signature or a single first-person identification. It also is substantively anonymous, in that it does not permit variation of patterns of formulation to accord with the traits of individuals or even to suggest that individuals who do occur have distinctive traits of speech, word-choice, or, in the final analysis,

---

[5]To be sure, mnemonic patterns make use of key words. Furthermore, we do find repetition of whole phrases and large-scale clauses, e.g., a fixed apodosis will serve diverse protases, or a uniform predicate, a range of subjects. But I think these external mnemonic devices are secondary to what is ubiquitous, which is the patterning of grammar and syntax, fundamentally autonomous of what actually is said and sounded.

even generative conception. This absence of individuation should not suggest that Mishnah to our Order is essentially neutral as to the imposition of a highly distinctive mode of discourse. The contrary is the case. Green states this matter as follows:

> These documents appear to be not accidental, inchoate collections, but carefully and deliberately constructed compilations. Each document has its own ideological or theological agendum; and it is axiomatic that the agendum of any document, though shaped to a degree by inherited materials, ultimately is the creation of the authorities, most of whom are anonymous, who produced the document itself. They have determined the focus, selected the materials, and provided the framework that unites the discrete pericopae and gives the document its internal consistency and coherence. The features of these documents suggest that their agenda transcend the teaching of any single master. First, rabbinic documents contain a substantial amount of unattributed material. This gives them an atemporal quality, and creates the sense that the document, or the tradition, is speaking for itself, independent of any individual mind. Second, rabbinic documents are not constructed around the sayings of any individual, but follow either a thematic, formal, topical, or scriptural arrangement in which the teachings or opinions of various masters are gathered together to address a single issue or to interpret a particular verse of scripture. This sort of arrangement points to a process of selection in which the teachings of individuals have been made subservient to the goals of the documents. Indeed, within the documents the comments of the masters and their disagreements with each other almost always focus on matters of detail. The larger conceptions which inform the documents themselves are never called into question. . . . Third, although every teaching in rabbinic literature originated in the mind of an individual, the continued vitality of those teachings depended on the rabbinic circles and communities who preserved and transmitted them. The chain of tradents, only occasionally mentioned by name, the redactors and the editors who stand behind the present form of both discrete pericopae and entire documents substantively revised, embellished and refined received materials, and sometimes invented new ones, to suit their various agenda. All of this means that we know about early rabbinic figures what the various authorities behind the documents want us to know, and we know it in the way they wanted us to know it. Consequently, the historical context, the primary locus of interpretation for any saying attributed to a given master or story about him, is the document in which the passage appears *not* the period in which he is alleged to have lived (n.d.).

What does the rhetoric of Mishnah leave unstated? The first thing we never are told, as I said, is who is speaking, where we are, and the purpose for which discourse is undertaken. These may be taken for granted, but nothing in Mishnah of our Order cares to tell us about the societal or concrete context of rhetoric. If this is a mode of communication, then to whom is communication addressed? Who is the speaker, and who the listener?

The sole evidence of the speaker is the use of the invariable attributive, ᵓWMR ("he says"), which bears no meaning particular to a saying and homogenizes all sayings. ᵓWMR states only that what follows bears the name of an authority and therefore is claimed to be authoritative. ᵓWMR is all we are told about the setting of a saying, where it was said, for what purpose, and, in all, in what social, spatial, temporal, and intellectual context. To put matters simply, ᵓWMR obscures all data of particularity and human circumstance. Yet ᵓWMR generally, though not always, is intellectually partitive. That is, once we have the presence of ꜥWMR, we know that a private authority, not the anonymous and unanimous consensus of the corpus represented by the speaker (the document), is at hand. The use of ꜥWMR establishes that the conception now to be stated is private. No claim is to be made for the consensus of the community for what is to be said. It follows that the silence of Mishnah on the authority behind a saying means to claim the consensus of the community (to speak in solely secular terms) for the stated proposition.

But is what is stated to be interpreted as transactional, in that relationships between speaker, listener, and topic are presupposed? Mishnah is remarkably reticent on that very matter. Its language invariably is descriptive, in the continuous participle. Its claim, through formal rhetoric that such-and-so is the way things are, describes and establishes the norms and forms of being. There is no speaker, nor person spoken-to, in the sense that a single individual to some other gives private expression to what is said (whether it reflects consensus or private opinion) or private context to what is heard. The acute formalization of all things detaches from the private person any claim that he alone says, in his own way, a particular and distinctive opinion. It imposes upon all sayings the authority of the document as a whole. The absence of differentiation among, and description of, the audience to what is said bears the same implication. This is how things are, without regard to the situation to which they are addressed, the condition, let alone the opinion of the people by whom they are heard. The abstraction of thought is carried over into the indifference to the nuanced situation of the people by whom and to whom thought is conveyed.

In this sense, the language of Mishnah and its formalized grammatical rhetoric create a world of discourse quite separate from the concrete realities of a given time, place, or society. The exceedingly limited repertoire of grammatical patterns by which all things on all matters are said gives symbolic expression to the notion that beneath the accidents of life are a few comprehensive relationships. Unchanging and enduring patterns lie deep in the inner structure of reality and impose structure upon the accidents of the world. This means, as I have implied, that reality for Mishnaic rhetoric consists in the grammar and syntax of language: consistent and enduring patterns of relationship among diverse and changing concrete things or persons. What lasts is not the concrete thing but the abstract interplay governing any and all sorts of concrete things. There is, therefore, a congruence between rhetorical patterns of speech, on the one side, and the framework of discourse established by these same patterns on the other. Just as we accomplish memorization by perceiving not what is said but how it is said and is persistently arranged, so we speak to undertake to address and describe a world in which what is concrete and material is secondary. But how things are said about what is concrete and material in diverse ways and contexts is principal. Mishnah is silent about the context of its speech because context is trivial. Principle, beginning in syntactical principles by which all words are arranged in a severely limited repertoire of grammatical sentences ubiquitously pertinent but rarely made explicit, is at the center.

Mishnah's ideas are shaped, in particular, as gnomic expressions. They deal with basic truths and make use of devices to create a pattern (if not one of sound). The vocabulary is invariably impersonal, *they do* or *one does* or *he who*. And the verb nearly always is in the present tense and always is in the present tense for descriptive rules. This, too, enhances the aura of universal application. So, too, "Constructions such as parallelism, symmetry, and reversal of the elements in the expression are common" (Farb, 1974: 118). Farb states, "These characteristics combine to produce a strategy of language manipulation for the particular purposes of teaching, conveying wisdom, and expressing a philosophy" (118). But all of this is attained, as we have seen, through formalization of language, not through word-choices and not through selection of exalted topics external to everyday life.

The skill of the formulators of Mishnah is to manipulate the raw materials of everyday speech.[6] What they have done is so to structure language as to make it strange, to impose a fresh perception upon what to others—and what in Tosefta—are merely unpatterned and ordinary ways of saying things. What is said in Mishnah is simple. How it is said is arcane. Ordinary folk cannot have had much difficulty understanding the words which refer to routine actions and objects. How long it must have taken to grasp the meaning of the patterns into which the words are arranged! How hard it was and is to do so is suggested (at the very least) by the necessity for the creation of Tosefta, the Talmuds, and the commentaries in the long centuries since Mishnah came into being. In this sense Mishnah speaks openly about public matters, yet its deep substructure of syntax and grammatical forms shapes what is said into an essentially secret and private language. It takes many years to master the difficult argot, though only a few minutes to memorize the simple patterns. That constitutes a paradox reflective of the situation of the creator of Mishnah.

Up to now we have said only a little about tense structure. The reason is that Mishnah exhibits remarkable indifference to the potentialities of meaning inherent therein. Its persistent preference for the plural participle, thus the descriptive present tense, is matched by its capacity to accept the mixture of past, present, and future tenses, which can be jumbled together in a single sentence and, even more commonly, in a single pericope. It follows that Mishnah is remarkably uninterested in differentiation of time-sequences. This fact is most clearly shown by the *gemisch* of the extreme-apocopated sentence with its capacity to support something like the following: "He who does so and so . . . the rain came and wet it down . . . if he was happy . . . it [is] under the law, If water be put." Clearly, the matter of tense, past, present, future, is

[6]The best current statement of the complex linguistic situation is Fitzmyer (1970: 501–31).

simply not relevant to the purpose of the speaker. If tense is irrelevant, however, then we find ourselves in the undifferentiated present. What is said is meant to bear no relationship whatever to the circumstance or particular time or context to which what is said applies. The absence of a powerful and recurrent system of tense-differentiation is strong evidence in favor of our conception that Mishnah describes a world detached from time.

The temporal and worldly authority of Mishnah's unspecified "speaker" likewise is curiously unspecified. Our Order contains scarcely a hint, either in how things are said or in what is said, about why we should take account of its rules. What is omitted is any reference to a system of institutional enforcement, political or supernatural. At no point is there an effort to give nuance to language to be used for one setting, as against some other, in the home as distinct from the Temple, the court, the school, or the street. The homogenization of thought and its expression in a limited and uniform rhetorical pattern impose the conception that the norms are axiomatic for, and expose the logic of, all situations in general, but pertain to none in particular. This again brings to the surface the notion, implicit in the way Mishnah says things, that it describes how things are, whether or not material-reality conforms. The absence of reference to a speaker and his role reenforces the conception that this-worldly details of identified teachers, with circumscribed and concrete authority, are not pertinent. The reason is that what comes under description does not depend upon the details of this-worldly institutions. That is why the document is so strikingly indifferent to the differentiation of rhetoric. Diverse ideational materials are reduced to a single rhetoric. The various contexts to which what is said is applicable are never given definition in the choice of words or rhetorical patterns. In the profoundly conventional discourse of Mishnah, the one thing left untouched by the effect of convention is the concrete world, which is to conform, whether in fact it does or does not conform.

It hardly needs saying that this sameness of rhetoric hardly is functional to the situation of ordinary people. If the language of Mishnah is ritual and private, its intent is quite the opposite: general and descriptive of all things. We have, therefore, to distinguish between the effects of formalization of thought, which produce a private framework of discourse among specialists, and the function thereof, which is to make discourse among individuals public and general, and abstract it from the ordinary life. Mishnah lacks abundant ways to speak in grammatical utterances, reducing to its handful of possibilities all truths about all things pertinent to Purities. A level of address has been chosen and, it is clear, is severely imposed upon all themes and all contexts. It is not possible for that aesthetic-mnemonic sameness to express the diverse things which need saying in ordinary circumstances.

In this sense Mishnaic rhetoric is anti-contextual but creates its own context of meaning. Its indifference to any other context but its own is suggested, as I said, by its partitive attributional formula, the same for all sayings of one genre, and also by its single honorific. Mishnah is remarkably uninterested in diverse honorifics, using the title Rabbi in all circumstances and for nearly all named authorities. The sole differentiation effected by the title is to omit from consideration the teachings of people who do not have that title, and this is solely in Tosefta. The homogenization of syntax is reflected in the unitary character of the document's honorifics. And, as I said, the absence of all reference to who is listening imposes an equivalent sameness upon the audience. What is said is said to whom it may concern, and the important parts of what is said are stated by people who are permitted neither individuation nor identification, who talk, as I have emphasized, in the same syntactical patterns about all subjects and in all settings.

In context it is trivial to notice that sexual differences play no role, except as demanded by the setting of a case or rule. Since women do the cooking, cases and examples of rules which deal with kneading dough will use the feminine form. In general, though, in Mishnah there is neither male nor female, nor is there the slightest suggestion that women speak differently from men. Where a woman is quoted, what she is made to say, hardly surprisingly, is in the familiar rhetoric. The reason is that differences of sex are as irrelevant to Mishnah's speech-world as differences of social status or institutional circumstance.

Outside of the precedents (*ma^{c}asim*), the formal characteristics of which are difficult to discern and which in any case occur seldom in Mishnah, our Order presents remarkably little living dialogue. (*X says* is not a dialogue, nor are disputes and debates dialogical in any natural sense.) Mishnaic syntax is based upon the monologue. Occasionally, two or more monologues are juxtaposed, but scarcely constitute dialogues. The reciter recites. No response is suggested within our document. In this sense, dialogue, a basic form of human speech, is noteworthy for its absence. Tosefta makes up for the matter, with its citation of Mishnah, as if to assume one side of a conversation, and its even more pronounced effort at interchange, its reference to something mentioned by Mishnah in the form, "What are . . . ?" or "Under what circumstances . . . ?" But in the main the document's highly formal character precludes the possibility of dialogue, there being only a few possible ways of uttering a thought, and these, as we have seen, not only formal but also gnomic.

The extraordinary lack of a context of communication—specification of speaker, hearer—of our document furthermore suggests that for Mishnah language is a self-contained formal system used more or less incidentally for communication. It is not essentially a system for communication, but for description of a reality, the reality of which is created and contained by, and exhausted within, the act of description. The saying of the words, whether heard meaningfully by another or not, is the creation of the world. Speech is action. It is creation. The speech-community represented by Mishnah stands strongly not only against nuance, but also against change. The imposition of conventional and highly patterned syntax clearly is meant to preserve what is said without change (even though we know changes in the wording of traditions were effected for many centuries thereafter). The language is meant to be unshakeable; and its strict rules of rhetoric are meant not only to convey, but also to preserve equally strict rules of logic or equally permanent patterns of relationship. What was at stake in this formation of language in the service of permanence? Clearly, how things were said was intended to secure eternal preservation of what was said. Change affects the accidents and details. It cannot reshape enduring principles, and language will be used to effect their very endurance. What is said, moreover, is not to be subjected to pragmatic experimentation. The unstated, but carefully considered, principles shape reality. They are not shaped and tested by and against reality. Use of pat phrases and syntactical cliches, divorced from different thoughts to be said and different ways of thinking, testify to the prevailing notion of unstated, but secure and unchanging, reality behind and beneath the accidents of context and circumstance.

Clearly, so far as Middle Hebrew served as a secular language, Mishnah has transformed a common speech to sacred language and has done so through peculiar formalization of syntactical structures in particular. Yet we cannot point to anything intrinsically sacred even in those structures and patterns. For example, there is no use of the divine name and no tendency to cite Sacred Scripture, let alone to model sentences after it. Indeed, Scripture is treated with remarkable disinterest. The treatment of leprosy in Leviticus 13–14 follows an illogical thematic scheme. Tractate Negaim revises that theme and introduces the appropriate correction. Our Order is remarkably uninterested in Scriptural proofs for its propositions. Accordingly, what serves as the vehicle of sanctification is the imposition upon common speech of fixed, secular patterns of syntax, which functionally transform talk about common things into sacred language solely through the employment of certain stereotype patterns. What is regular is sacred, is real. These patterns themselves on the surface, as I said, are routine and secular, yet in function accomplish the sanctification of language, its transformation into something other than, and different from, ordinary speech. We should expect distinctive word-choices, but I discern none.[7]

Two facts have been established. First, the formalization of Mishnaic thought-units is separate from the utilization of sound, rhythm, and extrinsic characteristics of word-choice. It depends, rather, upon recurrent grammatical patterns independent of the choices of words set forth in strings. The listener or reader has to grasp relations of words in a given sequence of sentences quite separate from the substantive character of the words themselves. Accordingly, second, the natural language of Middle Hebrew is

---

[7]Later on, the rabbinical estate did develop its own language for various objects. Babylonian Talmud Qiddushin 70a–b makes clear that rabbis called common objects by "their own" words.

not apt to be represented by the highly formal language of Mishnah. Mishnaic language constitutes something more than a random sequence of words used routinely to say things. It is meant as a highly formulaic way of expressing a particular set of distinctive conceptions. It is, therefore, erroneous to refer to *Mishnaic* language; rather, we deal with the Mishnaic revision of the natural language of Middle Hebrew. And, it is clear, what Mishnah does to revise that natural language is ultimately settled in the character of the grammar, inclusive of syntax, of the language. Middle Hebrew has a great many more grammatical sequences than does Mishnaic Hebrew; and, it follows, Mishnaic Hebrew declares ungrammatical—that is, refuses to make use of— constructions which Middle Hebrew will regard as wholly grammatical and entirely acceptable. The single striking trait of the formaliz ation of Mishnaic language, therefore, is that it depends upon grammar. And just as Chomsky says, "Grammar is autonomous and independent of meaning"(1957: 17), so in Mishnah, the formalization of thought into recurrent patterns is beneath the surface and independent of discrete meanings. Yet Mishnah imposes its own discipline, therefore its own deeper level of unitary meaning, upon everything and anything which actually is said.

Let us now ask about the ecology of Mishnaic modes of speech (Haugen, 1972: 336–37). What is its classification in relationship to other languages? A variety of Middle Hebrew, it is used in particular by people engaged in the memorization and transmission of teachings on behalf of which is claimed divine revelation. Accordingly, its users are religious specialists. What are the domains of use? So far as we know, Mishnah's distinctive modes of speech are particular to Mishnah. But this judgment must be qualified. Even in Tosefta the same modes do not consistently occur and scarcely serve to characterize intermediate divisions. Accordingly, what is particular to Mishnah is not the remarkably distinctive sentence-structures we have discerned, but recurrent use of such sentence-structures to give expression to sizable groups of cognitive units. That indeed is a limited domain of use. What concurrent languages are employed by the users of this mode of speech? Clearly, we may assume, Middle Hebrew in non-Mishnaic patterns was available to them. Whether in addition they spoke Aramaic or Greek is not equivalently clear, nor do we know that they spoke Middle Hebrew as a language of ordinary use. Accordingly, we do not know the dialinguistical data necessary to answer this question. Does Mishnah yield evidence of dialect? The answer clearly is that it does not. On the contrary, the speech is decidedly uniform and unnuanced. To what degree has the Mishnaic variety of Middle Hebrew been standardized, unified, and codified? Here the answer is clear. We have the highest degree of standardization. What kind of institutional support stands behind Mishnah? The answer is not wholly clear from the data we have examined. I am inclined to think that, if we take seriously the claim in behalf of Mishnah that it is Oral Torah, we have to assign to Mishnah an extraordinary sort of heavenly support for its variety of patterns of speech. In still other, this-worldly terms,

Mishnah probably also is supported through the activities of those who memorized the language and those who supported them, a wide circle of savants. What are the attitudes of the users toward the language? It certainly is public and ritualistic, not a language of intimacy. Its use assuredly confers upon the user a defined status, leading to personal identification as a *Tanna* in the schools and as a rabbi outside of them. Finally, how does the Mishnaic variety of Hebrew relate to other languages? The answer is, of course, that it is not a language at all but, rather, a variety of a language, limited and formalized for special purposes. Its ecology will then conform to the profile of cultic languages in general with the qualification that, if Middle Hebrew was widely used, it is a revision of a common language into a cultic language. Its relatedness to, and difference from, unpatterned Middle Hebrew serves to shape and express the ethos and world-view of a particular speech-community.

IV

The question is raised, "How and for what purpose was Mishnah edited into final form, and what is the nature of the sources used for the final product?" (Saldarini, 1976: 151). The consideration of Mishnah's external traits, of its limited repertoire of patterns of language, and of its single and uniform procedure for the conglomeration of materials into intelligible patterns—principal divisions, intermediate divisions, cognitive units—helps to secure the redefinition of these questions. We do not know the nature of the sources used in the formulation of Mishnah because Mishnah appears so completely to have reformulated whatever sorts of materials, in whatever kinds of antecedent collections, were available, as to obliterate their former character and distinctive traits. Accordingly, one fact about those who framed and formed Mishnah as we know it is that, while they drew upon diverse and ancient corpora of ideas, and while at their disposal were not simply ideas but ideas given particular and concrete form in words, sentences, paragraphs, and the like, the formal character of the antecedent heritage has been radically revised. We cannot specify extensive collections of antecedent materials preserved in Mishnah but revised therein. But we do know that Scripture—a collection of particularly authoritative character—assuredly did exist and was available. Yet its literary character produces no impact whatsoever on that of Mishnah.

Perhaps, along these same lines, there were catanae of sayings assigned to a given authority. Episodically, the existence of collections organized around a single name comes before us. Likewise, there were constructions of diverse sayings on a wide range of topics organized in terms of a single powerful syntactic and grammatical structure. These, too, are known. But we have too few of either sort of construction to propose that behind Mishnah were extensive collections of sayings in the name of a single authority or of rules on diverse topics in the model of a single grammatical-syntactical form. If there were, however, form by Mishnah is joined to, and revised by, substance and deprived of its antecedent organizing power. Authority is rendered secondary to the paramount confluence of substance and form. Accordingly, if we assume that the sherds in our hands testify to older corpora, then two earlier modes of redaction, by form and by authority, have been set aside. Mishnah, therefore, has its own theory of how sayings are to be stated and organized and that is, we have proved beyond doubt, in the union of theme and formulary pattern.

It follows that, in the absence of more than episodic evidence, we must speculate about the purpose of the editing of Mishnah in final form solely by systematically extrapolating, from the facts of its redaction, insight into the purpose of its redaction. What we learn from the character of the literature about the circle that produced the literature, so far as that character speaks of those who created it, is nothing whatsoever. The people who made Mishnah do not want us to know them because, I should imagine, nothing about them was deemed important in the understanding of what they did. That is why they do not organize materials around given names of authorities, though as I said, some such constructions do survive. To ask whether the redactors were lawyers, philosophers, wonder-workers, teachers, government officials, preachers, soldiers, priests, anointed messiahs, or any of the other things people who produce a holy document such as this might have been is futile. To ask whether they legislated for themselves or for all Israelites is equally hopeless because, silent as they are on themselves, so reticent are they about those to whom they seek to speak.

Yet they do take certain things for granted. In order to make sense of what they do tell us, there are things which we have to know and which are not told to us by them. But from the perspective of form and rhetoric the catalogue hardly is a long one. Mishnah presupposes the existence of Scripture. It is not possible to make sense of the details of any tractate without knowledge of Scriptural laws. Yet what, in rhetoric and grammar, is it about, and in, Scripture that is presupposed? It is not, I have stressed, the style and language of Scripture. These are ignored. Knowledge of Scripture's formal characteristics in no way facilitates our understanding and interpretation of Mishnah. It is simply certain facts of Scripture, e.g., that a corpse contaminates, that there is a dimension of the clean and the unclean. The knowledge even of facts of Scripture by themselves cannot, of course, suffice. Mishnah has distinctive conceptions even of the meaning of simple facts, data of Scripture themselves. In the present context, what is important is that knowledge of Scripture's forms and style in no important way improves understanding of those of Mishnah or even is relevant to interpreting them.

Yet there is a side to Scripture which, I think, is at the very bedrock of Mishnah's linguistic character and explains Mishnah's self-evident preoccupation with the interplay of theme and form. Scripture speaks of creation through words; and, we know, it is as much through how things are said as through what is said that Mishnah proposes to effect its own creative purpose. The priestly notion of creation by means of speech is carried through in Mishnah's most distinctive and ubiquitous attributive, X ᵓWMR, one *says*, just as at Gen 1:3, 6, 9, 11, 14, 20, 24, 29, at each of the stages of creation, God *says* (ᵓMR) something and it *is*.

The supposition of Mishnah that Scripture is known is, while not trivial, obvious. There is a second, less blatant supposition. It is that the language of Mishnah *will* be understood; its nuances appreciated; its points of stress and emphasis grasped. Our discussion of the cathectically neutral and indifferent style of Mishnah, its failure to speak to some distinct audience in behalf of some defined speaker, does not obscure the simple fact that Mishnah is not gibberish, but a corpus of formed and intensely meaningful statements, the form of which is meant to bear deep meaning. Accordingly, the gnomic sayings of Mishnah, corresponding in their deep, universal grammar to the subterranean character of "reality," permit the inference that the reality so described as to be grasped and understood by people of mind. Given the unarticulated points at which stress occurs, the level of grammar autonomous of discrete statements and concrete rulings, moreover, we must conclude that the framers of Mishnah expected to be understood by remarkably keen ears and active minds. Conveying what is fundamental at the level of grammar autonomous of meaning, they manifest confidence that the listener will put many things together and draw the important conclusions for himself or herself. That means that Mishnah assumes an active intellect, capable of perceiving inferred convention, and a vividly participating audience capable of following what was said with intense concentration. This demands, first, memorizing the message on the surface and, second, perceiving the subtle and unarticulated message of the medium of syntax and grammar. The hearer, third, is assumed to be capable of putting the two together into the still further insight that the cogent pattern exhibited by diverse statements preserves a substantive cogency among those diverse and delimited statements. Superficially-various rules, stated in sentences unlike one another on the surface and made up of unlike word-choices, in fact say a single thing in a single way. None of this is possible, it goes without saying, without anticipating that exegesis of the fixed text will be undertaken by the audience. Mishnah demands commentary. It takes for granted that the audience is capable of exegesis and proposes to undertake the work. Mishnah commands a sophisticated and engaged socio-intellectual context within the Israelite world. Mishnah's lack of specificity on this point should not obscure its quite precise expectation. The thing it does not tell us which we have to know is that Mishnah *will be understood*. The process of understanding, the character of Mishnah's language testifies, is complex and difficult. Mishnah is a document which compliments its audience.

Language serves the authorities of Mishnah as an instrument of power—

specifically, power to create reality. Wittgenstein said, "The limits of my language mean the limits of my world" (Farb, 1974: 192). What are the limitations of Mishnah's formalized modes of speech? What sort of reality is made possible within them and is constructed by them? To what degree, specifically, does Mishnaic language attain new possibilities for the containment and creation of reality precisely by its tendency to avoid explicit generalizations and its perpetual expression of precise, but abstract, relationships between things only in concrete terms? And, finally, we return to the central and inescapable question: For what purpose was Mishnah made?

We begin with the gnomic character of Mishnaic discourse. Clearly, Mishnah claims to make wise and true statements, statements which, moreover, apply at any time and in any place. It follows, second, that Mishnah proposes to describe how things truly are. And, third, accordingly, the people who made Mishnah did so in order to put together, in a single document and in encapsulated form, an account of the inner structure of reality: specifically, of that aspect of reality which, in their judgment, is susceptible of encapsulation in formally patterned words. When, fourth, we recall the exceedingly limited repertoire of ways by which statements are made, we recognize that, to the authorities of Mishnah, all of the diverse and changing things in the world can be reduced to a few simple, descriptive equations. These, fifth, are to be expressed in particular by the inner and deep traits of the interrelationships of words, by persistent patterns of grammar and of syntax, rather than by superficial traits of sound and repetition of concrete thought. The principle is to be derived by the listener's reflection upon any set of diverse rules or statements, his contributed perception of what unites the whole, which will be left unsaid but everywhere deemed obvious.

Relying entirely on the traits of syntax and grammar which are before us, what can we say about the deepest convictions concerning reality characteristic of people who spoke in the ways we have considered? There is a deep sense of balance, of the appropriateness of opposites in the completion of a whole thought. Many times do we hear: if thus, then so, *and if not thus, then not so*. Mishnaic rhetoric demands, because Mishnah's creators' sense of grammar requires, the completion of the positive by the negative and of the negative by the positive. The contrastive complex predicate is testimony to the datum that order consists in completion and wholeness. So, too, the many balanced declarative sentences reveal the same inner conviction that in the completion of a pattern, in the working out of its single potentiality through a sequence of diverse actualities, lies that besought order and wholeness. The fact that it is the intermediate division which constitutes the formulary context of Mishnah needs no further specification. Thought takes place in sequences of whole, matched, balanced, and contrastive thoughts, all of them, we need hardly repeat, about various specific things. Accidents do require specification and repetition. Mishnah is scarcely satisfied to give a single instance of a rule from which we may generalize. It strongly prefers to give us three or six or nine instances, on the basis of which we may then conclude that there is, indeed, an underlying rule. The singleton-case is not the rule solely for itself, nor, all by itself, for all things.

I do not perceive an equivalent meaning in the duplicated subject. When, however, we come to apocopation—beside sequentially balanced sentences, Mishnah's other remarkable formulary structure—we once more perceive something, from the external traits of expression, about the mind, the inner structure of which is subject to articulation. What do we have in apocopation? It is, first of all, a powerful sense of superficial incompleteness and disorder. Apocopated sentences are composed of disjoined phrases. The subject of such sentences generally is made up of two or more such phrases, each of them introducing its own actor and acted-upon, its subject and predicate. What unites the several clauses and imposes meaning upon all of them is the ultimate predicate. This, by itself, cannot always be asked to refer to any single one of the phrases of the subject. But it encompasses the result of all of them all together. It is, therefore, a construction, the meaning of which depends upon a context which is inferred from, but not made explicit by, its constituents. In a profound sense, the apocopated sentence, so distinctive to Mishnah, expresses that deep sense of a wholeness beneath discrete parts which Mishnaic language presupposes.

For it is the mind of the hearer which makes sense of the phrases and clauses of the subject and perceives the relationship, endowing the whole meaning, required by the predicate, upon the distinct clauses of the subject. The mind of the hearer is central in the process by which apocopation attains meaning. The capacity for perceiving the rational and orderly sense of things exhibited by that mind is the unstated necessity of apocopation. That, as we have seen in the preceding discussion, is characteristic of Mishnaic modes of expression, therefore of perception as well. Hearing discrete rules, applicable to cases related in theme and form but not in detail and concrete actualities, the hearer puts together two things. First is the repetition of grammatical usages. Second is the repetition of the same principle, the presence of which is implied by the repetition of syntactical patterns in diverse cases. These two, stable principle and disciplined grammar autonomous of meaning, are never stated explicitly but are invariably present implicitly.

So there are these two striking traits of mind reflected within Mishnaic rhetoric: first, the perception of order and balance; second, the perception of the mind's centrality in the construction of order and balance, i.e., the imposition of wholeness upon discrete cases in the case of the routine declarative sentence and upon discrete phrases in the case of the apocopated one. Both order and balance are contained from within and are imposed from without. The relationships revealed by grammatical consistencies internal to a sentence and the implicit regularities revealed by the congruence and cogency of cases rarely are stated but always are to be discerned. Accordingly, the one thing which Mishnah invariably does not make explicit but which always is necessary to know is, I stress, the presence of the active intellect, the participant who is the hearer. It is the hearer who ultimately makes sense of, perceives the sense in, Mishnah. Once more we are impressed by Mishnah's expectation of high sophistication and profound sensitivity to order and to form on the part of its impalpable audience.

In this sense Mishnah serves both as a book of laws and as a book for learners, a law-code and a schoolbook. But it is in this sense alone.

If our Order of Mishnah is a law-code, it is remarkably reticent about punishments for infractions of its rules. It rarely says what one must do, or must not do, if he or she becomes unclean and hardly even alludes to punishments or rewards consequent upon disobedience or obedience to its laws. *Clean* and *unclean* rhetorically are the end of the story and generate little beyond themselves.

If our Order serves as a schoolbook, it never informs us about its institutional setting, speaks of its teachers, sets clear-cut, perceptible, educational goals for its students, nor, above all, attempts to stand in relationship to some larger curriculum or educational and social structure. Its lack of context and unself-conscious framework of discourse hardly support the view that, in a this-worldly and ordinary sense, we have in our hands a major division of a law-code or of a schoolbook.

Nor is Mishnah a corpus of traditions which lay claim to authority or to meaning by virtue of the authorities cited therein. That is why the name of an authority rarely serves as a redactional fulcrum. The tense-structure is ahistorical and anti-historical. Sequences of actions generally are stated in the descriptive present tense. Rules attain authority not because of who says them but because (it would seem) no specific party at a specific time stands behind them. The reason, I think, that shortly after the promulgation of Mishnah, Mishnah gained for itself the place in the revealed Torah of Moses at Sinai, testifies against its capacity to serve as an essentially historical statement of who said what, when, and for which purpose. Mishnah, as I have emphasized, is descriptive of how things are. It is indifferent to who has said so, uninterested in the cumulative past behind what it has to say. These are not the traits of a corpus of "traditions." I am inclined to think that law-code, schoolbook, and corpus of traditions all are not quite to the point of the accurate characterization of Mishnah.

Yet, if not quite to the point, all nonetheless preserve a measure of proximate relevance to the definition of Mishnah. Mishnah does contain descriptive laws. These laws require the active participation of the mind of the hearer, thus are meant to be learned, not merely obeyed, and self-evidently are so shaped as to impart lessons, not merely rules to be kept. The task of the hearer is not solely or primarily to obey, though I think obedience is taken for granted, but to participate in the process of discovering principles and uncovering patterns of meaning. The very form of Mishnaic rhetoric, its formalization and the function of that form—all testify to the role of the learner and hearer, that is, the student, in the process of definitive and indicative description, not communication, of what is, and of what is real. Self-evidently, Mishnah's citation of authorities makes explicit the claim that some men, now dead, have made their contribution and, therefore, have given shape and substance to tradition, that which is shaped by one and handed onward by another. So Mishnah indeed is, and therefore is meant as, a law-code, a schoolbook, and a corpus of tradition. It follows that the purpose for which Mishnah was edited into final form was to create such a multi-purpose document, a tripartite goal attained in a single corpus of formed and formal sayings. And yet it is obvious that Mishnah is something other than these three things in one. It transcends the three and accomplishes more than the triple goals which on the surface form the constitutive components of its purpose.

To describe that transcendent purpose, we return to Wittgenstein's saying, "The limits of my language mean the limits of my world." Mishnah's formulaic rhetoric on the one side imposes limits, boundaries, upon the world. What fits into that rhetoric, can be said by it, constitutes world, world given shape and boundary by Mishnah. Mishnah implicitly maintains, therefore, that a wide range of things fall within the territory mapped out by a limited number of linguistic conventions, grammatical sentences. What is grammatical can be said and, therefore, constitutes part of the reality created by Mishnaic word. What cannot be contained within the grammar of the sentence cannot be said and therefore falls outside the realm of Mishnaic reality. Mishnaic reality consists in those things which can attain order, balance, and principle. Chaos then lies without. Yet, if we may extrapolate from the capacity of the impoverished repertoire of grammar to serve for all sorts of things, for the dozen topics of our Order, for example, then we must concede that all things can be said by formal revision. Everything can be reformed, reduced to the order and balance and exquisite sense for the just match, characteristic of the Mishnaic pericope. Anything of which we wish to speak is susceptible to the ordering and patterning of Mishnaic grammar and syntax. That is a fact which is implicit throughout our Order. Accordingly, the territory mapped out by Mishnaic language encompasses the whole of the pertinent world under discussion. There are no thematic limitations of Mishnaic formalized speech.

Yet reality, the world of clean and unclean, in the present context, is forced to surpass itself, to strive for a higher level of order and meaning through its submission to Mishnaic formalization. Implicit in the rhetoric of our document is the notion, now alluded to many times, of deep regularities which in principle unite cases, just as regularities in rhetoric unite cases. What is abstract need not be spelled out because it already is spelled out through recurrent, implicit relationships among words, among cases. In this context we note Green's statement:

If the performance of rituals within the Temple exposes the lines of God's revealed reality, then thinking . . . about these rituals outside the Temple, even without the possibility of performing all of them, has the same result. The Mishnaic rabbis express their primary cognitive statements, their judgments upon large matters, through . . . law, not through myth or theology, neither of which is articulated at all. Early Rabbinism took ritual beyond the realm of practice and transformed it into the object of speculation and the substance of thought. Study, learning, and exposition became . . . the basic Rabbinic activity . . . (n.d.).

Restating this view in terms of Mishnaic grammatical rhetoric, we may say that thinking about matters of detail within a particular pattern of cognitive constructions treats speculation and thought as themselves capable of informing and shaping being, not merely expressing its external traits. Language becomes ontology.

Language in Mishnah replaces cult, formalism of one kind takes the place of formalism of another. The claim that infinitely careful and patterned deeds are *ex opere operato* an expression of the sacred has its counterpart in the implicit character of Mishnah's language. Its rhetoric is formed with infinite care, according to a fine pattern for speech, about doing deeds of a particular sort. Language now conforms to cult then.

The formal cult, once performed in perfect silence, now is given its counterpart in formal speech. Where once men said nothing but, through gesture and movement in other circumstances quite secular, performed holy deed, now they do nothing but, through equally patterned revision of secular words about secular things, perform holy speech. In the cult it is the very context which makes an intrinsically neutral, therefore secular, act into a holy one. Doing the thing right with precision and studied care makes the doing holy. Slaughtering an animal, collecting its blood and butchering it, burning incense and pouring wine—these by themselves are things which can be, and are, done in the home as much as in the cult. But in the cult they are characterized by formality and precision. In Mishnah by contrast there is no spatial context to sanctify the secular act of saying things. The context left, once cult is gone, is solely the cultic mode of formalism, the ritualization of speech, that most neutral and commonplace action. Mishnah transforms speech into ritual and so creates the surrogate of ritual deed. That which was not present in cult, speech, is all that is present now that the silent cult is gone. And, it follows, it is by the formalization of speech, its limitation to a few patterns, and its perfection through the creation of patterns of relationships in particular, that the old nexus of Heaven and earth, the cult, now is to be replicated in the new and complementary nexus, cultic speech about all things.

What the limitation of Mishnaic language to a few implicit relational realities accomplishes, therefore, is the reduction of the world to the limits of language. In ritual grammar the world therein contained and expressed attains formalization among, and simplification by, the unstated but remarkably few principles contained within, and stated by, the multitudinous cases which correspond to the world. Mishnaic language makes possible the formalization of the whole of the workaday world. It accomplishes the transformation of all things in accord with that sense for perfect form and unfailing regularity which, as I said, once were distinctive to the operation of the cult. Mishnaic language explores the possibility of containing and creating a new realm of reality, one which avoids abstractions and expresses all things only through the precision of grammatical patterns, that is, the reality of abstract relationships alone.

Have we come closer to a perception of the purpose for which, according to the internal testimony of our Order, Mishnah was created? In a concrete sense, of course, we have not. Mishnaic rhetoric says nothing explicit about the purpose of the rhetoric. In the simplest sense, as we noted long ago, the proximate purpose of formalization was to facilitate the mnemonic process. Yet it is to beg the question to say that the purpose of facilitating memorization is to help people remember things. Mishnah wants to be memorized for a reason. The reason transcends the process, pointing rather to its purpose. Nor do we stand closer to the inner intentions of Mishnah's authorities when we raise the polemical purpose of memorization. This was to act out the claim that there are two components of the one whole Torah which "Moses, our rabbi," received from God at Sinai, one transmitted in writing, the other handed on by tradition, in oral form only. True, the claim for Mishnah, laid down in tractate Abot, Mishnah's first and most compelling apologetic, is that the authority of Mishnah rests upon its status as received tradition of God. It follows that tradition handed on through memory is valid specifically because, while self-evidently not part of the written Torah which all Israel has in mind, it is essential to the whole Torah. Its mode of tradition through memory verifies and authenticates its authority as tradition begun by God despite its absence from the written part of Torah. Both these things—the facilitation of memorization, the authentication of the document through its external form—while correct, also are *post facto*. They testify to the result of Mishnaic rhetoric for both educational-tradental and polemical-apologetic purposes. Once we memorize, we accomplish much. But why, to begin with, commit these gnomic sayings to such language as facilitates their memorization?

In a world such as Mishnah's, in which writing is routine, memorization is special. What happens when we know something by heart which does not happen when we must read it or look for it in a scroll or a book is that when we walk in the street and when we sit at home, when we sleep and when we awake, we carry with us in our everyday perceptions that memorized gnomic saying. The process of formulation through formalization and the co-equal process of memorizing patterned cases to sustain the perception of the underlying principle, uniting the cases just as the pattern unites their language, extends the limits of language to the outer boundaries of experience, the accidents of everyday life itself. Gnomic sayings are routine in all cultures. But the reduction of all truth to gnomic sayings is not.

To impose upon those sayings an underlying and single structure of grammar corresponding to the inner structure of reality thus is to transform the structure of language into a statement of ontology. Once our minds are trained to perceive principle among cases and pattern within grammatical relationships, we further discern in the concrete events of daily life both principle and underlying autonomous pattern. The form of Mishnah is meant to correspond to the formalization perceived within, not merely imposed upon, the conduct of concrete affairs, principally the meaning and character of concrete happenings among things in the workaday life of people. The matter obviously is not solely ethical, but the ethical component is self-evident. It also has to do with the natural world and the things which break its routine, of which our Order speaks so fully and in such exquisite detail. Here all things are a matter of relationship, circumstance, fixed and recurrent interplay. *If X, then Y, if not X, then not Y*—that is the datum by which minds are shaped.

The way to shape and educate minds is to impart into the ear, thence into the mind, perpetual awareness that what happens recurs, and what recurs is pattern and order and, through them, wholeness. How better than to fill the mind with formalized sentences, generative of meaning for themselves and of significance beyond themselves, in which meaning rests upon the perception of relationship? Pattern is to be discovered in alertness, in the multiplicity of events and happenings, none of which states or articulates pattern. Mind, trained to memorize through what is implicit and beneath the surface, is to be accustomed and taught in such a way to discern pattern. Order *is* because order is *discovered*, first in language, then in life. As the cult in all its precise and obsessive attention to fixed detail effected the perception that from the orderly center flowed lines of meaning to the periphery, so the very language of Mishnah, in the particular traits which I have specified, also in its precise and obsessive concentration on innate and fixed relationship, effects the perception of order deep within the disorderly world of language, nature, and man.

What we have said about matters of form and language has now to be set into the appropriate context of our document, which is, the realm of the sacred. The memorization and repetition of Mishnah from the time of the creation of Mishnah are perceived as holy, an intrinsically sacred action, not merely an informative and functionally useful one. Indeed, given the subject matter of our Order, why should someone want the information of Mishnah? What function thereby is to be served? Accordingly, we turn at the end to a discussion of the character of religion, so far as religion conveys a world-view, as Mishnah's formal character certainly does. Clifford Geertz states:

> In a recent anthropological discussion, the moral (and aesthetic) aspects of a given culture, the evaluative elements, have commonly been summed up in the term "ethos," while

the cognitive, existential aspects have been designated by the term "world-view." A people's ethos is the tone, character, and quality of their life, its moral and aesthetic style and mood; it is the underlying attitude toward themselves and their world that life reflects. Their world-view is their picture of the way things, in sheer actuality, are, their concept of nature, of self, of society. It contains their most comprehensive ideas of order. Religious belief and ritual confront and mutually confirm one another; the ethos is made intellectually reasonable by being shown to represent a way of life implied by the actual state of affairs which the world-view describes, and the world-view is made emotionally acceptable by being presented as an image of the actual state of affairs of which such a way of life is an authentic expression. This demonstration of a meaningful relation between the values a people holds and the general order of existence within which it finds itself is an essential element in all religions, however those values or that order be conceived. Whatever else religion may be, it is in part an attempt (of an implicit and directly felt rather than explicit and consciously thought-about sort) to conserve the fund of general meanings in terms of which each individual interprets his experience and organizes his conduct. . . . Sacred symbols thus relate an ontology and a cosmology to an aesthetics and a morality: their peculiar power comes from their presumed ability to identify fact with value at the most fundamental level, to give to what is otherwise merely actual, a comprehensive, normative import. The number of such synthesizing symbols is limited in any culture, and though in theory we might think that a people could construct a wholly autonomous value system independent of any metaphysical referent, an ethics without ontology, we do not in fact seem to have found such a people. The tendency to synthesize world-view and ethos at some level, if not logically necessary, is at least empirically coercive; if it is not philosophically justified, it is at least pragmatically universal. . . . It is a cluster of sacred symbols, woven into some sort of ordered whole, which makes up a religious system. . . .

For those who are committed to it, such a religious system seems to mediate genuine knowledge, knowledge of the essential conditions in terms of which life must, of necessity, be lived. . . . Religion supports proper conduct by picturing a world in which such conduct is only common sense.

It is only common sense because between ethos and world-view, between the approved style of life and the assumed structure of reality, there is conceived to be a simple and fundamental congruence such that they complete one another and lend one another meaning (1957: 421–37 passim).

I have cited Geertz at length because he serves to complete the present discussion. What I have tried to show is that intrinsic and essential to the ethos of that life represented and formed by Mishnah is an aesthetic which also is an ontology, an aesthetic which contains within itself a profound and implicit, but never articulated, world-view.

There is a perfect correspondence between what Mishnah proposes to say and the way in which it says it. An essential part of the ethos of Mishnaic culture is its formal and formulaic sentence, the means by which it makes its cognitive statements and so expresses its world-view. Not only does ethos correspond to world-view, but world-view is expressed in style as much as in substance. In the case of Mishnaic form, the ethos and world-view come together in the very elements of grammatical formalization which, never made explicit, expresses the permanence and paramount character of relationship, the revelatory relativity of context and circumstance. Life attains form in structure. It is structure which is most vivid in life. The medium for the expression of the world-view is the ethos. But for Mishnah, ethos neither appeals to, nor as far as I can see, expresses emotion. Just as there is no room for nuance in general in the severe and balanced sentences of Mishnah, so there is no place for the nuance of emotion or "commitment" in general. The rhetoric of our document makes no appeal to emotion or to obedience, describing, not invoking, the compelling and ineluctable grounds for assent. This claim that things are such and so, relate in such and such a way, without regard or appeal to how we want them to be, is unyielding. Law is law, despite the accidents of workaday life, and facts are facts. The bearer of facts and the maker of law is the relationship, the pattern by which diverse things are set into juxtaposition with one another, whether subject and predicate, or dead creeping thing and loaf of heave-offering. What is definitive is not the thing but the context and the circumstance, the time, the condition, the intention of the actor. In all, all things are relative to relative things.

The bridge from ethos to world-view is the form and character of the sentence which transforms the one into the other. The declarative sentence through patterned language takes attitude and turns it into cognition. Mishnaic "religion" not only speaks of values. Its mode of speech is testimony to its highest and most enduring, distinctive value. This language does not speak of sacred symbols but of pots and pans, of menstruation and dead creeping things, of ordinary water which, because of the circumstance of its collection and location, possesses extraordinary power, of the commonplace corpse and the ubiquitous diseased person, of genitalia and excrement, toilet seats and the flux of penises, of stems of pomegranates and stalks of leeks, of rain and earth and wood, metal, glass and hide. This language is filled with words for neutral things of humble existence. It does not speak of holy things and is not symbolic in its substance. This language speaks of ordinary things, of things which everyone must have known. But because of the peculiar and particular way in which it is formed and formalized, this same language not only adheres to an aesthetic theory but expresses a deeply-embedded ontology and methodology of the sacred, specifically of the sacred within the secular, and of the capacity for regulation, therefore for sanctification, within the ordinary.

To conclude: World-view and ethos are synthesized in language. The synthesis is expressed in grammatical and syntactical regularities. What is woven into some sort of ordered whole is not a cluster of sacred symbols. The religious system is not discerned with such symbols at all. Knowledge of the conditions of life is imparted principally through description of the commonplace facts of life, which symbolize, stand for, nothing beyond themselves and their consequences for the clean and the unclean. That description is effected through the construction of units of meaning, intermediate divisions composed of cognitive elements. All is balanced, explicit in detail, but reticent about the whole; balanced in detail but dumb about the character of the balance. What is not said is what is eloquent and compelling as much as what is said. Accordingly, that simple and fundamental congruence between ethos and world-view is to begin with, for Mishnah, the very language by which the one is given cognitive expression in the other. The medium of patterned speech conveys the meaning of what is said.

PART THREE
FROM RELIGION TO THEOLOGY

CHAPTER VIII

The Tasks of Theology in Judaism

The principal task of theology in Judaism is to draw out and make explicit the normative statements of the acknowledged sources of Judaism and to learn how to renew discourse in accord with these norms.[1] It is, specifically, to delineate the world-view shaped within the experience and aspirations of the community of Judaism and to perceive the world within that view. The goal is that, in time to come, the sight of ages to come may be made yet more perspicacious, too. Vision received, vision reformed, vision transmitted—these are the tasks of theology in Judaism.[2]

I

The beginning of the work is to state what it is that Judaism teaches, to define both its principal concerns and its methods of expressing its ideas. The work of definition is to discover what it is that theology to begin with wishes to say. This descriptive task—the perception of the vision received—is theological in its purpose. But it requires the disciplines of hermeneutics, history of religions, and history. The tasks of theology in Judaism will be carried out at the intersecting frontiers among these useful disciplines, even though, as I shall explain, merely working along lines laid out by them will not yield a significant theological result.

[1] Because of the occasion for which this paper is prepared, the awarding to me of an honorary degree, Doctor of Humane Letters, by the University of Chicago, I have formed the paper in response in some small way to the thought of Professors Jonathan Z. Smith (parts I and II) and David Tracy (parts IV, V). The context of the whole, of course, is the difficult question of the role of theology in the humanities, this provoked for me by the character of the degree. Part III derives its basic perspectives from my *Purities* (1974–77), *Holy Things* (1978–79), and *Women* (1980f.). I enjoyed the critical counsel of Professors Wendell S. Dietrich, John Giles Milhaven, John P. Reeder, Jr., Sumner B. Twiss, and Richard S. Sarason, Brown University; William Scott Green, University of Rochester; David Blumenthal, Emory University; and Marvin Fox, Brandeis University; to all of whom I express thanks and, for all, absolution as well for my sins.

[2] It is a commonplace that *halakhic* statements are normative, and theological statements represent the private opinion of an individual. This paper is meant to restate the theological task in such a way that theology, too, may be perceived, within the communities of the faithful of Judaism, as part of public discourse, not merely private opinion. At this time, however, I do not wish to enter into issues of Judaic dogmatics. The reason that the work of dogmatics, the restatement of available and required truths for the current age, need not now be done is that it is

Let us start with hermeneutics. The reason to begin here is that when we wish to define Judaism, we have to locate and encompass that whole range of texts which find a place in the canon of Judaism. For to define a religion is to state the substance of its canon, that is, to spell out the canonical ideas found in the canonical literature. And, second, the work of coming to grips with that range of canonical texts with which the theologian of Judaism must reckon is an exercise in the exegesis of exegesis. The theologian had to explain how these texts have been so read as to be received as everywhere pertinent. For Judaism is a religion of great age and diversity. To uncover the fundament of ultimate conviction everywhere present, and to do so with full reverence for diversity in the history of Judaism, we have to look for what is ubiquitous. And that, I think, is the process and the method: how things are made to happen ubiquitously and consistently. Discernment of process yields the rules which we may extract from the happening and the substantive convictions which lie behind the rules. For when we ask about process and method, our interest is in both formal and substantive traits. Axiomatic to the "how" of process and method is the "what" of substance: the elements of world-view which generate both the process and the method.

At this stage in the work, it is not the task of the theologian to declare the truth. The truth, Judaism everywhere holds, is revealed in Torah. It therefore is to be discovered in Torah. The theologian has to locate that point within the intellectual structure of the faith at which discovery may take place. The work is to lay out the lines of the truth, the frontiers of Torah. Now if, in the present age, we take seriously the commonplace proposition that Judaism is a way of life, we are not going to find it easy to choose those people whose way of life defines Judaism and reveals Torah. The diversity among the Jews as a group is too great. Some Jews do not see themselves as engaged in an essentially religious mode of being at all. Others, whom we shall have to call by a separate name, Judaists, do see themselves as participants in a religious mode of being, Judaism. These religious Jews are themselves diverse. The way of life of all those who are Judaists is not uniform. In this regard, therefore, the sustained effort to uncover the fundament of the true faith by description of the way of life of the Judaists is fruitless. The *status quo* does not contain within itself the fundament of the true faith. To turn the way of life into a statement of

premature. For a long time we were told that, in any event, Judaism has no theology; and it certainly has no dogmas. While the dogma of dogma-less Judaism has passed away with the generation to whom it seemed an urgent and compelling proposition, it has left discourse about and within Judaism in disarray. There is a poverty of philosophical clarity and decisive expression amid a superfluity of conviction, too much believing, too little perspicacious construction. As one person put it, "There is no God, but Israel is his sole, chosen people." Of still greater weight, dogmatics lays the groundwork for the exercise of advocacy and apologetic. That exercise is a work of mediation between culture and revelation, between where the people are and where Torah wishes them to be. It seems to me self-evident that until we have a richer and more responsible conception of what it is that awaits both advocacy and mediation, Torah or Judaism, formulation of dogmas for defense is unimportant.

theology or a source for deeper meaning is hopeless. All we should gain is a statement—at best—of culture. Once we admit that fact, we no longer have the choice of speaking of Judaism as a way of life in a this-worldly and merely descriptive sense. If, on the other hand, we turn to historical descriptions of the "authentic" way of life of Judaism, for instance, the *Shulḥan ʿArukh*, we no longer speak of the way of life of all of the living at all, but of a holy book which is part of a holy canon. We might, therefore, just as well turn forthwith to the canon. Or, to state matters more bluntly, Judaism is not going to be described by sociology. But Judaism must be described and interpreted.[3]

And yet, how the holy books are to be read for the work of theology is not clear. For they already have been read for a very long time, and remarkably little theology has come forth. The work of definition remains primitive. So, it is clear, the canon has to be read in some way other than the way in which, under the current auspices, it presently is read. The established hermeneutics of *yeshivot* and Talmud departments, philosophers of Judaism, and ideologists as well, proves arid and productive mainly of contention, when it is of any intellectual weight at all. And the exercise in repeating the holy words without understanding much, if anything, of what they say and mean cannot in this context be taken seriously. It is not reading or learning at all. Pretense and ritual are not the same thing, and ritual-learning must include learning. So we have to find a way of reading the holy books congruent to both their character and our interest in them.

It seems to me that that requirement is met with two questions: First, *how* do these texts convey their message? What is it that we learn from the way they say things and the way in which people have learned and are taught to hear what they say? Second, *what* do they say which is pertinent to living as a Judaist today? That is, once the text comes into being, leaving its own particular moment of history and undertaking a journey beyond its concrete and specific context, the canonical text has to discover new life in other contexts. And the way that happens is through the urgent work of exegesis. The task is the comparison of the words of one text to the ways of another world and the finding of modes of harmonization and mediation between the one and the other.

Now when the theologian comes along, it is not to do the work of descriptive hermeneutics, of explaining solely how the diverse texts have been made to speak. What the theologian requires, for the much more complex work of generalization, is information about commonalities amid the

---

[3]Obviously, I cannot concede that Judaism is practiced today only by those who now carry out the teachings of Jewish law, e.g., as summed up in the *Shulḥan ʿArukh*. It does not seem to be descriptively valid since vast numbers of Jews also regard themselves, and are generally regarded as, Judaists, who do not live in accord with all of the law of Judaism all the time or ever. The choice then is (1) to declare that Judaism has no *halakhah* or (2) to declare that all who do not keep the *halakhah* are not Judaists. Both propositions seem to me factually so far from the truth as to have to be set aside. The problem explored here then becomes urgent and unavoidable.

diversities of exegesis, the exegesis of exegesis, so to speak. The theologian has to uncover the processes and modes of thought. To know how a given text has been received is interesting. To know how the methods of reception, transmission, interpretation, and application of that text correspond to methods to be located in the reading of other texts is to know something important: the deeper structure of the processes of hermeneutics, the method within the diverse methods of the received exegesis. The work of generalization must come. What is available for generalization, it is clear, is what is common among exegetical techniques of diverse and discrete documents. That is, as I have said, how all of them are read, through all times, and in all places.

When, of course, we speak of times and places, we arouse the interest of the historian of religions. For what do we know about the exegesis of a text if we cannot describe the contexts of ideas and circumstances of visions in which that exegesis is done, that is, the particular choices which have been made among a broad range of possibilities? Surely, the impulse and motivation of the exegete have to enter into the account of the results of exegesis: What was the question which had to be answered in those times and for those groups of people? It is not enough to wonder what it is that we learn from hermeneutics, i.e., *how* people say things about the commonalities of faith. We have also to know what it is that, under diverse circumstances, they wish to say: the *substance* matters as much as the method. Here is the point at which comparative and historical studies in religions come to the fore.

When it comes to the work of description, not only does context have its part to play, so too does consideration of choice, that is to say, comparison. What things people *might* have said we must know in order to understand the choices which they *have* made and the things they *do* choose to say. So these two go together: the consideration of form, language, mode of interpreting and applying the canon which, all together, I hope we may call hermeneutics, and attention to the range of the choices selected for serious consideration, the work of comparison of diverse contexts and expressions of a given continuum of religion, or diverse religions, for analysis of which we generally call upon the historian of religions.

There is yet a third kind of thinking about religions which is to be invoked: an interest in the larger, concrete, social, and historical framework in which Judaism comes to particular expression and definition, an interest characteristic of historians. When we have some clear picture of the procedures and methods of exegesis of the texts and of the choices available and made, we have yet to link our results, our conception of the dynamics of Judaism and of its processes, to that world of the Jewish people which took shape in these processes and out of these dynamics.

There is, I mean, an ecology of Judaism: a natural framework in which all elements interact with all other elements to form a stable, coherent, and whole system. For if Judaism is to be described as it has endured, it has to be described where it has endured: in the political-social and imaginative life of the Jewish people, in its mind and emotions. And that part of the task of description and interpretation is best done by historians of the Jewish people, those who (in the present context) take on the work of relating the social and historical framework of the group to its inner life of feeling, fantasy, and imagination. The question to be asked in this setting is how it is that the distinctive myths and rites of Judaism—its way of living and way of shaping life—continued to possess the power to form, and to make sense of, an enduring world in diverse and changing contexts. When we consider that Judaism continued in a single, remarkably persistent system for nearly two thousand years from the second century to the nineteenth and even the twentieth, we must ask what has so persisted, amid time and change, to have continued to make sense of the world to the Jews, and of the Jews to their world. That perennial and enduring congruence between myth and circumstance, context and system, surely will enter into our definition of Judaism alongside the elements of process described and choice explained.

My main point is that the defining of the received vision of Judaism is through processes of exegesis which govern feeling and imagination, make sense of context and situation, and persist with remarkable stability for a very long time. It is the discovery and statement of these rules of process which permit us to speak of Judaism. The received vision of Judaism is to be defined as those distinctive processes of exegesis of the canon which yield coherent choices, made time and again through the ages and repeated in one circumstance after another. The work of description is to be done through the disciplines of hermeneutics, history of religions, and history. But in the end, these through their combination do not constitute theology. They only define the parameters within which theology is to be done (see parts IV and V).

II

Our three-part assignment, then, is to work out the hermeneutics of texts; to uncover the choices before the ones who wrote the texts (and the many who received them) and understand what the religious community selected against the background of what it thereby rejected; and, finally, to analyze the concrete contexts in which the processes of exegesis and selection took place.

First, we must determine what is the text, or the kind of text, upon which the theological work is to be done.

It seems self-evident that, in nineteenth and twentieth century theological discourse, a wrong choice has been made. For when we ask about the canon upon which theologians of Judaism draw in modern and contemporary times, the answer is twofold: modern philosophy of religion, on the one side, and the Hebrew Scriptures, the written Torah, on the other. (A few particularly learned theologians cite Talmudic sayings, too.) Proof of this proposition is through a simple mental experiment. When you read the work of nearly all modern and contemporary voices of Judaism, what books must you know to understand their thought? And what do you *not* need to know? It is commonplace that you must know Kant and will do well to know Hegel. You also should know some stories and sayings of the Hebrew Scriptures, the written Torah, and some tales of the Talmud and midrashim, the oral Torah. Except for Abraham J. Heschel and Joseph B. Soloveichik there is not a single important theologian of the present or past century who cannot be fully and exhaustively understood within the limits just now stated—modern philosophy of religion, written ·Torah, and a few pithy rabbinic maxims— because none draws systematically and routinely upon the other resources of the canon of Judaism. But the entire range of the holy books of Judaism speaks, in particular, through Heschel.

In my judgment Judaism cannot draw for definition solely upon the written Torah and episodic citations of rabbinic *aggadah.* This is for two reasons. First, it has been the whole of the dual Torah, written and oral, of Moses, "our rabbi," which has defined Judaism through the ages and which must therefore serve today to supply the principal sources of Judaism. Second, the whole (dual) Torah in fact is many, for the canon of Judaism— Torah—has received new documents in every age down to our own.[4] If, therefore, we conclude that the correct sources of Judaic theology are formed of the one whole Torah of Moses, "our rabbi," we once more find ourselves at that point at which we began, with the question of canon and hermeneutics of canon—how it is delineated and interpreted.

The canon of Judaism defines the sources of theology of Judaism and sets forth the field within which the work of theological inquiry must be undertaken. One part of that canon is well known to, and shared by, others: the written Torah. That part is not to be neglected because it is not unique to

---

[4]This is the principal point of my conference address at The University of Chicago, April, 1977, printed as "Transcendence and Worship through Learning. The Religious World View of Mishnah," (1978). I was genuinely surprised that the Reform theologians and rabbis at that meeting did not see the congruence between this description of the open-ended canon of Torah and the Reform conception of progressive revelation. Instead I found myself criticized for laying too much stress on the importance of reason and learning, as against emotion, in the processes of the unfolding of revelation. But since when is the announcement of how we feel today a revelation of God's will and word for the world? Further, a definition of Judaism which draws principally upon the written Torah read other than through the perspective of the oral Torah, its full and exhaustive interpretation, is not Judaism either. That is to say, so far as there are rules which permit us to speak of Judaism, these rules must be observed. Otherwise what we do is make things up as we go along and call our invention Judaism. But so far as we claim to communicate with other ages and other people in our own age, we cannot simply make things up as we go along. When there is no shared realm of discourse, past and present, there is that capricious alternation of noise or silence which is, in the life of emotions, the prelude to death and, in the life of the intellect, the symptom of the end of reasoned discourse. Since theology is the work of and for intellectuals pursued through reasoned discourse about, in part, a realm of distinctive and rich emotions and educated feelings, we cannot afford the costs of ignorance and capriciousness. People who live by their own rules cannot be called social or, ultimately, even sane.

Judaism. Heschel, for his part, understood that despite all that has been done to make the written Torah alien to Judaism, the "Old Testament" remains the *Tanakh*, the written Torah of Judaism. He deemed his most important book to be the *Prophets*. The second half of the Torah, the oral part, *aggadah* and *halakhah*, however, is not to be neglected—just as Heschel, for his part, understood it: the Mishnah, the Talmud, and the great corpus continuous with the Mishnah and the Talmud. Here, too, Heschel undertook work of surpassing intellectual ambition in his *Torah min hashshamayim beaspaqlaria shel haddorot*, an essay in the conceptions of revelation of the authorities of Mishnah and, in a still larger framework, in the character of religious epistemology in Judaism.[5]

Thus far I mean to stress two points. First of all, the sources of theology of Judaism are the whole and complete canon of Torah. That canon is defined for us by the shelves of books deemed by the consensus of the faithful to be holy and to warrant study in religious circumstances, that is, to be part of Torah. The canon of Torah is sufficiently open so that the words of even living men may be received in faith and recorded in piety. Torah is an open canon: *The processes by which books find their way into that canon define the convictions of Judaism about the character and meaning of revelation.*

Second, I am able to point even in our own day to a theologian whose *oeuvres* do conform to the criterion of breadth and rigorous learning in the Judaic canon by which all theology is to be measured and by which most theologians, alas, are found shallow and ignorant.

Having indicated through the corpus of Heschel's work the character of the canon of theology in Judaism, I may now come to a further point. Even the

---

[5]To complete our definition of the theological canon through our sketch of Heschel's remarkable choices, we have to refer to the entire intellectual range formed of the philosophers of Judaism of the Middle Ages: Maimonides and Judah Hallevi being Heschel's particular, but not sole, choices; the metaphysics of the Zohar, which Heschel fully grasped; and those doctors of the heart and soul who created the Hasidic tales. Into this comprehensive framework of the Judaic canon, Scripture, oral Torah, Zohar, philosophy, mysticism, prayerbook—rationality and feeling, revelation and reason—which Heschel took into his mind and made his own, Heschel also received the achievements of the nineteenth and twentieth century theologians of Christianity and philosophers of religion. His last book, and in many ways his most sophisticated, brought together the Kotzker and Kierkegaard, a *tour de force* not likely to have its parallel in our day. See Heschel, *Torah min hashshamayim beaspaqlariah shel haddorot* (1962, 1965). On the Prophets: *Die Prophetie* (1936). See also *God in Search of Man. A Philosophy of Judaism* (1955) and *The Sabbath. Its Meaning for Modern Man* (1951)—with wood engravings by Ilya Schor. I once told Heschel I thought the center of his work lay in religious epistemology, the sources of religious truth. He said to me, "No, you are wrong. The center is the question of ontology." This is stated by Fritz A. Rothschild (*Encyclopaedia Judaica* 8:425), as follows: "Heschel's own work attempts to penetrate and illumine the reality underlying religion, the living and dynamic relationship between God and man, through the objective, yet sympathetic understanding of the documents of Israel's tradition and of the experience of the pious Jew." Note especially Heschel, *A Passion for Truth* (1973).

most productive, and by far the best, theological mind in modern and contemporary Judaism missed the principal theological canon of Judaism. For Heschel neglected the chief source of Judaism, which is its *halakhah*.

III

The center of Judaism is its way of life. No accurate and careful description of Judaism omits that obvious point. We already have noted that merely describing how Jews now live is not to define the way of life of Judaism. That is a sociological fact. But it is now to be balanced against a theological conviction everywhere affirmed in the history of Judaism from the second century to the nineteenth and twentieth centuries: Judaism expresses its theology through the pattern of deeds performed by the practitioner of Judaism. We are what we do. Judaism is what Judaists are supposed to do. I cannot think of a proposition more widely held in ages past and in our own time than that the theology of Judaism *is* its *halakhah*, its way of living. If, therefore, we want to describe what Judaism teaches, we have to make sense of what Judaism requires the practitioner of Judaism to practice.[6] But what is the meaning of the practice, and how is that meaning to be uncovered?

Under some circumstances Judaism borders upon orthopraxy (eat *kosher* and think *teraif* [unkosher]) and, under others, upon what Herschel called "religious behaviorism." That is, we find robots of the law, who will do everything required by the law and think nothing about the law, that is, religious behaviorists. And we also find nihilists of the law, who do everything by the law and think the law allows thinking anything we like, ortho-practitioners. These corruptions of the faith are revealing. What seems to me worth noticing in them is that orthopraxy is deemed an acceptable option while religious behaviorism is rarely recognized, let alone condemned. It is surprising that there is little effort (Soloveichik here is definitely the exception) and no wide-ranging, systematic, and *sustained* effort whatsoever

---

[6]Joseph Dov Soloveitchik certainly is to be invoked as a principal exponent of the position outlined here, e.g., in his "Ish halakhah" (1944: 651–735) and "The Lonely Man of Faith" (1965: 5–67): "The man lives in accordance with the *halakhah*, he becomes master of himself and the currents of his life . . . he ceases to be a mere creature of a habit. His life becomes sanctified, and God and man are drawn into a community of existence, 'a covenantal community,' which brings God and man together in an intimate, person-to-person relationship. It is only through the observance of the *halakhah* that man attains this goal of nearness to God," so Aaron Rothkoff, *Encyclopaedia Judaica* 15:132–133. It is no criticism to observe that Soloveitchik's observations, while profound, thus far are episodic and not systematic. Despite his formidable insights, *the work of interpretation of the halakhah as a theological enterprise simply has not yet begun.* Nor do I think it can be done by *halakhists* within the intellectually impoverished resources of their training. They are, to begin with, in no way humanists. Perhaps had Rosenzweig lived he might have done this work, just as he—nearly alone—turned to the *Siddur* as a principal source of theology.

(with no exception) to state the theology of Judaism principally out of the sources of the *halakhah*.[7]

The fact is, however, that so far as Judaism today is a living religion, it continues its life through *halakhah*. One authentic monument to the destruction of European Jewry likely to endure beyond the present fad is contained in the *responsa* literature of the ghettos and the concentration camps.[8] That is where Judaism is lived, defined in the crucible of life and death. There is a theology of Judaism emergent from and triumphant over the "Holocaust." But we have yet to hear its message because we scarcely know how to listen to Judaism when Judaism speaks idiomatically, as it always has spoken, in accord with the methods and procedures of *its* canon; in obedience to *its* rules; and, above all, in the natural course of the unfolding of *its* consistent and cogent processes of thought and expression. The *halakhah* endured in the crucible of Warsaw and Lodz when *aggadah* and theology fell dumb.

The coming task of theology in Judaism is to define Judaism through the theological study of the now-neglected canon of the *halakhah*. To begin with, the canon must be allowed to define its literary frame for theological expression. One of the chief reasons for the persistent failure of the philosophers of *halakhah* down to the present time to accomplish what they set out to do is the confusion of their categories. They work through the whole of *halakhah* on a given subject. They therefore present results entirely

---

[7]My description of Heschel's corpus seems to me probative. I can point in his works to systematic and profound reflection upon the theology of the whole of the canon of Judaism except for the *halakhic* part; that is, that part which, speaking descriptively, all concur, forms the center and the core. The fact that Heschel lived wholly and completely in accord with the *halakhah* is beside the point, just as it is beside the point that another great theologian of modern Judaism, Martin Buber, did not. What the two have in common is that through them *halakhah* did and does not speak; and, in the case of Buber, what to begin with is heard from *halakhah* is simply a negative fact, the existence of something *against* which theology will find its definition. What we do have as theology of *halakhah* in Heschel and Soloveichik is sermonic and not sustained; it is episodic and not systematic. (Here I shall mercifully leave unnamed a fair number of Orthodox and Conservative *halakhist*-theologians.) I say this of Heschel, however, (in full awareness of the unkept promise of it) his *The Sabbath: Its Meaning for Modern Man* comes as close as any essay in contemporary theology of Judaism to take up in a systematic and existentially profound way (as against the intellectual ephemera of sermons) the intellectual premises of *halakhah*. There is in the corpus of Heschel no work which draws upon and responds to the *Shulḥan ᶜArukh*, Maimonides' *Mishneh Torah*, the Talmud as Talmud (not merely as a storehouse of interesting sayings and stories), or, above all, and the source of it all, Mishnah and its companion, Tosefta. If it is not in Heschel, then, as I have said, it is nowhere else. I cannot point to a single systematic and sustained work of theology out of the sources of Mishnah and Tosefta, out of the Talmud as a *halakhic* monument or any significant part thereof, or out of the monuments formed by the medieval commentaries and codes down to the present day. For historical study of the social-religious meaning of *halakhah*, see Jacob Katz, *Masoret ummashber* (1958), *Tradition and Crisis* (1961), *Exclusiveness and Tolerance* (1961).

[8]Some of this has been translated into English as, *The Holocaust and Halakhah*, by Irving J. Rosenbaum (N.Y., 1976).

divorced from context, on the one side, and from dynamic processes of exegesis, on the other. So they tell us things, mere facts. That is, they end up with a description of merely what "the *halakhah*" has to say, without analysis or explanation of meaning, a clear account of the context in which, and setting to which, *halakhah* framed its message and how the message was framed. They therefore tell us about *halakhah*. They do not, however, convey a shred of wisdom or insight into the processes and methods of *halakhah* relevant to any given age of Judaism, past or present. But the *halakhah* did not, and does not, take shape in a timeless world. It is meant to *create* a world beyond time— a different thing. Its genius was to take shape in a very specific and concrete moment, yet to transcend that moment and to address ages to come as well. We shall not know how that was done if we persist in ignoring the diversity of the context and canon of the *halakhah*. We have to confront the specificities of its books and their diverse messages and methods, in all, the historicity and religiosity of the *halakhah*.[9]

Once the canon is suitably defined in its diversity and specificity, what is it that we wish to know *about* these documents? The first thing is to grasp the processes of their unfolding: the hermeneutics generative of the exegetical processes which occupy the *halakhic* thinkers of the ages. One significant issue must be how the *halakhic* process expanded its range and so was able to encompass and take as its own each and every circumstance confronted by the Jewish people. For Judaism is a world-creating and world-explaining system. The system, as is obvious, works through law. The law, moreover, functions through processes of argument and discussion. These processes make intelligible and bring under control of rules all of those fresh data of the world which together, at a given point, constitute time and change. The system persists because it makes sense of all data and draws within its framework the newest facts of life. When it can no longer deal credibly with the new world

---

[9]Just as Heschel could address himself to the issues of religious ontology of the prophets, the rabbis named in Mishnah, Maimonides and Judah Hallevi, the Zohar, Hasidic literature, prayerbook, and on down to our own time, so the theologian of *halakhah* will have to allow each and every document of *halakhah* to emerge in all its concrete specificity. But where to begin? Self-evidently, it is to Mishnah and its tractates and divisions that we look for *one* beginning. But if we do not also look to Scripture and its many and diverse codes of law, clearly etched along the lines of the Priestly Code and the Holiness Code, on the one side, and the earlier thinking of the Deuteronomical schools, on the other, we shall miss yet other beginnings. And I think it obvious that, for theology in Judaism to be compelling in our own time, it will have to contend with the testimonies of documents standing on the threshhold of the canon even now: the Dead Sea scrolls (see Lawrence H. Schiffman, *The Halakhah of Qumran* [Leiden, 1976]), the Targumim, and the other documents important to our own day and unknown or neglected before now. In outlining the limits of the *halakhic* canon, we want to inquire after the processes of thought and the reaching of concrete conclusions of the masters of *halakhah*, early and late. They who expressed their theology through law, and only through law, so shaped the norms, social and psychological, of age succeeding age. They surely must define Judaism, not merely the epiphenomena called its "way of life."

within its vast, harmonious framework of rational inquiry and reasoned dispute, of exegesis of the canon in light of the newest concerns of the age, and of the newest concerns of the age in the light of the canon, the system collapses. That is to say, faced by two facts which could not be brought within the intelligible framework of the system of Judaism, Emancipation and modern, political anti-Semitism, Judaism has considerable difficulty. Specifically, it did not succeed in shaping meaningful issues for argument in accord with its established methods and its rational agendum for reasoned debate. So the theologian will want to reflect upon both how the system works and how it does not work. There is a clear frontier delineated by the end of inner plausibility. There is a border defined by the cessation of self-evidence.[10]

IV

At the outset I specified the first two principal tasks of the theologian in Judaism as those of definition and correlation: definition of Judaism—vision received, correlation of Judaism with the life of Jewish people—vision reformed. At the end let me point out that these tasks are not to be done in isolation from one another because the sources of definition of Judaism, the *halakhic* sources, address themselves to the life of the Jewish people and propose to reshape that life in accord with the paradigm of the holy: *You shall be holy, because I am holy.* In this context, there are two sources for theology in Judaism: first, Torah, whole, unending, a never-to-be-closed canon; and, second, the human experience of the Jewish people raised to the level of Torah

[10]Alongside description and interpretation of the processes of exegesis must come a second arena for delineation: the range of choice permitted by the system and prohibited within the system. One may eat only certain few foods, but the problems connected with the eating of those foods are rich and engaging. Stated more broadly, the proposition does not change. There is a given way of life defined by the processes of exegesis of the law and through its diverse literature. That way of life has to be described in the context of humanity and of the humanities: what sorts of people, society, and culture emerge when life is lived in this way, and not in some other. The *halakhic* literature awaits this kind of attention: description of the life of emotion and of relationship; of the society of home, family, and town; of the choices made—and the alternatives avoided—by the individual and by the group. The whole is best framed by the *halakhic* corpus. Since, moreover, we have access to other great systems of religion expressed through distinctive ways of life—I refer, for one instance, to Islam, with its legal literature, its processes of exegesis, and its way of life; but I do not exclude reference to Buddhism, on the one side, and to Christianity, on the other, both of them profoundly *halakhic* constructions at important points in their history—there is a sizable task of comparison to be worked out. So alongside, and cogent with, the exegesis of exegesis, that is, the description of the processes of Judaism, another task must be done. It is the comparison of the results, the description of the history of Judaism within the history of religions. Through this work there is a chance to gain that perspective upon which definition must depend. And I need hardly dwell upon the centrality of the work of the historian of the Jews, able to relate the *halakhic* process to the concrete social and historical circumstances of the Jewish people. For the historian and sociologist of the Jews in the end provide the most interesting evidence about the concrete workings of Judaism.

through *halakhah*.[11] Theology in Judaism makes sense of life already lived. But theology in Judaism has to reflect upon a particular mode of life already lived: the life lived in accord with Torah, therefore, with *halakhah*. What is to be defined and explained is the correlation between the (ideal, normative) human images of the *halakhah* and the actual shape of life lived in accord with the *halakhah*. What is this particular kind of humanity which is shaped within the disciplines and critical tensions of the law? What are the larger human meanings to be adduced in interpretation of this particular kind of humanity?

To answer these questions the texts which constitute the sources of theology in Judaism have first to be reread, systematically, thoroughly, and at the outset, historically, one by one. A fresh set of questions has to be devised, questions about: first, the inner issues addressed by the *halakhic* texts; second, the human meaning of those issues, when interpreted; third, against the particular times and settings in which the texts are framed; and fourth, also against the continuing and enduring social and historical realities of the Jewish people. These are the four criteria of meaning yielded by correct interpretation.

To start at the end, we have to know about those on-going considerations which must be taken into account by all normative statements on behavior and belief, those traits of society and imagination which characterize every context in which Judaism comes to expression and which, therefore, define the outer limits of Judaism.

Next, we need to discern those particular and distinctive concerns of a given situation and to isolate what is fresh and unanticipated therein.

For once we have uncovered the concrete and specific context in which a major conceptual initiative is given shape in *halakhah*, thirdly, we are able to enter into the human circumstance which will help us to understand the question—the existential problem—dealt with by a given initiative.

And, finally, it is at that point that we may bring to full articulation the inner issues addressed by the *halakhic* text. Then we do not reduce them to accidents of a given context. We confront them in their ultimate and whole claim to speak in the name of Torah and to talk of holy things, of God and humanity in God's image.

---

[11]What follows is a response to David Tracy (1975: 43ff.). I hasten to clarify that it is the model, not the substance, which I invoke as a clarifying exercise of intellect. Tracy describes the revisionist model as "philosophical reflection upon the meanings present in common human experience and language, and upon the meanings present in the Christian fact." Of acute relevance is Tracy's first thesis, "The two principal sources for theology are Christian texts and common human experience and language." If I may rephrase in this setting the outcome of my earlier propositions, it is that the principal sources for theology in Judaism are, first, the *halakhic* texts as they are lived out in ordinary life and, second, the common human experience and language which will help to make sense of the inner meanings of those lived texts. This is, I hasten to say, not a translation of Tracy's propositions into the setting of Judaism. It is an effort to respond to what seems to me a sound insight, arising, on its own, within the context of Judaism.

It is principally in the great *halakhic* texts that the humanistic concerns of theology in Judaism are encapsulated and awaiting discovery. So far as Judaism proposes to express itself through the deeds of the Jewish people and the society which they construct together, we require access to two things. First is philosophical reflection upon the meanings present in common human experience, and second is the language prescribed and expressed within Torah. That common human experience, so far as it is accessible to Torah, is shaped by *halakhah*—when *halakhah* is understood for what it is. So at the end let us state what it is and what it is not.

Halakhah is Judaism's principal expression of theology. But of course it, too, is not theology. The work of theologians, too long set aside since the splendid philosophical-*halakhic* accomplishment of Maimonides, is to express the theology of *halakhah* in its fullness and complexity. If we take *halakhah* as the crucial category for the world-view and ethos defined as Judaism, in contrast to the other definitions of the principal sources of Judaism, then we want to know the range and perspectives of the vision of the *halakhah*. What the world-view is which shapes, and is shaped by, the ethos of the *halakhah*, the conceptions of humanity, and of the potentialities of human society—these things await definition. But, I wish now to suggest, theology is something more than merely the making explicit of what is implicit and constitutive.

The work of the theologian—as distinct from that of the scholar of history or hermeneutics—must be constructive and creative. For we must grant to theologians what we do not want for scholars, the freedom as constructive religious thinkers to propose fresh perspectives on, and even alterations in the world-view and ethos of, the law. This freedom, we know, has been assumed and vigorously exercised by the great thinkers of the *halakhah*, who understood the deep paradox of the famous play on words, *ḥerut ᶜal halluḥot*, "freedom [is] incised upon the tablets of the law." If, as we tell ourselves, in discipline there is freedom, then to the theologians we cannot deny the greatest freedom of all: to speak in fresh and original ways within the *halakhic* frame, as they do within the frame of biblical and aggadic materials all the time. For, it is self-evident, affirming a *halakhic* definition of Judaism is a theological decision, in the rich sense of the term: the doing of normative and constructive theology.

Having specified the historical and hermeneutical work to be done, we therefore turn to adumbrate the constructive task. For, as I implied, theology is not solely the description of theology, the evocation of worlds past and remembered. If it also is not the invocation of worlds here now and coming in time, it is hardly needed. It is the first task of the theologian to describe and interpret that world of meaning. But it is the second, and still more important, task to carry forward the exegesis of the world-view of Judaism by continuing *halakhic* reflection upon the world. That is, theologians have the work of viewing the world and shaping a vision of what we are and can be.

For, in its way, *halakhah* in the end lays before us a conception of who the community of Israel is and what the community of Israel can be. *Halakhah* speaks of the holiness of the community of Israel within the holiness of God. Its themes and issues then focus upon the way of life of the community of Israel, to the end that the community of Israel may fulfill its promise and potential as the people of the Lord, the kingdom of priests and the holy people. Now when theologians look at the world today and see the world within the disciplines of *halakhah* and the perspectives of the holiness *halakhah* means to nurture, their creative and constructive work begins. It is to lay down statements of continuing norms for a new context. It is to renew the ancient norms through the lessons of a new age. What, after all, do we deal with, if not an exploration of human nature and of the divine image impressed within human nature? And what is at the heart and soul of Judaism, if not the inquiry into the image of God in which we are made, therefore into the potential sanctity of us and of the world we make?

We cannot, therefore, concede that the theological work is done for all time in the pages of Maimonides' *Mishneh Torah* or *Shulḥan ᶜArukh*. We insist that the work is to be done in our own days when decisions are made which bespeak a vision of who we are and what we can be, of what it means to be in God's image and to live in a community meant to express God's will. The ancient, medieval, and modern rabbis did and do more than a work of history and hermeneutics. On the basis of what their eyes are trained to see and their minds to perceive, in age succeeding age they forge a new and contemporary understanding of a new and unprecedented world. That was what was original for them: Maimonides does not merely quote the ancient sources, though *Mishnah Torah* is a melange of quotations. Through his reflection and arrangement he says something new through something a thousand years old. What we have to learn is that the *halakhic* process contains the theological process of Judaism. When we understand how that process works, we shall gain access to Judaism. The reason is that the *halakhic* corpus contains such vision as we have, and have to share, about the sacred potentialities of humanity and of the human community. The tasks of theology today begin in the exegesis of exegesis done. But they lead to the doing of the exegesis of this time, the interpretation of our world and of its days. The creation of worlds goes on in world without end. That is what, as Rashi says, it means to be "like God"—to create worlds.

Judaism is a religion about this world and about the human being. Its encompassing conceptions concern the human being, made in God's image and little lower than angels, and the community framed and formed by human beings, which is the arena for the working out of God's word and will. Distinctive to Judaism is the intensely practical and practiced law. The word is not abstract. The will is for the here and now. But the word is yet a word, the will is not solely about what I eat but how I understand and feel—and what I am. In the end, we always are what we are, that is, we are mortal and die. But before that, we may become something "in our image, according to our likeness," like God—only that we die. And there, in that painful tension between death and living, between our mortality and the promise and vision of the sacred in ourselves, is the sanctuary of life, the arena for our struggles and our anguish. In the pain and the suffering, in the living in the face of the dying is the sacred. The achievement, the vanquishing and the being vanquished, too, are sacred. Holiness is the pathos; holiness, the triumph.

V

It remains briefly to address two questions, usefulness and relevance. At the outset there is a three-fold set of tasks of theology in Judaism: (1) to define Judaism, (2) to discover the human situation to which Judaism responds, and, finally, (3) to create those modes of advocacy and apologetics which will permit contemporary Jews to gain renewed access to that Judaism subject to definition. This third task may be captured in the question: To whom is such a theological enterprise as I have described going to be useful? And alongside there is a second question, important to those will want to study, and even interpret, the theology of Judaism in the setting of universities, therefore in discourse with a diverse and plural intellectual constituency: To whom, outside of Judaism, are the results of this kind of theology going to be relevant?

The obvious fact is that the two questions are one. For Jews seeking to define and understand Judaism and scholars of religions with the same fundamental questions—What is this thing? How does it work?—part company only at the end. Jews have yet a Jewish question, not shared by others, which is: How shall I find my way inside; or, if inside, what does it mean to *be*, to live, inside? But these are the same questions once again. The study of religions must encompass attention to the study of theologies; and, given the situation of teacher and student, the study of religions is going to include much effort (perhaps too much) given to the understanding of theologies.

Now I think it is everywhere understood as a datum that in our classrooms there will be no advocacy, but the academic kind, and surely no active theologizing. But there must be understanding, an exercise in interpretation, in the framework of the common humanity or the study of religions collapses into the recitation of facts, a rubble of trivial observations. To prevent the ruin of the work, we quite properly turn to anthropology and sociology, philosophy and psychology, drama, poetry, and art—indeed to each and every source of insight available to us in humanistic learning. But if my proposal is a sound one, then we find yet another source of insight to which to turn: theology itself. If the work is done with a decent respect for the diversity of our students and for the rights of all of them to be what they are without our interference, then surely the insights sought in descriptive theological inquiry and exposition—the human meaning of the law—may turn out to crown the construction of meaning (if not the search for truth) at which we labor.

WORKS CONSULTED

Alon, Gedalia
    1954–55   *Toledot hayyehudim be'ereṣ yisra'el betequpat hammishnah vehattalmud.* 2 vols. Tel Aviv.
    1957–58   *Meḥqarim betoledot yisra'el.* 2 vols. Tel Aviv. Trans. Israel Abrahams: *Jews, Judaism and the Classical World. Studies in Jewish History in the Times of the Second Temple and Talmud.* Jerusalem, 1977.

Avi-Yonah, Michael
    1976   *The Jews of Palestine. A Political History from the Bar Kochba War to the Arab Conquest.* Oxford: Basil Blackwell.

Banton, Michael, ed.
    1966   *Anthropological Approaches to the Study of Religion.* London: Tavistock Publications.

Baron, Salo W.
    1952   *A Social and Religious History of the Jews.* Vol. II. New York: Columbia University Press.

Bayer, Bathja
    1972   "Talmud: Musical Rendition." *Encyclopaedia Judaica* 15:753.

Beauvoir, Simone de
    1953   *The Second Sex.* Trans. and ed. H. M. Parshley. New York: Knopf.

Biderman, Israel M.
    1976   *Mayer Balaban. Historian of Polish Jewry.* New York.

Boyce, Mary
    1975   *A History of Zoroastrianism.* Leiden: E. J. Brill.

Brandon, Samuel G. F.
    1951   *The Fall of Jerusalem and the Christian Church.* London: S.P.C.K.

Brown, Peter
    1971   *The World of Late Antiquity. From Marcus Aurelius to Muhammad.* London: Thames and Hudson.

Buchsel, Friedrick
    1964   "Paradosis." pp. 172–73 in *Theological Dictionary of the New
                Testament* II. Ed. G. Kittel. Trans. G. W. Bromiley.

Buechler, Adolf
    1912   *The Economic Conditions of Judaea after the Destruction of the
                Second Temple.* London: Jews' College Publications, No. 4.
    1928   *Studies in Sin and Atonement in the Rabbinic Literature of the First
                Century.* London: Jews' College Publications, No. 11.
    1956   *Studies in Jewish History.* Ed. I. Brodie and J. Rabbinowitz. London:
                Oxford.

Cherniss, Harold
    1935   *Aristotle's Criticism of PreSocratic Philosophy.* New York: Octagon.
    1944   *Aristotle's Criticism of Plato and the Academy.* New York.
    1945   *The Riddle of the Early Academy.* Berkeley and Los Angeles: Uni-
                versity of California Press.

Chomsky, Noam
    1957   *Syntactic Structures.* The Hague: Mouton.

Cohen, Gerson D.
    1973   "The Blessings of Assimilation in Jewish History." pp. 251–58 in
                *Understanding Jewish Theology. Classical Issues and Modern
                Perspectives.* Ed. J. Neusner. New York: KTAV.

Donaldson, James
    1907   *Woman: Her Position and Influence in Ancient Greece and Rome,
                and Among the Early Christians.* New York: Longmans, Green, & Co.

Douglas, Mary
    1966   *Purity and Danger.* London: Routledge & Kegan Paul.
    1973   "Critique." pp. 137–42 in J. Neusner, 1973b.
    1975   *Implicit Meanings: Essays in Anthropology.* London: Routledge &
                Kegan Paul.

Evans-Pritchard, Edward E.
    1965   *The Position of Women in Primitive Societies and Other Essays in
                Social Anthropology.* London: Faber and Faber.

Farb, Peter
    1974   *Word Play. What Happens When People Talk.* New York: Knopf.
                (Used: Bantam edition, 1975.)

Finkelstein, Louis
    1936   *The Pharisees.* Philadelphia: The Jewish Publication Society of
                America.

Fitzmyer, Joseph A.
    1970   "The Languages of Palestine in the First Century A.D." *Catholic
                Biblical Quarterly* 32:501–31.

Geertz, Clifford
    1957   "Ethos, World-View, and the Analysis of Sacred Symbols." *The*

> *Antioch Review* 17/4:421–37.
1973   *The Interpretation of Cultures.* New York: Basic Books.

Gereboff, Joel
1973   "The Pioneer: Zecharias Frankel." pp. 59–75 in *The Modern Study of the Mishnah.* Ed. J. Neusner. Leiden: E. J. Brill.
1979   *Tarfon.* Brown Judaic Studies. Missoula: Scholars Press.

Gerhardsson, Birger
1961   *Memory and Manuscript.* ASNU 22. Uppsala, Lund: C. W. K. Gleerup.

Ginzberg, Louis
1955   "The Significance of the Halachah for Jewish History." *On Jewish Lore and Law.* Philadelphia: The Jewish Publication Society of America (orig. 1929).

Green, William S.
1977   *Men and Institutions in Earlier Rabbinic Judaism.* Brown Judaic Studies. Missoula: Scholars Press.
1978   "What's in a Name?—The Problematic of Rabbinic 'Biography.'" pp. 77–96 in *Approaches to Ancient Judaism.* Missoula: Scholars Press.
1979   *Joshua ben Hananiah.* 3 vols. Leiden: E. J. Brill.

Guttmann, Alexander
1940   "The Problem of the Anonymous Mishnah." *Hebrew Union College Annual* 16:137–56.

Halivni, David Weiss
1968,   *Meqorot ummesorot.* ET: I. *Sources and Traditions. A Source*
1975   *Critical Commentary on Seder Nashim*; II. *A Source Critical Commentary on the Talmud. Seder Moed. From Yoma to Hagiga.* Tel Aviv.

Harlow, Jules, trans.
1963   "Tanḥuma Qedoshim 10." p. 143 in *Judaism.* Ed. A. Hertzberg. New York: Washington Square Press.

Harris, Marvin
1968   *The Rise of Anthropological Theory. A History of Theories of Culture.* London: Routledge & Kegan Paul.

Haugen, Einar
1972   *The Ecology of Language: Essays by Einar Haugen.* Stanford: Stanford University Press.

Heschel, Abraham J.
1936   *Die Prophetie.* Krakow: Polish Academy of Sciences and Berlin: Erich Reiss. E.T.: *The Prophets.* New York: Harper & Row: 1962.
1951   *The Sabbath. Its Meaning for Modern Man.* New York: Farrar, Straus, and Young.
1955   *God in Search of Man. A Philosophy of Judaism.* New York: Farrar, Straus & Cudahy.

1962,   *Torah min hashshamayim beaspaqlariah shel haddorot.* E.T.:
1965   *Theology of Ancient Judaism.* 2 vols. London and New York:
            Soncino.
1973   *A Passion for Truth.* New York: Farrar, Straus and Giroux.

Hubert, Henri and Marcel Mauss
1964   *Sacrifice: Its Nature and Function.* Trans. W. D. Halls. Chicago. (=
            "Essai sur la fonction du sacrifice," *L'Année sociologique,* 1898.)

Humphreys, S. C.
1975   "Transcendence and Intellectual Roles: The Ancient Greek Case."
            Daedalus 104:91–117.

Isaksson, Abel
1965   *Marriage and Ministry in the New Temple. A Study with Special
            Reference to Mt. 19:13–22 and I Cor. 11:3–16.* Lund.

Jensen, Adolf E.
1963   *Myth and Cult Among Primitive Peoples.* Trans. Marianna Tax
            Choldin and Wolfgang Weissleder. Chicago: University of Chicago
            Press.

Jousse, Marcel
1925   *Études de psychologie linguistique. Le style oral rythmique et
            mnémotechnique chez les Verbo-moteurs. Archives de philosophie.* II,
            iv. Paris: G. Beauchesne.
1930   *Les rabbis d'Israël. Les Récitatifs rythmiques parallèles. I. Genre de la
            Maxime.* Paris: Editions Spes.

Kadushin, Max
1964   *Worship and Ethics. A Study in Rabbinic Judaism.* Evanston: North-
            western University Press.

Kanter, Shamai
1979   *Gamaliel of Yavneh.* Brown Judaic Studies. Missoula: Scholars Press.

Katz, Jacob
1958   *Masoret Ummashber.* Tel Aviv.
1961a   *Exclusiveness and Tolerance. On Jewish-Gentile Relations in
            Medieval and Modern Times.* New York: Schocken.
1961b   *Tradition and Crisis.* Glencoe: Free Press.

Kosovsky, Binyamin
1942   *Oṣar lashon hattosefta.* Jerusalem.
1957   *Oṣar lashon hammishnah.* Jerusalem.

Kraus, Hans-Joachim
1956   "Zur Geschichte des Uberlieferungsbegriffs in der alttestamentlichen
            Wissenschaft." *Evanglische Theologie* 16:371–87.

Lasch, Christopher
1977   *Haven in a Heartless World. The Family Besieged.* New York: Basic
            Books.

Leach, Edmund
    1970   "The Legitimacy of Solomon." pp. 248–92 in *Introduction to Structuralism*. Ed. Michael Lane. New York: Basic Books.

Levine, Baruch A.
    1974   *In the Presence of the Lord. A Study of Cult and Some Cultic Terms in Ancient Israel*. Leiden: E. J. Brill.

Lewin, Benjamin M., ed.
    1921   *Igeret Rab Sherira Ga'on*. Haifa.

Lieberman, Saul
    1950   "The Publication of the Mishnah." pp. 83–89 in *Hellenism in Jewish Palestine. Studies in the Literary Transmission, Beliefs, and Manners of Palestine in the I Century B.C.E.—IV Century C.E.* New York: Jewish Theological Seminary of America.

Lightstone, Jack N.
    1979   *Yose the Galilean*. 3 vols. Leiden: E. J. Brill.

Lord, Albert B.
    1948   "Homer, Parry and Huso." *American Journal of Archeology* 52:36.

Montefiore, C. G. and H. Loewe, eds.
    1938   *A Rabbinic Anthology*. Philadelphia: The Jewish Publication Society of America.

Moore, George Foot
    1921   "Christian Writers on Judaism." *Harvard Theological Review* 14:197–254.
    1927   *Judaism*. 3 vols. Cambridge: Harvard University Press.

Neusner, Jacob
    1962   *A Life of Yohanan ben Zakkai. Ca. 1–80 C.E.* Leiden: E. J. Brill.
    1965–70   *A History of the Jews in Babylonia*. 5 vols. Leiden: E. J. Brill.
    1970a   *Development of a Legend: Studies on the Traditions concerning Yohanan ben Zakkai*. Leiden: E. J. Brill.
    1970b   *Formation of the Babylonian Talmud: Studies on the Achievements of Late Nineteenth and Twentieth Century Historical and Literary-Critical Research*. Leiden: E. J. Brill.
    1971   *The Rabbinic Traditions about the Pharisees before 70*. 3 vols. Leiden: E. J. Brill.
    1973a   *Eliezer ben Hyrcanus. The Tradition and the Man*. 2 vols. Leiden: E. J. Brill.
    1973b   *The Idea of Purity in Ancient Judaism*. Leiden: E. J. Brill.
    1973c   *Invitation to the Talmud. A Teaching Book*. New York: Harper & Row.
    1973d   *Modern Study of the Mishnah*. Leiden: E. J. Brill.
    1974–77   *A History of the Mishnaic Law of Purities*. 22 vols. Leiden: E. J. Brill.
    1975   *The Academic Study of Judaism. Essays and Reflections*. New York: KTAV.

1976   "Essay Review of Urbach's *The Sages.*" *Journal of Jewish Studies* 27/1:23–35.

1977a   *The Academic Study of Judaism. Essays and Reflections. Second Series.* New York: KTAV.

1977b   "The Meaning of Torah Shebe^{c}al Peh." pp. 29–41 in *The Solomon Goldman Lectures. Perspectives in Jewish Learning.* Vol. I. Eds. Stanley Kazan and Nathaniel Stampfer. Chicago: The Spertus College of Judaica Press.

1978a   "Comparing Judaisms." *History of Religions* 18/2:177–91.

1978b   "From Scripture to Mishnah: The Case of Niddah." *Journal of Jewish Studies* 2.

1978c   "Learning and Transcendence in Judaism." *Journal of Reform Judaism*, Spring:15–29.

1978–80   *A History of the Mishnaic Law of Holy Things.* 6 vols. Leiden: E. J. Brill.

1979a   "From Scripture to Mishnah: The Exegetical Origins of *Maddaf.*" *Fiftieth Anniversary Festschrift of the American Academy for Jewish Research.*

1979b   "From Scripture to Mishnah: The Origins of Mishnah's Fifth Division." *Journal of Biblical Literature* 98:2, June.

1979c   *Way of Torah: An Introduction to Judaism.* 3rd ed. Belmont, CA: Wadsworth.

1980f.   *A History of the Mishnaic Law of Women.* 5 vols. Leiden: E. J. Brill.

Nielsen, Eduard
1954   *Oral Tradition. A Modern Problem in Old Testament Introduction.* Foreword by H. H. Rowley. Studies in Biblical Theology 11. London: SCM Press.

Otwell, John T.
1977   *And Sarah Laughed. The Status of Women in the Old Testament.* Philadelphia: Westminster Press.

Parry, Milman
1930   *Harvard Studies in Classical Philology* 31:138.

Pautrel, R.
1934   "Des abréviations subies par quelques sentences de Jésus dans la rédaction synoptique." *Recherches de science religieuse* 24:344–65.

1936   "Les canons du mashal rabbinique." *Recherches de science religieuse* 26:1–45.

Peters, F. E.
1970   *The Harvest of Hellenism. A History of the Near East from Alexander the Great to the Triumph of Christianity.* New York: Simon and Schuster.

Porton, Gary
1976   *The Traditions of Rabbi Ishmael.* 4 vols. Leiden: E. J. Brill.

Primus, Charles
1977   *Aqiba's Contribution to the Law of Zera'im.* Leiden: E. J. Brill.

Rabin, Chaim
    1958   *The Zadokite Documents. I. The Admonition. II. The Laws.* Oxford: Clarendon Press.

Rahula, Walpola
    1962   *What the Buddha Taught.* New York: Grove Press.

Reuther, Rosemary R.
    1974   *Religion and Sexism. Images of Woman in the Jewish and Christian Traditions.* New York: Simon and Schuster.

Rosaldo, Michelle Zimbalist and Louise Lamphere, eds.
    1974   *Woman, Culture, and Society.* Stanford: Stanford University Press.

Rosenbaum, Irving J.
    1976   *The Holocaust and Halakhah.* New York: KTAV.

Rothkoff, Aaron
    1972   "Joseph Dov Soloveitchik." *Encyclopaedia Judaica* 15:132–33.

Rothschild, Fritz A.
    1972   "Abraham Joshua Heschel." *Encyclopedia Judaica* 8:425.

Saldarini, Anthony J.
    1976   "Review: *History of the Mishnaic Law of Purities I–III.*" *Journal of Biblical Literature* 95/1:151.

Sandmel, Samuel
    1978   *Judaism and Christian Beginnings.* New York: Oxford University Press.

Sarason, Richard S.
    1979   *A History of the Mishnaic Law of Agriculture. Demai.* Leiden: E. J. Brill.

Schechter, Solomon
    1970   *Studies in Judaism.* 3 vols. Paterson, NJ: Atheneum.

Schiffman, Lawrence H.
    1976   *The Halakhah of Qumran.* Leiden: E. J. Brill.

Scholem, Gershom
    1960,   *Jewish Gnosticism, Merkabah Mysticism, and Talmud*
    1965   *Tradition. Based on the Israel Goldstein Lectures, Delivered at the Jewish Theological Seminary of America.* New York: Jewish Theological Seminary of America.

Schorsch, Ismar
    1975   *Heinrich Graetz. The Structure of Jewish History and Other Essays.* New York: Jewish Theological Seminary of America.

Schürer, Emil
    1885   *A History of the Jewish People in the Time of Jesus Christ.* Trans. J. Macpherson, S. Taylor and P. Christie. Edinburgh: T. & T. Clark. Rev. and ed. Geza Vermes and Fergus Millar, 1973.

Smallwood, Mary
    1976   *The Jews under Roman Rule.* Leiden: E. J. Brill.

Smith, Jonathan Z.
    1978   *Map is Not Territory. Studies in the History of Religions. Studies in Judaism in Late Antiquity.* Leiden: E. J. Brill.

Smith, Morton
    1963   "A Comparison of Early Christian and Early Rabbinic Tradition." *Journal of Biblical Literature* 82:169–76.
    1968   "Historical Method in the Study of Religion." *History and Theory. Studies in the Philosophy of History, Beiheft 8. On Method in the History of Religions.* Ed. James S. Helfer. Middletown: Wesleyan University Press.

Soloveitchik, Joseph D.
    1944   "Ish hahalakhah." *Talpiyot*: 631–735.
    1965   "The Lonely Man of Faith." *Tradition* VII/2:5–67.

Spiro, Melford
    1972   *Buddhism and Society.* New York: Harper & Row.

Stuhlmueller, Carroll
    1958   "The Influence of Oral Tradition upon Exegesis." *Catholic Biblical Quarterly* 20:299–326.

Swidler, Leonard
    1976   *Women in Judaism; The Status of Women in Formative Judaism.* Metuchen, NJ: Scarecrow Press.

Tracy, David
    1975   *Blessed Rage for Order. The New Pluralism in Theology.* New York: Seabury.

Turner, Victor
    1977   "Sacrifice as Quintessential Process: Prophylaxis or Abandonment?" *History of Religions* 16:189–215.

Urbach, Ephraim
    1975   *The Sages. Their Concepts and Beliefs.* 2 vols. Jerusalem: Magnes Press.

Williams, Raymond B.
    1970   "Historical Criticism of a Buddhist Scripture: The Mahāparinibbāna Sutta." *Journal of the American Academy of Religion* 38/2:156–67.

Yadin, Yigael
    1971   *Bar Kokhba. The Rediscovery of the Legendary Hero of the Second Jewish Revolt against Rome.* London: Weidenfeld and Nicolson.

Zahavy, Tzvee
    1977   *The Traditions of Eleazar ben Azariah.* Brown Judaic Studies. Missoula: Scholars Press.

INDEX

GENERAL INDEX

BIBLICAL AND TALMUDIC REFERENCES

Friday

monday